Insightful and thought-provoking. Martyn Drake's book provides a clear focus on the reality of a 21st-century non-profit; what it actually does, how it operates and why the need to balance commercial and charitable practices to achieve maximum social value creation.
**Alex Skailes, Director at the Centre for Charity Effectiveness, Cass Business School, London**

With an increasing focus from the private sector on business with a social purpose, plus the growing need to diversify income, Martyn Drake's book is absolutely essential reading for anyone working or aspiring to work in the modern charity sector.
**Richard Williams, Director of Enterprise and Development, NCVO (National Council for Voluntary Organisations)**

An indispensable guide... Any third-sector senior leader will find something new and inspiring in this book.
**Mark Lever, CEO, Helpforce**

The chasm between commerce and charity needn't seem so great, nor so murky and perplexing. This book acts as a bridge between those two worlds... I wish I'd read [it] before I made that transition.
**Martin Halliwell, CFO, British Red Cross**

It challenges conventional thinking in the sector in a really engaging and motivating way. It brings fresh thinking and uses great case studies and research to reinforce its key points... I have already ordered copies of this book for everyone in my organization.
**Richard Hawkes, CEO, British Asian Trust**

# The Commercial Charity

*How business thinking can help non-profits grow impact and income*

Martyn Drake

**KoganPage**

**Publisher's note**

Every possible effort has been made to ensure that the information contained in this book is accurate at the time of going to press, and the publishers and authors cannot accept responsibility for any errors or omissions, however caused. No responsibility for loss or damage occasioned to any person acting, or refraining from action, as a result of the material in this publication can be accepted by the editor, the publisher or the author.

First published in Great Britain and the United States in 2020 by Kogan Page Limited

| | | |
|---|---|---|
| 2nd Floor, 45 Gee Street | 122 W 27th St, 10th Floor | 4737/23 Ansari Road |
| London | New York, NY 10001 | Daryaganj |
| EC1V 3RS | USA | New Delhi 110002 |
| United Kingdom | | India |

www.koganpage.com

Kogan Page books are printed on paper from sustainable forests.

© Martyn Drake, 2020

**ISBNs**

| | |
|---|---|
| Hardback | 978 1 78966 330 3 |
| Paperback | 978 1 78966 328 0 |
| Ebook | 978 1 78966 329 7 |

**British Library Cataloguing-in-Publication Data**

A CIP record for this book is available from the British Library.

**Library of Congress Cataloging-in-Publication Data**

Names: Drake, Martyn, author.
Title: The commercial charity : how business thinking can help non-profits
   grow impact and income / Martyn Drake.
Description: London ; New York : Kogan Page Inc, 2020. | Includes
   bibliographical references and index.
Identifiers: LCCN 2019039965 (print) | LCCN 2019039966 (ebook) | ISBN
   9781789663280 (paperback) | ISBN 9781789663303 (hardback) | ISBN
   9781789663297 (ebook)
Subjects: LCSH: Nonprofit organizations–Management. |
   Charities–Management. | Nonprofit organizations–Finance. |
   Charities–Finance.
Classification: LCC HD62.6 .D73 2020 (print) | LCC HD62.6 (ebook) | DDC
   658/.048–dc23
LC record available at https://lccn.loc.gov/2019039965
LC ebook record available at https://lccn.loc.gov/2019039966

Typeset by Integra Software Services, Pondicherry
Print production managed by Jellyfish
Printed and bound by CPI Group (UK) Ltd, Croydon, CR0 4YY

# CONTENTS

# FOREWORD

*by Mark Lever, CEO, Helpforce*

Over the last 25 years of working in the third sector, I have seen massive changes in both the way our work is financed and in the nature of the relationships between charity and funder. Having spent 12 years leading the Royal Voluntary Service, I became CEO of the National Autistic Society (NAS) in 2008. Both organizations are proud service delivery charities, and up to 2010, like most charities of that type, they'd grown and benefitted from the increasing investment that was going into health and social care as the government moved from giving grants to offering increasingly large contracts. On reflection, it's clear that I joined the NAS at 'the top of the market'.

Since 2010, we have seen significant downward pressure on funding for those contracts, and an increasing proportion of the money coming from central rather than local government. Austerity has taken its toll on local services in general and health and social care in particular, which has resulted in the closure of many services, and third-sector providers continually having to deliver more with less. The gaps in provision from this lack of funding have also been expected to be filled by the sector, whose street fundraising activity has often been curtailed by the very local authorities they have been seeking to support.

Alongside this, we have seen greater private sector involvement – not in itself a bad thing – but the distribution of profits outside the sector has led to a further funding drain for those 'uncommercial' charitable services. On top of that, the funding itself has become much more closely linked to the government of the day's priorities, which continue to change, adding yet more uncertainty and unpredictability to an already challenging situation.

It was in this context, in 2013, that I first met Martyn Drake. I have met and worked with many consultants, all of whom have come equipped with their own glossy methodologies and approaches into which they've attempted to shoehorn whatever challenges you face, irrespective of how unique, and in this case, unprecedented, those challenges were. Martyn was refreshingly different. He started by gaining a deep understanding of our situation by listening to all parts of the organization. He helped us to think through the complexity of the situation and the opportunities that we had. He completely understood the balance we had to strike between real commercial acumen and decision-making, while at the same time, remaining utterly focused on our charitable mission and social purpose. Having benefited from his support and approach and knowing many of my CEO colleagues were in very similar situations, I encouraged Martyn to become more involved in the wider sector, and I'm very glad that I did.

This book reflects the way that Martyn has since helped many third-sector organizations to thrive: to find that balance and blend of business thinking and charity mission, to navigate the challenging environments that we still face, and to find new, different ways to succeed.

The book starts by acknowledging the evidence that shows that earned income accounts for over half of all the money received by UK charities. It then proceeds to explore how this vital funding stream can be increased and made more sustainable. Firstly, by considering how some of the barriers presented by culture, history and language can be overcome, and then by drawing parallels with lessons learned from the world of business.

In reading the book you are frequently challenged to think about those fundamental but inherently challenging questions that we often seek to avoid: 'Why do you do what you do?', 'Why should people use your services?', 'What really makes you different?'

The book persuasively guides you from developing your understanding of why you need earned income and how to use it for greatest impact, through the development of a strategy that carefully balances the relationship between profit and purpose and then proceeds to set out how you build the capability, commitment and focus that are essential to delivering a successful social change programme underpinned by a commercial strategy.

To help you analyse your own situation, Martyn has pulled together a range of frameworks and models that others have found helpful – they are presented as optional tools rather than a panacea.

For me, what makes this book stand out is the sheer volume of practical case studies and examples drawn from both the world of business and charity to illustrate how others have successfully tackled the particular challenges being discussed.

Martyn has produced an indispensable guide for any leader looking to transform their approach to developing sustainable commercial income streams to support the mission and purpose of their charity or social enterprise. Any third-sector senior leader will find something new and inspiring in this book.

*Mark Lever became the inaugural Chief Executive of Helpforce in 2019. Prior to that, he was Chief Executive of the National Autistic Society, Chair of the Disability Charity Coalition, Co-chair of the Care and Support Alliance and Chief Executive of the Royal Voluntary Service.*

# FOREWORD

*by Martin Halliwell, CFO, British Red Cross*

As anyone who has taken the step across the void that often appears to exist between the commercial and charity sectors will know, it comes with its challenges.

Like the author, I moved from the world of commerce into civil society and – just like Martyn – I was inspired to do so because of the work I had seen being done to help the most vulnerable of people.

I wish I'd read this book before I made that transition.

When I first started my role as chief finance officer at the British Red Cross – having worked for 30 years in global businesses including most recently Unilever – I felt I might be required to change my perspective entirely. I was baffled by the differences in the language used and by apparent anomalies in the principles that drive strategic direction.

This book unravels the mystery. It shows just how many principles apply directly to both sectors. Martyn recognizes that many learnings and techniques can be transferred from the commercial to the charity sector and how that can be done without compromising the sector's core purpose. We all understand the necessity for new ideas and creative solutions if we are to tackle the many challenges we face and Martyn successfully takes themes from the commercial world and shows how they apply in the non-profit sector.

By keeping it simple, the book explores opportunities – from improving income to making better strategic decisions – in an intuitive way and it is a fascinating journey full of anecdotes. Martyn comes equipped with a toolbox of innovative ideas that he has gained from his extensive commercial experience and his last six years working across a wide breadth of organizations in the charity sector.

I am lucky because I have had the opportunity to talk with Martyn while he was researching and writing this book and, now that I have read it, I can see just how well it conveys his energy and breadth of knowledge. He is as thought-provoking on the page as he is in conversation. This book also conveys his genuinely held passion and a personal desire to bring new thinking to the charity sector.

The sector certainly needs new ideas and to be exposed to alternative perspectives – the speed of change and the organizational challenges we face are as demanding as anything I have seen in the commercial world. That said, Martyn recognizes that we cannot be prescriptive – there is no generic formula that will guarantee success – and different organisations must find their own solutions to the diverse challenges they face. While there are no easy answers, Martyn is a reliable and creative guide, helping us all to identify the questions we need to ask of our organizations and acting as a catalyst when it comes to looking for the areas of our business that we need to better probe if we are to improve performance.

Perhaps most importantly, Martyn can see clearly the many strengths in the charity sector and he never loses sight of the fact that we are in the business of improving people's lives. Together, he and the reader can hold up a mirror so that we can see what we do well and what we can do better. Just as commercial entities need to be agile, adapt to changes and increasingly deliver outcomes with more limited resources, so do charities.

The chasm between commerce and charity needn't seem so great, nor so murky and perplexing. This book acts as a bridge between those two worlds.

*Martin Halliwell is the Chief Financial Officer of British Red Cross. He is a former Vice President of Finance at Unilever and held senior finance roles at Alberto Culver, Kingfisher and Proctor and Gamble.*

# FOREWORD

by Richard Hawkes, CEO, British Asian Trust

I have always believed that charities and charity leaders are stronger if they are more commercial, but it is no exaggeration to say that taking over as CEO of the British Asian Trust in 2015 really opened my eyes to the enormous potential value of business thinking in the third sector.

It has been a great privilege for me to have worked in the charity sector for over a quarter of a century. During this time, I have been fortunate to hold leadership positions in a number of extremely well-known organizations and sector bodies. Before joining the Trust I spent five years as CEO of Scope, much of whose income was commercial; I chaired the Care and Support Alliance, most of whose members relied heavily on earned income from services; and, I had thought I was fairly commercially astute myself.

But the British Asian Trust was a step-change, as the Board is made up of hugely successful entrepreneurs, and a business philosophy and approach has run through the DNA of the organization since it was created. The organization is not afraid of taking risks to achieve greater impact, it sees the private sector as a partner with whom social change can be delivered together and it constantly looks for innovative ways of using finance to achieve its goals.

Many of us in the sector think that we are more commercially astute than we probably are, and those of us who do want to take a more business-like approach to generating income or creating a more sustainable form of change, often find ourselves constrained by the expectations and the culture of our organizations. What *The Commercial Charity* does is help us to understand the kinds of things we could all apply to our organizations, with thought-provoking ideas and easy to understand examples.

What I love about this book is how it challenges conventional thinking in the sector in a really engaging and motivating way. It brings fresh thinking and uses great case studies and research to reinforce its key points and messages. As someone who has long argued that the sector overall needs a serious shake-up, I especially enjoyed the section on 'reshaping the sector'. But this is also a very practical book, with many suggestions that sector leaders could consider and embrace. The section on 'redefining your role' brings this to life by challenging organizations to give serious thought to why they actually exist.

I have already ordered copies of this book for everyone in my organization! And I know that once they have all read it, it will help us become even more successful.

*Richard Hawkes is the Chief Executive of the British Asian Trust and Chair of Motivation Charitable Trust. He is a former Chair of the International Development Network, Bond, Chair of iPartner India, Member of the BBC Appeals Advisory Committee and Chief Executive of Scope and Sense International.*

# ACKNOWLEDGEMENTS

I'm deeply grateful to Martin Halliwell and Richard Hawkes for reviewing the manuscript and contributing such thoughtful forewords for the book, and particularly to Mark Lever who, in addition to the foreword, stoically ploughed through several early drafts and provided invaluable insights and encouragement.

I could not have written a single page of this book, however, without the gracious and generous help and support of the many people who've shared their experiences both on and off the record, who've bravely hired me as a consultant or a coach over the last six years, and who've allowed me to learn so much about their organizations and the broader non-profit sector. My insights into what drives it and how it can improve are entirely down to them, and it is a privilege to be able to share their stories.

In particular I would like to thank Nic Alderson, Sharon Allen, Paul Anticoni, Amanda Batten, Sally de la Bedoyere, Henny Braund, Hanah Burgess, David Elliott, Steve Ford, Alastair Graham, Jane Harris, Helena Herklotz, Neil Heslop, Mark Hislop, Petra Ingram, Paul Jackson-Clark, David Jessop, Richard Kramer, Kamran Malick, Gill Morbey, Mark Salway, Jonathan Senker, Alex Skailes, Madeleine Starr, Jacob Tas, Andy Tilden, Jan Tregelles, Andrew Vale, Peter Wanless, Chris Wright and Richard Williams, along with the rest of the team at NCVO.

Of no less value have been all those conversations, whether in seminars, over coffee, lunch or a beer, with many more friends across the sector, all of whom have opened my mind, challenged my preconceptions, and helped to shape my ideas. I've no doubt you know who you are. I'm also indebted to Jenny Volich and Helen Kogan at Kogan Page for their wonderful enthusiasm for the idea of this book, and to Lachie Humphreys for making the publishing process so painless.

Finally, and I realize this is a fairly standard line for authors, I am eternally grateful to my wife, Gaynor, not merely for supporting and encouraging me to write this book, or for looking after everything else while I did, but for tirelessly reading and re-reading my earliest drafts and helping to make this book passingly readable. Her patience in correcting innumerable errors and tactfully making me aware of a myriad pointless rambles, dry expositions and nonsensical paragraphs, has been above and beyond the call of duty. All of those that remain are nobody's fault but mine.

# Introduction

*A commercial journey*

In early 2013 I wrote and sent a speculative letter, the response to which changed the course of my business and my life.

At the time I'd been running my consulting practice for about four years; a career I'd stumbled into following the turbulence of the 2008 financial crash. Those first few years had been very busy, with a succession of lucrative but all-consuming projects for various blue-chip businesses, and when they came to an end, I found myself with an empty diary and a desire for a different challenge.

During that same four-year period, we'd also undergone a transition within the family, with both of our sons diagnosed with various autism spectrum disorders. And it was that combination of circumstances that prompted me to write to Mark Lever, CEO of the National Autistic Society (NAS), whose website had been so useful for us while we were going through the various diagnoses and emotional roller-coaster rides that accompanied them. I had no great expectations that the work I did for businesses would be of any relevance whatever to a charity, but nevertheless, in my letter I shared what I did, and offered, should it ever be of use, my pro-bono support to the NAS.

A week later I was facilitating them through a comprehensive strategy review, and discovering that UK charities, especially the large ones, were not at all as I expected them to be. I thought that charities sent out letters, e-mails and people in branded bibs with buckets, all to garner donations and direct debits, which they then spent on helping people in difficulty. As it turns out, that's a surprisingly small part of what they do.

The NAS, for instance, gets less than 20 per cent of its income from donations. The majority of its £100 million annual turnover is from contracts with local authorities and the Department for Education, to run schools and services for autistic adults and children. And furthermore, it turns out that the NAS isn't at all unusual in that regard (Figure 0.1).

Earned income, as it is generally termed within the sector, accounts for over half of all the money received by UK charities – 52 per cent according to the latest figures, or around £25 billion a year, compared to about £8 billion a year from public donations and £3 billion a year from legacy gifts.

The National Council for Voluntary Organisations (NCVO) produces an Almanac[1] each year, breaking down income and expenditure for the sector, and while most years show a modest increase in voluntary donations, the

FIGURE 0.1   UK charity sector income overview (£ million)

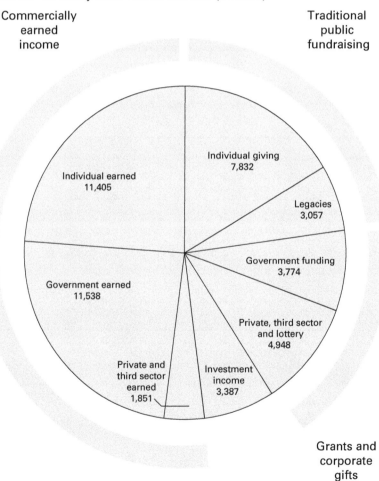

SOURCE  NCVO UK Civil Society Almanac[2]

largest source of income growth, in 11 of the 15 years on record since 2000, has been earned income. Contrary to many people's preconceptions, commercial trading has, for the past two decades, been the primary engine of growth for the charity sector.

That reliance on commercial income was the first of three big surprises. The second was how awkward that situation seemed to feel for many of the people in the sector, to which I'll return shortly. But my third surprise was the sheer level of commitment to collaboration, often between charities who are in direct competition. Maybe it shouldn't have been surprising, but as someone who until that point had worked only in competitive industries, it certainly went way beyond my expectations.

As we came towards the end of that pro-bono engagement, and we began preparing for the final review with trustees, Lever asked me if I would be interested in continuing to support him and his team for another six months, as an adviser and coach. 'I don't want you to do this pro-bono,' he said, before I had time to react, 'I think you're providing a lot of value, and I'm happy to pay for it. Plus,' he added, 'I think you can bring a lot to the sector, and you won't be able to keep doing that if you don't charge for it.'

He was right. Modesty aside, it was clear I'd added a lot of value, and as he listed half a dozen other charity CEOs he knew, and talked a little about their situations, it was hard to argue that they wouldn't benefit from similar support. And as he'd said, there was no way on earth I could do all that pro-bono. It was a watershed moment.

Since that day, I've worked with NAS on a variety of other projects, and I'll use some of them as examples later on, but through introductions and recommendations, first by Lever and subsequently by others, I've worked with, spoken with and advised dozens of other charities and non-profits. Examples of those projects and the insights they've provided are spread through the rest of this book. Some have kindly given me permission to use their names, others I've anonymized or combined, to illustrate the relevant points while protecting their confidentiality.

Consistent with the philosophy of this book – that a sustainable, commercial approach can have a key role within the non-profit sector – the overwhelming majority of those engagements have been for a fee that's not that much less than the fees I would charge any of my business clients. My rule of thumb is that if a project will return a charity's investment five or ten times over, I'll work for a fee; if not, I'll suggest ways they could do it themselves without charge. That rule ensures that I'm always adding far more into the sector than I'm taking out, and so far, it seems to have served all parties very well.

Throughout that work I've noticed consistent themes – themes I will examine throughout this book – one of which I've already mentioned: the discomfort with commerce. It's easy to trivialize it, to assume that it will dissipate as projects progress, but a degree of change is inevitable in any serious attempt at developing more commercial income, and when change starts to ramp up, that discomfort, as we will see later, can quickly harden into a major barrier.

Techniques for drawing out, understanding, and getting past that 'awkwardness' around commerce have been among the most useful things I have learned as my charity client portfolio has grown. And one of the main elements of that learning has been around the cultural barrier that is language.

Language is incredibly important and individual words can have deep connotations. For instance, I've yet to meet anyone in the sector whose job title includes the word Sales, despite it being, from any objective perspective, a critical function within many charities' operations. The word 'sales', and particularly 'salesperson', carries a huge amount of baggage (baggage that I'll attempt to unpack in Chapter 7), which is why most charities avoid the word, and instead use titles and department names with less challenging descriptions, like Bid Writing or Contracts. The same is true for the word 'profit'. Instead, most charities prefer the word 'surplus'. And that's a problem.

Bid writing is not sales, nor are surplus and profit synonyms. They have subtly different meanings and significantly different connotations. Surplus implies that a service brings in more than it costs to provide, that it makes more money than it needs to. Surplus implies a windfall, a luxury that we can do without if we must. It implies a method of pricing that starts with covering costs and adds a little where it can. Our job is to pay for ourselves; anything more is just surplus.

Replacing the word surplus with the word profit shifts the dialogue and drives a more ambitious way of thinking. It creates an expectation, a way of looking at pricing, value and income generation, that goes far beyond the concept of 'cost plus a bit'. Changing that expectation, from making a reliable surplus to making a significant profit, opens up the concept, and the opportunity, of generating much more unrestricted income, creating faster routes to increasing reach, scale and, above all, the impact that a charity can have.

I'll return to the profit issue and how to address it shortly, but there are many other examples – I've found them in most charities – where this deliberate or unconscious aversion to using overtly commercial language can form a similar barrier to growing impact. But its roots are deep. There is a palpable cultural difference between most charities and most businesses, and it's for good reason. It's what makes charities the organizations that they are. It's what drives them to do the things that only they can do. It's why donors and supporters voluntarily give £8 billion a year and leave another £3 billion of charity legacies in their wills. And for most people working in the sector, the choice of language is born out of that cultural identity, that deep history of giving, not selling; of being here, not to make money, but to make a difference.

However, the reality is, whether they recognize it or not, that most charities, under the surface, are also businesses. Social enterprises if you prefer, but commercial entities nonetheless. That so many charity professionals feel such discomfort around the disciplines that underpin over half of their income has implications. Few charities have the skills and expertise to make the most of the opportunities in front of them; to open the throttle on their commercial engine; to use the valuable knowledge and assets they have to drive the rapid growth of profitable income streams that could fund a greater, more sustainable impact in the world. It's hard to have conversations about those skills gaps, let alone to start addressing them, if the language and concepts that describe them are anathema within the culture.

The biggest single lesson that I've learned, the fundamental tenet of this book and of almost all my work within the sector, is that these two things are not mutually exclusive. Commercial language, attitudes and behaviours can be adapted, developed, and indeed can thrive, within a charity culture that remains deeply in touch with its roots, and unwaveringly focused on its mission. It just needs a little thought and care.

But for the increasing number of charities who are willing to open the dialogue around commercial concepts, to find a narrative that allows them into their culture and to set out on the journey of developing the necessary skills and expertise, the future is one of immense opportunity.

## Endnotes

**1** NCVO (2018) UK Civil Society Almanac, *NVCO*, https://data.ncvo.org.uk/documents/11/ncvo-uk-civil-society-almanac-2018.pdf (archived at https://perma.cc/S2EE-Y6SY)

**2** NCVO (2018) UK Civil Society Almanac, *NVCO*, https://data.ncvo.org.uk/documents/11/ncvo-uk-civil-society-almanac-2018.pdf (archived at https://perma.cc/S2EE-Y6SY)

# 01

# The business of charity

## The power of commerce

The most obvious way that commerce benefits a charity's mission is the income it generates. Commercial income, unlike most grants and donations, has no inherent restrictions on how it can be used. When a charity wins a grant or receives a large philanthropic donation, there's usually a pretty well-defined project that the money must be spent on – in fact, it's usually the biggest part of the pitch.

With individual donations, there are no formal restrictions, but there is an inherent expectation from the donor that the money will go directly to the beneficiaries of the charity's work. It's a perception regularly reinforced and used as a beating-stick by many in the popular press.

On 2 February 2014 the *Daily Mail*[1] started one such round of beatings with a story tearing into the £234,000 salary reportedly earned by Jasmine Whitbread, then CEO of Save the Children International. What it didn't say was that in the prior year, her organization and its members had collectively reported 21 per cent growth to $1.9 billion of income.[2] It had responded to 119 humanitarian crises in 48 countries, given life-saving medical treatment to 3.1 million children and directly supported over 50 million children around the world.[3] Nor did it point out that, in the same year, the *Daily Mail*'s parent group had reported that its entire media portfolio, including the *Daily Mail* and *Mail on Sunday*, had declined by 6 per cent to £793 million,[4] less than half that of Save the Children. Or that the *Mail*'s then editor, Paul Dacre, was rewarded for it with £1.8 million plus benefits, over seven times the salary Whitbread received. Many of its readers vocally expressed, through online comments and social media, their disgust and loss of faith in all charity giving, while at the same time renewing their subscriptions to the *Daily Mail*. They saw no hypocrisy in that, and they're not alone.

For many donors there is an unspoken but very clear agreement – I'm not giving you this money to pay for accountants and project managers, to redecorate your head office or give a fat salary to your Chief Exec – I'm giving it to you so that you can spend it on clean water and mosquito nets; on counsellors and research programmes; on helping the vulnerable, the victimized and the abused. One of their biggest concerns is how their money is spent; specifically, how much will get through to the beneficiary. Conversely, one of the biggest challenges for charities is how their infrastructure, their head office staff, their organizational development, all of which are critical to the effectiveness of their work, will be paid for.

Some of the sector's most contentious topics revolve around this issue. To combat the perception that donated money is being syphoned off, charities are becoming increasingly transparent, publishing information in their annual reports and supporter marketing to show exactly where the money goes, with pie charts and percentages for overheads, for fundraising and for the charitable activities themselves. And while transparency is a good thing, by itself it does nothing to change the donor expectation of where those numbers should be, which consequently drives many charities towards a mindset of underinvestment, of running on a shoestring, of sackcloth and ashes.

A couple of years ago I had lunch with the Chair of one of the UK's biggest and best-known charities, and I asked him what frustrated him most. He turned immediately to that perception of 'what charities should be' – a perception not just in the media and the public mind but also in the minds of trustees and staff; and he went on to give a painful example.

A few years previously, his charity had invested heavily in a new customer relationship management (CRM) system. 'We lost a lot of money on that project,' he explained. 'It would have cost around £200,000 to get someone really good to deliver it, but we knew we'd risk our reputation if we paid a salary like that, so we took the traditional charity approach. That decision probably cost us nearer £2 million in the long run.'

Every organization should continually seek to become more efficient, more productive, and more effective in achieving its aims. But that process requires investment, it requires talent and it requires good leadership and management capability, all of which cost money. When a charity can't pay for the infrastructure and systems it desperately needs, when it can't recruit really good people unless they're willing to sacrifice their own standards of living, when it can't get trustees or non-executives of the calibre and variety it needs because it's unable to pay them, its impact will suffer, its potential will remain unrealized, and it will fail the people who work there, the people they're trying to help, and ultimately the people who donate to its cause.

None of this is news to those brave enough to step into a leadership role within the sector. These are perennial talking points, unrelenting challenges, apparently insurmountable barriers for CEOs and their teams. And as that charity Chair accurately pointed out, they are barriers primarily of our own making, as donors, as trustees and as charity workers, clinging to a Victorian ethos of what it means to be a charity, rather than asking what a charity needs to become in order to succeed in its aims.

Generating more unrestricted income from trading that can be invested, without qualm or concern, in developing the infrastructure and the organization itself can be a major part of that solution. To be able to tell a donor that 'every penny you give goes directly to the front line because our commercial income pays for everything else' is a powerful argument and it's one potential solution to a complex and heavily constraining issue.

That's not the only benefit of applying a commercial approach to mission delivery, nor is it potentially the most powerful. Finding a commercially sustainable way to address a social problem, a way that's both impactful and profitable, can start a chain reaction that goes way beyond anything a single charity could ever do on its own.

When two of the UK's best-known charities, Scope and the National Autistic Society, first set out to change the world for their beneficiaries, neither of them expected they could do it on donated funds alone. From the beginning, both of those organizations started setting up services and institutions that could be paid either privately or by the state but, most importantly, could be sustainable without the constant reliance on fundraising from individual donors.

The NAS, founded in 1962 by a group of parents of autistic children, created the first autism-specific residential school, and were assisted by one of Scope's early members. Scope, or The Spastics Society as it was then known, was formed 10 years earlier, by three parents of disabled children, to enable them to have the same access to education as their able-bodied peers. In their powerful 1952 short film,[5] the Spastics Society highlighted the huge gap in provision for 'spastic children' – or as we'd now describe them, children with cerebral palsy. The film ends with a call for a thousand-fold increase in educational provision for spastic children, and points specifically to local authorities as a key source of funding.

Both charities created and championed facilities that hadn't previously existed, to meet needs that nobody was meeting, and over time both proved that those needs could be met, those social gaps addressed, and that with the right contracts in place for funding them, good money could be made from doing it. In so doing, they created new commercial markets, ones that have since been entered by many more organizations, both non-profit and for-profit. Today, those markets are worth millions, if not billions, of pounds and serve thousands, if not millions, of people in need.

I recently had a final update with the outgoing CEO of a client organization, whom I'd previously helped develop several new commercial income streams. I asked her how things were going, and if the early positive signs we'd seen at the end of our project together had gone on to bear healthy fruit. It turned out they had just had a record year for commercial income, and she would be leaving the organization in better shape than it's ever been.

'Probably the only challenge that I'm leaving for my successor to sort out,' she said, 'is that we're becoming so successful that other people are noticing, and they're starting to set up similar enterprises to ours. I've a feeling there could be some stiff competition coming our way.'

'But actually,' she continued, unprompted, 'now I think about it, that's probably a good thing. I guess the more people who are doing it, the more impact it will have.' And what she said was absolutely true. In reality, the biggest challenge her successor should be thinking about is which market to create next.

## The morality of profit

I touched earlier on the problematic concept of profit and made the point that the tendency towards substituting it with the word 'surplus' brings preconceptions and associations that severely limit both thinking and ambition.

By definition, non-profits don't make a profit, and just like sales, the word profit brings with it a whole raft of subconscious associations. For many in the charity sector it triggers images of corporate greed, sharp-suited business people with no conscience, and of 'all that's wrong with our society'. Yet the concept of profit generation is essential if a charity is to make enough unrestricted income to drive the organization forward. So how do we square the circle? How do we defuse the discomfort?

The key is to separate what we mean by a profitable venture and what we mean by a non-profit organization. Within a charity's strategy there will be plenty of activities that will never make for a commercial business model, things that will only ever run at a loss, and that's as it should be. The government will never pay for someone to lobby it. People who desperately need help to understand how to claim benefits are in no position to pay for such a service, and the authorities from whom those benefits will be claimed have no incentive to pay either. There may be creative business models that could meet those needs, but I'm yet to see them and have no idea what they could be.

The opportunity, therefore, is for activities that can make a profit to make as much as they ethically and practically can, so the charity can use it in those other areas. As one CEO exhorted his team during one project kick-off meeting, 'Making a profit on this is not optional, it's a moral imperative if we want to reach all of those people who can't access our services today.'

'We profit wherever we can' might sound like the mantra of a ruthless corporate business but, ironically, within a clear ethical framework, in an organization committed to using those profits to literally change the world for the better, it's a far more defensible philosophy for a charity to hold than it is for just about anyone else.

That doesn't mean it's going to be easy to get a charity's people on board with what's a pretty challenging concept. But what it does show is that crafting a narrative that links the profitability of ventures to the overall impact the organization can have, is a critical element in developing the cultural readiness of the charity to begin looking at commercial opportunities in a more positive light. Another element that can help with that transition is normalizing the conversation around profit, and one process that can be extremely helpful for that is to use the Profit/Impact Matrix in Figure 1.1.

It's a simple 2 × 2 chart, with profit on the vertical axis and impact on the horizontal. Anything below the horizontal axis loses money, or makes a net loss, while anything above it makes a profit. Similarly, everything to the right of the vertical axis has a positive impact in line with the charity's mission, while anything to the left of it would have a negative impact and would detract from the mission. Few right-minded charities would do anything to undermine their mission, which is why that side of the chart is shaded out.

For a 'traditional' charity, there's very little above the line beyond fundraising. Most fundraising activities provide no direct benefit to the charity's mission, but they're very profitable, so sit high in the top left. A chain of charity shops could provide some impact, if the shops employ people the

FIGURE 1.1  Profit/Impact Matrix

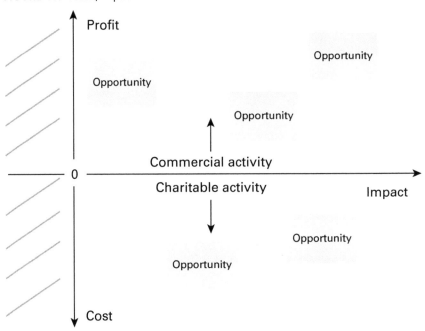

charity is there to serve, for example, or act as a hub for local support groups or for information and advice. And one of the immediate benefits of using the process is to trigger precisely those questions. Does this activity have a positive impact? Could it have a bigger one? Could it generate more profit?

It's a quick and simple filter for new commercial ideas, and as a process it can begin to deconstruct those instant negative reactions to commercial concepts such as profit, but it's also a powerful strategic tool for asking the big questions. Why are we doing each of these things? Is this the best way to spend our money, time and effort? Could we evolve any of these activities to be more impactful, or more profitable? And most importantly, are there things on here that we should stop doing, so we can redirect our resources into others that will obviously bear more fruit?

Tools like the Profit/Impact Matrix, and others I'll introduce throughout this book, aren't there to be blindly followed. They don't tell you what to do, but they do prompt you to think very deeply about what you *are* doing, and what you potentially *could* do, that would increase, in some cases dramatically, the effectiveness of your organization. And they often have unexpected benefits on the side.

One of the most interesting dynamics I usually see when using the Profit/ Impact Matrix, for example, is how the conversation shifts very rapidly, from concerns over the word profit to deep discussions about the word impact; specifically, how it's evaluated, how it can be compared across very different activities, and whether the charity actually has an internally consistent view about what 'impact' even means.

Understanding and measuring impact is not easy, but it's an area in which many charities have made great strides over recent years. But comparing impact across different activities, even with sophisticated measurement, is not always straightforward. One charity I worked with was dedicated to alleviating the suffering of working equines – horses, donkeys and mules – around the world. The charity is called Brooke, after its founder, Dorothy Brooke, and they estimate there are over 100 million working equines, providing daily support to around 600 million people, in some of the poorest and toughest environments in the world. And a good portion of those equines are vulnerable, in poor health and, at times, living with a great deal of pain and suffering.

Many of the people I met within Brooke had scientific backgrounds, often trained in veterinary college, and they had a laser-sharp focus on the effectiveness of their programmes, the condition of the animals that came through them, and the impact they were having. But even so, the idea of comparing cost and impact across different programmes and activities was complex and challenging. Not because they didn't have the data, but because the questions it raised went beyond data.

Which is more important: the number of animals whose wellbeing gets improved, or the degree of the improvement? Is it better to take 100 donkeys that are in a truly terrible state and help them recover, change the practices that created the problems and enable them to live longer, healthier, happier lives; or to help 100,000 donkeys who are in a milder state of suffering to get to that same place? Or is it better to invest in influencing policy, social norms and cultural expectations at a national level, to drive awareness and catalyse a demand for change in a much broader way? Given that there is a limit to the funds that can be raised and therefore spent, which has most priority?

That same 'breadth versus depth' trade-off exists in many charity organizations at many different levels. These are essential conversations to have, but they are incredibly complex, nuanced, and often emotionally charged. At Brooke we were lucky – we hit this question shortly before their global leadership conference, in which programme leaders from all over the world would be spending three days together with the fundraising and support teams in London. We got to spend an entire morning talking it through with all of them.

Those wider, inclusive debates can also unlock another subtle benefit of the matrix. There is often a deep organizational divide within charities between those who make the money and those who spend it; between the fundraisers and practitioners. That divide invariably extends to those who bring in money through commercial means, and it can form yet another internal barrier to their success.

Putting the concept of profit squarely alongside impact helps bring both sides together, making explicit the relationship between the two. It demonstrates, simply and visually, how an organization's activities are intimately intertwined with its financials; and how, whether an activity is above or below the line, improving its profitability and financial contribution is one of the most powerful ways to fund a greater impact. This is the realization that invariably emerges from these sessions, and it's the narrative story that needs to be told, and widely accepted, if a charity is to break down its mental barriers and embrace a more proactive, professional and unashamed approach to commerce.

The narrative will vary by situation, but its components are simple. Increased profit from one venture can pay for others that may fail; for new ideas that need to be tested; for a rapid expansion in scale and reach to help more people live better lives. It can provide for better salaries for innovative, creative, ambitious recruits. It can act as a force for modernization, for organizational and professional development. It can reduce a charity's dependency on vulnerable income, and it can potentially attract an array of other organizations to do the same thing, accelerating the pace of change.

Crafting a narrative that makes those links and normalizing those commercial concepts within everyday discussions across the organization are the two basic steps for overcoming the awkwardness, for realigning people's attitudes and for defusing the cultural resistance that will undermine a charity's commercial potential. The average executive has between five and ten meetings a day, in each of their two hundred or so working days a year – a thousand opportunities a year to draw those connections and to tell that story.

Culture change is never simple, and for every three steps forward there's often a step back, but one thing is for sure: compared to some of the impact debates I've seen, getting people comfortable with the notion of profit as a force for good is a comparative walk in the park.

## The trends reshaping the sector

In the opening pages I touched on the fact that, for much of the past 20 years, charity funding in the UK has grown predominantly through increased commercial income. However, that trend hides a tale of two halves. For the first 10 of those years, the trend wasn't driven by the sector itself. It was mainly driven by successive UK governments, through a consistent policy of outsourcing.

The aftermath of the Second World War saw Winston Churchill famously voted out of office, and the Labour government that followed created a range of nationalized institutions in areas such as telecommunications, rail, waterways and healthcare. By the 1970s, when Margaret Thatcher became Prime Minister, those institutions had grown enormously, and questions were being asked as to whether it was still the government's business to own and operate them.

Thatcher's initial projects to privatize British Aerospace and British Telecom aimed to spin those institutions out into the private sector, as publicly listed companies. But as the policy of outsourcing progressed through successive governments, the approach evolved towards a much wider variety of models – models that also included non-profits. A good example of that is public transport.

The British Transport Commission was created in 1948 through the nationalization of the rail and waterways networks. In 1962 it was split into three independent, government-owned corporations: British Rail, London Transport and British Waterways, of which London Transport is the only one still publicly owned and operated. The privatization of British Rail assets began under Thatcher in the 1980s, starting with its hotels and engineering divisions, before full privatization under John Major's Conservative government in 1993.

In contrast, British Waterways was 'mutualized' under an agreement set out by the Labour government of Gordon Brown in 2010. The Canal and Rivers Trust was formed as a registered charity, to take over all the assets and liabilities of the corporation in England and Wales. Funding was agreed in time for its launch in 2012 under David Cameron's Conservative–Lib Dem coalition, which will see it through until 2027, by which time it is expected to have developed its own independent income streams to continue delivering its services and fulfilling its mission.

In between the privatization of rail and the mutualization of waterways, the UK's Health Service went through its own outsourcing revolution.

The NHS was formed in July 1948, the same year as the Transport Commission, and operated largely intact for almost 40 years, until the 1990 NHS and Community Care Act. The Act, agreed under Major's Conservative government, transformed the NHS from two organizations (primary and secondary care) into a vast 'internal marketplace', spinning out a multitude of independent non-profit trusts, all of whose services would be commissioned and funded by regional and local commissioning bodies, who would collectively be financed, monitored and assessed by other layers of independent, arm's-length bodies, ultimately answerable to the Department of Health.

The Blair/Brown era saw a dramatic increase in funding for the burgeoning health and social-care market, rising from just over £60 billion in 1997 to almost £130 billion by 2009. In parallel, successive governments gave the commissioning groups more flexibility to bring in other providers, including both private and third-sector organizations. Many charities won good business contracts during that expansion, many of which included the transfer of services and staff (and their public-sector pension liabilities). That combination of outsourcing and investment was a major contributor to the growth of third-sector commercial income throughout the first decade of the 21st century. But change was on its way in the shape of the 2008 financial crash, the ensuing bank rescues and spiralling government debt.

There is no doubt that the austerity policies pursued following the subsequent 2010 General Election seriously damaged the UK's government-outsourced economy. During its growth phase, the outsourced economy had attracted a huge variety of participants. The market contraction that followed intensified their competition, often pitting local and national charities against global corporations such as Serco and G4S.

Government outsourcing markets are no different from any other: when they start to shrink there's a race to the bottom on price, and margins across the board are the first casualty. Having invested and expanded rapidly during the growth years, and often with big pension liabilities from TUPE'd staff, many service delivery charities are now in a tight spot, with some being pushed to the brink of financial viability. But so far, the sector seems to have avoided the more spectacular declines of some of the larger private-sector providers, such as Capita and Carillion. And yet, the outsourcing of government services, and their associated costs, liabilities and risks, continues.

Catch22 is a £57 million turnover charity that proudly self-identifies as a social business. It was formed through a merger in 2008 and operates primarily in the government service markets of education, children's social care, justice and employability. In 2015, about a year after the launch of the government's 'Transforming Rehabilitation' initiative to outsource probation services, I interviewed its CEO, Chris Wright. The outsourcing approach for probation had been different again from those used for the NHS, Waterways, Rail and others, and was designed to be far more competitive from the outset. The Ministry of Justice explicitly encouraged third-sector organizations to participate in the competitive bidding process, which, as Wright explained, meant investing quite a lot of money, but none of the four social-sector organizations that made it through the selection process were awarded any contracts.

'I think that was largely as a consequence of the dissonance,' he explained, 'between the policy intent and rhetoric, and the reality of government commercial procurement, which ultimately wanted to shift all the risk to the provider. Clearly, if you haven't got a very large balance sheet, it's very difficult to carry that risk.' As it transpired, they may well have dodged a bullet.

In the 2017 Annual Report[6] from HM Inspectorate of Probation, Chief Inspector Dame Glenys Stacey was deeply critical of the programme, saying: 'I question whether the current model for probation can deliver sufficiently well.' 'I find it inexplicable that, under the banner of innovation, these developments were allowed.' 'We should all be concerned, given the rehabilitation opportunities missed and the risks to the public if individuals are not supervised well.' 'Regrettably, none of government's stated aspirations for Transforming Rehabilitation have been met in any meaningful way.'

In March 2018, following a review,[7] the Public Accounts Committee similarly found that the programme had not achieved its stated aims. According to the committee's Labour MP Chair, 'The so-called "rehabilitation revolution" is showing worrying signs of becoming a contracting catastrophe.' Three months later, a Justice Committee report,[8] led by Conservative MP Robert Neill, reinforced those conclusions. According to Neill, 'The Transforming Rehabilitation reforms had some laudable aims but these reforms have failed to meet them. We are unconvinced that transforming rehabilitation will ever deliver the kind of probation service we need.'

In February 2019, three of the community rehabilitation companies (CRCs) operated by contract-winning Working Links went into administration. Shortly afterwards, the Ministry of Justice decided to end the CRC contracts 14 months early, in 2020. The National Audit Office (NAO) reported[9] the following month that the incremental cost of stabilizing the CRCs and cancelling the contracts would approach £500 million. In the report's conclusions, the NAO was scathing:

> The Ministry set itself up to fail in how it approached the Transforming
> Rehabilitation reforms. Its rushed implementation introduced significant
> risks that its chosen commercial approach left it badly placed to manage.
> The consequences of these decisions are far-reaching. There is little evidence of
> hoped-for innovation and many of the early operational issues, such as friction
> between the NPS [National Probation Service] and CRCs, persist. Transforming
> Rehabilitation has achieved poor value for money for the taxpayer.

In May 2019, it was finally announced that the management of probation services would be renationalized.[10]

It's possible that the inclusion of non-profit expertise within the mix might have helped mitigate some of the problems, although it's more likely that the charities had a narrow escape from what has turned out to be a fatally flawed approach. Whatever the reality, the environment for most service delivery charities today is dramatically different from the one they enjoyed before the crash. Charities operating in any of these markets today need to be far more astute and make more informed, hard-nosed strategic choices about where to participate, where to invest and where to exit.

These choices aren't easy; they demand deep considerations about beneficiaries, the mission of the charity, the financial and reputational implications. They also demand different ways of thinking about the opportunity, different skills and more sophisticated decision-making processes.

The initial expansion of these service markets explains, to a large degree, the sector's overall commercial income growth from 2000 to 2010. But that market's contraction in the years since has done nothing to slow earned income's trajectory. So, what has been driving that growth through the second decade? What is the other half of the story?

The answer is broadly a combination of two trends: international development and domestic social enterprise. In both areas, charities are pioneering a powerful shift towards market-based models and commercially derived income.

Social enterprise as a concept has been around for many years but is now rapidly gaining ground. In the social justice arena, for example, there are myriad charities, social enterprises and ethical businesses creating training and employment opportunities for ex-offenders and for people living with addiction, mental health issues and disabilities who would otherwise find it difficult, if not impossible, to get jobs. And most of those enterprises aspire to, and in many cases succeed in, running on a purely commercial model.

The House of St Barnabas, for example, was originally founded as The House of Charity in 1846. It supported the homeless and destitute, providing at one time as many as 800 beds in its remarkable baroque building in Soho Square, until regulatory and financial pressures finally forced it to close its doors in 2006. Seven years later it reopened as a fashionable and exclusive private member's club, but House of St Barnabas is by no means a normal club. Continuing its 160-year-old purpose, it remains a registered charity, but one that now operates as an out-and-out social enterprise, using the profit it derives from its membership subscriptions, its bars, restaurant and events to support cohorts of previously homeless people into stable employment. Its beneficiaries, referred to them through a network of homelessness charities, get training and paid work in all aspects of the club's operations, before being supported to find jobs within the hospitality industry, often through the club's own membership network.

Social enterprise is not just for start-ups; it's also becoming an increasingly important element for many existing charities. It might be conferences and training courses for autism professionals, consultancy and materials for medical researchers, support for global retailers whose store staff are also carers at home, and so on. Enterprise can offer a sustainable model for both income and impact, and, increasingly, established charities are also recognizing that the opportunity is constrained only by their creativity.

A second, separate trend of commercial concepts rapidly gaining importance is within international development. For much of the 20th century, the developed world's approach to developing-world crises was based around relief – the 'give a man a fish' part of the timeless proverb. But over recent decades that approach has been transformed, and the predominant model now is to 'give a man a fishing rod', or more often, a portfolio of microloans, training and infrastructure investments, to set up a thriving fishing economy. Activities around employment, livelihoods and economic development are increasingly being included within most development charities' programmes, and indeed, in their broader 'theories of change' (more about this in Chapter 4).

These activities and models aren't just about alleviating suffering; they represent an holistic approach to creating social change. They help to stabilize societies and lay the foundations for new infrastructure investment, and more often than not, they are predicated on achieving sustainable economic development. In turn, that makes them more attractive to a broader range of funders and, increasingly, investors.

In September 2018, the British Asian Trust, along with an extensive coalition of partners (including UBS Optimus Foundation, Tata Trusts, the Michael & Susan Dell Foundation, Comic Relief, the Mittal Foundation, the UK Government's Department for International Development, the Lawrence Ellison Foundation and British Telecom), launched an $11 million Education Development Impact Bond (DIB). This was just the latest example of the growth of social finance and impact investing as powerful financial instruments for charities.

At a social finance event[11] a year before the DIB's launch, Sir Ronald Cohen, described by some as the father of social finance, explained how DIBs demonstrate the principle that 'you can link a social improvement to a financial return'. He went on to say, 'We've all heard of the hidden hand of markets. But if he [Adam Smith] were alive today, I think he would agree that bringing impact, alongside risk and return, brings the invisible heart of markets to guide their invisible hand.'

Speaking at the same event, Richard Hawkes, British Asian Trust's CEO, reinforced the interrelationship between charity and business that sits at the heart of social finance and the British Asian Trust. '[It's] been in our DNA since we were created as an organization: the desire to challenge the accepted way of doing things, to think boldly about the way that we approach our work, and really importantly, to apply business principles to the work that we do.'

The model for the Trust's DIB is to raise investment capital from a variety of philanthropic and commercial sources, and to invest those funds, through a lead charity, in entrepreneurs and others on the ground, who can come up with innovative approaches to improve learning outcomes across India's education system. While the mechanics and sources of repayment are different, the goal for DIBs, as with micro-loans and the broader social investment market, remains a measurable impact *and* measurable financial return.

This represents a profound evolution from the traditional image of charities, but the benefits of that shift are manifold. Harnessing markets and entrepreneurs, lending and investing instead of giving, has the potential to be far more sustainable, because it creates a repeatable, often profitable model, and provides a more powerful route to developing agency, empowerment and self-determination.

Mark Salway is the Director of Social Finance at the Centre for Charity Effectiveness within London City University's Cass Business School.

Salway was heavily involved in Care International's development of their peer-to-peer lending platform (online at lendwithcare.org), and as he explained to me:

> Receiving aid is not always great for self-esteem. If you ask the people what they want, nine times out of ten, it's to help themselves. Often, they want money to build a business or consolidate existing debt. It's a loan that they will want to pay back and will be focused on doing so above all else. At Care International our loan default rates were tiny – and they still are. It's a huge source of pride for most people who take a loan, when they get to the day that they've paid it all back. And for us too, because then we can lend that money to someone else.

In Bangladesh, the Grameen Bank has been a pioneer of micro-finance. In October 2018 alone, it lent $279 million to the poorest of the poor, mostly through community groups, over 95 per cent of whom are women. In the same month, it received the exact same amount, $279 million of repayments from existing loans. Over its 40-year history, it has lent a cumulative total of over $26 billion, mostly with interest, always without collateral, entirely based on trust; almost $24 billion has already been repaid. This is a commercially sustainable model that has had enormous social impact directly, and indirectly, as a demonstration of what an ethical, market-based model can achieve. In 2006, the bank and its founder, Muhammad Yunus, were jointly awarded the Nobel Peace Prize.

A few years ago, I was at a reception for the fundraising industry. The speaker was a high-profile, well-respected fundraiser of many years' standing. During his talk, he explained, to the audience's surprise, that the best way to grow rice is not to grow it in water, but to plant the rice seed in dry earth and to soak it on a regular, but infrequent basis. Apparently, by using this technique, rice yields can increase six-fold, transforming the lives of rice-farming communities. He talked with pride about how, in one of his projects, a trained expert would visit a village to teach and demonstrate these principles to the women and children, and would return a year later to a warm welcome, and stories of new saris, new school books and a chance for them to finally move from absolute poverty to relative prosperity.

He concluded with an appeal: all that it cost was £12 per family to change their lives, and the more we could engage donors with these stories, the more communities we could transform. All of that is true, but it's an approach that's tightly constrained by the capacity to recruit affluent Western donors. It will take an awful lot of banquets, soirées and auctions to transform agricultural practices across half a continent.

What if there was a business model behind the training: one that recouped a small percentage of the extra income from that improved yield? Could that return pay for a local recruit to pass on that training, radiating out the impact from that initial seed? Could the future of fundraising be to focus on planting more of those seeds in different communities, kick-starting a locally driven, commercially powered model to expand the benefits in a self-sustaining way? Is there a micro-finance model that could increase the reach and pace exponentially?

I suspect there is, and I'd be amazed if, five years on from hearing that presentation, one hadn't already emerged and started to dramatically accelerate that change. Micro-finance, livelihoods and social investment are powerful development tools, but they aren't the only ways that business principles are being used by international charities. Some are creating waves of change, not by developing new local markets, but by reshaping established global ones.

In the environmental space, Greenpeace has had some success in using campaigns against individual corporations to drive them to the table, then offering to help them change practices to reduce their environmental damage. It hasn't always been plain sailing; in May 2018, Greenpeace cancelled its engagement with Indonesian conglomerate Sinar Mas Group for allegedly reneging on its environmental policies. Greenpeace had helped it to draft those policies in 2013, after two decades of campaigning had forced the business to work with them and to finally pledge to stop clearing forests and peatland on Sumatra. Nevertheless, for those intervening years its work had a tangible impact, and I doubt this setback will deter Greenpeace from continuing to develop the model.

International non-profits such as Fairtrade Foundation, Forest Stewardship Council and Rainforest Alliance have arguably had a greater impact by using their certifications and marketing platforms to raise consumer awareness and to affect buying behaviour, which in turn exerts commercial pressure on businesses to effect change. Their impact has changed forestry and land management practices, supply chains and supplier contracts, public awareness and customer expectations. They've had broader indirect impacts as well. Hotel Chocolat is just one example of the multitude of responsible, ethical start-ups whose success has partly been enabled by the awareness those charities raised. The impact of market-based actions often reaches far outside the immediate footprint.

Each of those non-profits found ways to harness the power of consumer markets to deliver lasting societal change, and many UK organizations are using similar market-shaping tools to raise the bar on ethics and standards closer to home. The National Autistic Society, for example, has an independent certification team. It's managed entirely separately from the NAS portfolio, and it not only audits NAS's own schools, but can be commissioned by other organizations, including direct competitors of NAS. The team will audit their schools and offer advice, consultancy or training, whatever is needed, to bring them up to the same quality standard, and provide them with a valuable recognized accreditation which they can use for marketing and sales.

Each of these very different types of initiative, developed by charities internationally and domestically, demonstrates the vast range of ways that individual impact and sustainable change can be delivered by working with markets, by embracing business principles, by making a desired outcome commercially attractive and economically beneficial. These are new models and, to realize their potential, they all demand a much deeper understanding, within the charity community, of business and commerce.

Without that understanding, the journey is difficult and can often be dangerous. I know many charities who have aborted their attempts to develop commercial income, or failed expensively by going about it in the wrong way. It's those experiences that have prompted me to write this book. But if the sheer number of successes and the scale of their impact demonstrate one thing, it's that it absolutely can be done.

This book will show how non-profits can succeed in these endeavours. To be successful, aspiring leaders first need to bring two things to the table: commitment and focus. Commitment is essential, to work through the potential cultural resistance and the inevitable skills gaps that will stand in the way of success. But focus is critical, both in terms of leadership focus, to keep commercial development high on the agenda, and organizational focus, to keep the breadth of activities tightly controlled. Indeed, the road to commercial income has various pitfalls, but lack of focus is one of the deadliest.

## Finding your focus

In August 2017, the Royal National Institute for the Blind (RNIB), one of the UK's biggest charities, announced that it was drastically reorganizing its commercial division, RNIB Solutions, with the likely loss of around 50 jobs.[12] The division was set up to try to reduce the charity's deficit, but instead of contributing a profit it had lost money every year. The 2017 loss alone was £4.2 million on a turnover of less than £17 million, and the total loss over its three-year existence was around £10 million.

Following the announcement, I wrote an article for *Third Sector* magazine[13] on what I thought had gone wrong, the most obvious of which was uncontrolled proliferation caused by the absence of any strategic focus. Following the article, I was surprised by the number of e-mails I got, including from people who'd worked within the organization at the time, who thought that I'd hit the nail on the head. Quite an achievement, considering they'd never been a client, I had no insider contacts and I'd only ever visited their offices once.

In an interview with the same magazine later that year,[14] incoming Managing Director of the Solutions Division, Scott Lynch, confirmed: 'What happened is that our ambition was greater than what we achieved... Some of the income we got was one-off in nature – consultancy, for example. When I joined earlier this year it became clear that some of the income wasn't repeatable and the scale of it wasn't what we expected.' Lynch's plan was to refocus Solutions on just five key areas, adding: 'You should diversify cautiously. You can't add lots of cost into your business if you are not sure about the income that will be coming in.'

My 'diagnosis at a distance' wasn't a complete shot in the dark, nor was it some mystic ability to see through walls. It was simply that it's a pattern I've seen again and again in charities who want to expand their trading, and nothing I'd seen, in their actions, press releases or annual reports, suggested that RNIB was any different.

Three months prior to that announcement, I'd been working with an organization that had been born out of an 'arm's length' body of government that was abolished with the introduction of the Care Standards Act 2000. That body's replacement, named Skills for Care, was formed as an independent charity and company limited by guarantee, with the aim of improving skills in the care sector.

Skills for Care's purpose is to help social-care employers get, keep and develop their workforce. As Sharon Allen, the CEO, explained, 'We know that a competent, confident and values-led workforce is the key to quality care and support.' Thus, the organization has a wide remit: to support all social-care providers across all sectors (of which there are over 21,000 operating across England) with recruitment and retention, standards and learning, leadership development, and provision of workforce intelligence, all aimed at the outcome of improving the quality and standard of care.

When I first met the team in 2015, most of Skills for Care's income still came from an annual contract with what was then the Department for

Health (DH), but that contract, in line with austerity across public expenditure, was already experiencing annual reductions. To address this fall in income, Skills for Care had decided to explore social entrepreneurship, aiming to generate income from other sources and through other means that might ensure that investment in the social-care sector was not impacted by the cuts.

My remit was to help them to make the shift, more consciously and proactively, from 'We do what the DH pays us to do' to 'We do what the sector needs, some of which the DH will pay us to do'. It was clear from the outset that this would be something of a cultural journey for the people within the organization, that they'd need a broader set of skills themselves: to listen even more closely to employers within the sector; to see them as clients and customers, rather than simply beneficiaries; to help them define the outcomes they wanted; and to offer them solutions on a proper, commercial basis.

That need for change became even clearer when, as we started the engagement, they shared with me the list of commercial ideas that the team had identified so far. The list was long, running to at least five pages, and it was almost entirely what I'd describe as line-extensions: add-ons to something they already did, that some employers had paid for in the past.

For example, they'd had success with some training courses, and although they had been priced primarily to cover costs, they'd been very well received by those who attended. So, on the list there was a big section on other courses that they could run. Similarly, they'd had some success with a number of publications and workbooks, where they'd covered their costs and got very positive feedback, so another section listed a range of new publications and workbooks they could develop. And so on, down the list.

As I started to ask more questions about what they'd done in the past, and how they'd come to these views, a consistent pattern emerged. The early courses attracted plenty of interest and attendees, but when they started adding more, fewer people came. In fact, some of the suggested courses on the list had been tried before and not broken even. The view from the proposers was that they'd not marketed them very effectively, and if they'd invested more in publicity, they'd have got better attendance. And that may be true, but it was a big assumption, and one that was probably based more on hope than evidence.

Training courses in most disciplines can often be picked up at rock-bottom prices. They're frequently offered by ex-professionals, sole traders, the retired and part-timers, as much because of their passion for the topic as for the pocket money they earn. In much the same way, RNIB's Braille translation and website services, for example, were competing with private individuals, small social enterprises and dozens of shoestring operators, all of whom were passionate about providing the same solution. Without any real differentiation, an innovative capability, a far deeper understanding of client needs and so forth, they were never going to make much money. Nor, in effect, would they bring any fresh impact to the landscape that others weren't already bringing.

The fundamental flaw is not the choice of markets or activities; it's a lack of clear, strategic focus on the unique value an organization can provide. In the case of Skills for Care, the entire initial list of ideas came from the question 'What else can we do?' rather than 'What is it that customers really need but don't seem able to get?'

I have to say that, to their enormous credit, the team at Skills for Care responded incredibly well to my feedback and observations. They got it, they threw themselves into the project, and they ended up with a small, focused set of big opportunities that probably only they could exploit, and that did indeed have the potential to dramatically change their clients' lives for the better.

This is what I call the 'more is less' paradox: the idea that by doing more and more low-value stuff, you will make more and more money, whereas the converse is more often true. Line-extensions are attractive because they're easy to deliver and they feel low risk: another training course, another workbook, another conference. But each one adds complexity, increases workload and will invariably provide diminishing returns. Every new extension eats up more and more time to develop, market and maintain, and will probably create less and less incremental value and impact. That's what created the RNIB situation, which the charity itself summed up in the announcement as 'highly complex, very manual, built on outdated infrastructure and neither efficient nor scalable'.

Diversification of income has been a hot topic in the charity sector for many years, as a way to mitigate the risks of over-reliance on one or two major sources of funds. Commercial trading is a great way to spread that risk, to diversify away from those dependencies. But within the commercial sphere, diversification can be a double-edged sword: the more things you try to do, quite often the less successfully you do any of them. Charities are especially at risk from over-diversifying commercially, because they rarely have the management experience and expertise to keep a grip on that evolution, to define the boundaries, to drill into performance on a regular basis, to keep asking the big questions about their portfolio and their customers.

Questions like: Who will be the paying customers? What are the problems we can help them solve? And why should they choose us?

They're simple questions, but their power is in the way they shift the focus away from 'What else can we sell?' and onto 'What is the unique value we can provide?' It's often easy to tell from which of those two questions an organization has developed its thinking. The first question ends up with marketing that essentially says 'These are all the things we can do', the second with a message that reads 'These are the valuable outcomes we help you achieve'.

I keep in pride of place on my website a short video, which I recorded with the executive team at Skills for Care to help them launch the rollout of the changes that we agreed and shaped during our project together. In it, they talked about the approach they'd developed, the need to engage with and listen to employers, to adapt to their situations, to help them define the outcomes they wanted to achieve, and only then to start talking about the ways Skills for Care might help them.

In 2015/16, the year in which we first met, Skills for Care reported income from their trading subsidiary of £1.5 million. By the following year that income had grown to £2.1 million and had grown again to £2.5 million the year after, providing an incremental, unrestricted contribution to the charity of approaching £2 million across the three years. That growth came about because the entire team focused on a small number of things that could make the biggest difference and add the most value to the organizations they were there to serve.

Meanwhile, as late as 2017, RNIB Solutions was losing twice that amount each year, and its website was sagging under the weight of an ever-growing list of things they could do. Don't get me wrong; they can do great things. But as a client, I'm not interested in how many things you can do, I'm interested in the value you can provide to me.

## The road to success

St Bernard of Clairvaux once wrote, 'L'enfer est plein de bonnes volontés ou désirs', a phrase which has likely morphed into the modern aphorism, 'The road to Hell is paved with good intentions'. Hope is not a plan; nor will a goal, without a plan, be anything more than a pipe-dream.

Earlier, I said that the two ingredients necessary to make any of the ideas and techniques in this book effective are commitment and focus. If a journey of 1,000 miles begins with a single step, then the first step on this journey is commitment. The second step is to create focus, a process that is not unlike strategy development.

That process has three broad phases. It starts with outlining an ambition, a future that fits with the potential of the organization and the changing needs of the wider world; a direction of travel, and some sense of the boundaries: things that you'd look at, and things that you wouldn't – principles that will shape and inform the process. All of those things will probably get challenged, and may get changed as the process unfolds, but they provide a starting point and some way-markers to help along the route.

The next phase is one of expansion, of opening up the opportunities and alternatives that could be explored, developing ideas and insights about how that future could be realized, identifying where commercial opportunities might exist, or could be created, and what would need to be true in order for the organization to realize them. It's a creative phase, and in later chapters I'll introduce some creative tools that can help.

The third phase was once described to me, by a client, as like 'wrestling an octopus'. It's where all those ideas and options are combined, filtered, refined, shortlisted and coalesced into a small number of focused areas for development, and ultimately, a programme of work that can be delivered. However, the process does not stop there.

As Prussian Field Marshall Helmuth von Moltke the Elder once said, 'No plan of operations extends with any certainty beyond the first contact with the main hostile force.' Or as Mike Tyson put it, 'Everyone has a plan 'till they get punched in the mouth.'

Innovation, by definition, means doing something that hasn't been done before. If your process is successful, the programmes that emerge will all be about doing things you've not done, working in ways you've not worked, selling to customers you don't yet know, in markets that may not yet exist. Many of those initial ideas will fail, or at least will need to change significantly if they're to succeed. It's essential to understand this, right from the outset, to design an approach that will be able to adapt to the unknown.

One of the most underappreciated and counterintuitive facts about market research is that, in general, the more easily you can find information about a market, the less attractive that market will be. The more information there is, on customer behaviour, competitive dynamics, market valuations and the like, the more it demonstrates that the market is established, it is already being supplied, customers have predictable buying patterns, and it will take something very special, something highly distinct and extremely appealing, to chip away business from those pre-existing relationships. That's not to say it can't be done, but it's not easy, nor is it without risk. Simply adding another copycat alternative into an already competitive market is as unlikely to further a charity's purpose as it is to generate a profit.

Conversely, a lack of data could point to a much bigger opportunity. Where information is hard to find, where a suspected need appears to be unmet, where competitors are hard to identify, let alone to assess, if an opportunity does exist, it's far more likely to be impactful, profitable and realizable. There is still a risk, but of a very different type.

Whether it's about an innovative idea that will disrupt an existing market or an unproven idea that will create a new one, hitting a home run with the first swing is a rare event. Hence, the ideas that emerge from the process will need to be refined in the crucible of reality, to be metaphorically punched in the mouth by potential customers.

The output from the strategy process will therefore not be a single, well-thought-through investment case to build a multi-million-pound income stream. It will be a small number of tightly defined, but flexibly planned projects, to explore an opportunity, to prototype ideas and engage them with customers, to refine, and potentially redefine, what the real opportunity may be. It will be a suite of high-risk, small investment requests, to finance and resource an exploratory phase, with the aim of establishing some customers, creating a proposition for them, proving a delivery model and building a business case, validated by experience, for a larger investment to scale it up.

It's important to set this expectation, right from the outset, because it goes against the grain for each of the three groups that need to get on board with it. In most organizations, the Board will want a robust business case before they sign off investment, the staff will want to know what they can offer before they talk to customers, and the leadership will want confidence that if they put good people on it, their time will pay off. The reason so many charities get stuck when trying to develop commercial income is that meeting all three needs is like squaring a circle – it's logically impossible.

New ideas, new innovations, are inherently uncertain and are rarely right first time. Boards will need to allocate funds 'at risk' to explore an opportunity that may not prove viable. Staff will need to get out there without a defined offer, to have unprejudiced conversations with potential customers, who themselves may need help to understand what they want and what difference it would make. And the leadership will have to live without firm evidence for the opportunity, and instead, put their faith in the process and the team to find the unmet need and suggest, often quite novel, solutions.

It sounds risky, but it's far less risky than the 'big-bet' or 'do-nothing' alternatives. By starting small, staying focused and working flexibly, the individual risks are small and easily managed, the potential rewards are huge, and the chances of ultimate success are, in my experience, pretty high. As one of my clients said, a month into our project to explore an opportunity, 'We've learned far more in the last four weeks, from just getting out there and trying to make sales, than we got from six months of research. And it's sounding more and more like there's a market for us here, even if it's not the one we thought it would be.'

In Chapters 2, 3 and 4, I'll look at where those big new ideas can come from. For charities that already have some commercial income, Chapter 5 looks there as well, with more ideas about how to secure it, grow it, and get more impact and contribution from it. All these ideas then feed into Chapter 6, where I walk through the full process for opening them up, focusing down on the best, and turning them into a comprehensive commercial strategy.

## Endnotes

1  Seamark, M (2014) Fury over £234,000 Salary of the Top Boss at Save the Children: Charity Chiefs' Huge Wages Must be Reined in, Say MPs, 2 February 2014, *Daily Mail*, www.dailymail.co.uk/news/article-2550648/Fury-234-000-salary-boss-Save-Children-Charity-chiefs-huge-wages-reined-say-MPs.html (archived at https://perma.cc/RGJ7-GPSH)

2  Save the Children International (2013) Trustees' Report and Financial Statements for 2013, *Save the Children International*, www.savethechildren.org.uk/what-we-do/policy-and-practice/resource-centre/annual-report-2013 (archived at https://perma.cc/HR7E-M9R4)

3  Save the Children (2013) Results for Children: Annual Review 2013, *Save the Children International*, https://www.savethechildren.net/sites/default/files/libraries/Annual%20Review_2013_English.pdf (archived at https://perma.cc/X95X-EM6J)

4  DMGT (2014) Daily Mail and General Trust plc Annual Report, 30 September 2013, filed with Companies House 17 February 2014 (see page 20 for DMG Media performance and page 52 for Directors' Remuneration), *DMGT*, https://www.dmgt.com/~/media/Files/D/DMGT/reports-and-presentations/100-31110.pdf (archived at https://perma.cc/8RP2-N6J9)

5  The National Spastics Society (1952) *The Chance of Their Lives* [film], A Sovereign Production

**6** HM Inspectorate of Probation (2017) Annual Report 2017, *HM Inspectorate of Probation*, www.justiceinspectorates.gov.uk/hmiprobation/corporate-documents/annualreport2017/ (archived at https://perma.cc/R6TK-J4L5)

**7** UK Parliament Public Accounts Committee (2018) Government Contracts for Community Rehabilitation Companies Inquiry, 21 March 2018, *UK Parliament Public Accounts Committee*, www.parliament.uk/business/committees/committees-a-z/commons-select/public-accounts-committee/inquiries/parliament-2017/contracts-community-rehabilitation-companies-17-19/ (archived at https://perma.cc/4M2H-UY5G)

**8** UK Parliament Justice Committee (2018) Transforming Rehabilitation, 22 June 2018, *UK Parliament Justice Committee*, https://publications.parliament.uk/pa/cm201719/cmselect/cmjust/482/48202.htm (archived at https://perma.cc/YL42-KQGA)

**9** National Audit Office (2019) Transforming Rehabilitation: Progress Review, 1 March 2019, *UK National Audit Office*, www.nao.org.uk/report/transforming-rehabilitation-progress-review/ (archived at https://perma.cc/LLW5-CP4F)

**10** Financial Times (2019) Probation Services Renationalised after Chaotic Privatization, 16 May 2019, *Financial Times,* www.ft.com/content/c5935758-7730-11e9-bbad-7c18c0ea0201 (archived at https://perma.cc/9KY4-VWXY)

**11** Highlights of the London speeches are available on the British Asian Trust's website and on YouTube, entitled 'In conversation with Sir Ronald Cohen'.

**12** Cooney, R (2017) Jobs at Risk at RNIB after Commercial Venture Struggles, 22 August 2017, *Third Sector,* www.thirdsector.co.uk/jobs-risk-rnib-commercial-venture-struggles/management/article/1442632 (archived at https://perma.cc/NY8W-8HND)

**13** Drake, M (2017) What We Must Learn from the RNIB, 29 August 2017, *Third Sector,* www.thirdsector.co.uk/martyn-drake-learn-rnib/finance/article/1443042 (archived at https://perma.cc/RMQ2-SW2J)

**14** Kay, L (2017) Why RNIB Solutions Became a Problem, 5 December 2017, *Third Sector,* www.thirdsector.co.uk/why-rnib-solutions-became-problem/finance/article/1450105 (archived at https://perma.cc/BJG3-VRZB)

# 02

# Developing earned income

## Inspiration, ideas and perspectives

In 1931, Harry Beck was a 29-year-old temporary contractor, working at London Transport drawing electrical circuit diagrams. He showed one to the publicity department, suggesting that it might make Underground maps easier to read if they straightened the lines and spaced the stations more evenly apart, like in a circuit diagram. He was laughed out of the office.

Two years later, a persistent Beck finally persuaded them to trial a print run of 1,000 copies. They sold out within an hour. Within six months there were a million in circulation and almost every tube system in the world now uses Beck's circuit diagram style of map. Beck didn't invent circuit diagrams, they'd been around for decades, but he was the first to think of using them for maps.

Anyone who has studied innovation will have come across the story of James Dyson and the bagless vacuum. Dyson famously made around 5,000 prototypes of his cleaner before he landed on the model that worked the way he wanted it to. That's almost five times as many prototypes as Edison's team went through for the lightbulb. What few people know, however, is that cyclonic extraction, Dyson's central innovation, had already been around for a century. Dyson first came across it while visiting sawmills, where cyclones have been used to extract and separate sawdust since at least the 1920s. His innovation was to bring it into the living room.

Likewise, Steve Jobs didn't invent the laptop, nor did he invent the MP3, the touch screen, the mobile phone or the digital camera. All those things were already out there, in different industries, in different disciplines. He was the first to start packaging them together, into the iPod, iPhone, iPad; the innovations that collectively make up over 70 per cent of Apple's turnover today.

Each of these stories illustrates two things. First, the most innovative ideas rarely land perfectly straight out of the box – some ideas will be immediately dismissed; others will take a great deal of work and a great many iterations and revisions before they succeed. Innovators must be flexible and resilient, because they may be in for a long haul. Second, the best ideas probably already exist, somewhere else, in a different form, being applied in different circumstances, in a different way.

Inspiration is everywhere, which is why, throughout this book, I will draw examples from charities, social enterprises and commercial businesses alike. For any given non-profit, some of these examples will have obvious application, others will never be relevant. But there will also be some that sit in between, in the gap of creativity. These are the radical ideas, the transformational possibilities, like the circuit diagrams that inspired the Underground map. These are the ones I would encourage the reader to seek out and harvest, not to the exclusion of the obvious, but to raise the level of ambition and to broaden the scope for innovation.

One of the biggest barriers in any innovation process is our tendency to stop looking once we've found a couple of ideas we like. Overcoming that tendency can be harder than it sounds, particularly as we become older and more experienced in our fields. When my kids were young, if we were travelling, I'd often use games to provide us with temporary relief from the boredom-inspired, incessant bickering with which they would invariably fill any vacuum. The one of which I'm most proud was: 'Give me 10 different ways you could....' Be it a brick, a balloon or a paperclip, they would have to come up with 10 different ways you could use the object.

Over time, their indulgence of me lessened, and responses shifted from the creative 'You could use a paperclip to scratch your initials on a cup, link them into a chain, wear one as an earring...' to the more brusque 'Clip 10 different lots of paper together... now can I play on your phone?' It was good while it lasted, but within that small vignette is a broader illustration of how most of us develop from the open-minded inventiveness of inexperienced youth to the decisive impatience of adulthood.

I regularly host seminars for groups of leaders, where I'll present a specific problem or case study and split them into small teams to come up with solutions. Invariably, each small team proposes a single solution, a 'silver bullet' they believe is the best way forward. The irony is that the teams will all have come up with different silver bullets, from which I draw out and share three lessons: there are many ways to crack a nut; they are rarely mutually exclusive; and we all have an overwhelming tendency to stop thinking once we've come up with the first one that could work.

Partly this is because we love silver bullets. In fact, we find them so attractive that once we think we've found one, we genuinely can't bring ourselves to wipe it from our minds and come up with another equally good alternative – even when we're asked to. I've lost count of the number of proposals I've seen submitted to executive teams and boards, which purport to have three 'options' but only actually have one, bracketed by the 'do nothing' option and the outrageous alternative.

But it's also because once someone tables an idea, the rest of the team tend to focus on discussing it: reinforcing with their own thoughts and experiences or critiquing with contrary views. Particularly if a suggestion receives a negative response, it becomes riskier for members of the team to make more of them, and more comfortable to discuss those already on the table. Like the silver bullet dynamic, the aversion to likely critique forms another bias within groups, which stifles new ideas.

There are simple ways around these biases, but they need to be consciously adopted. A series of private calls with attendees prior to a workshop can generate a variety of ideas to kick-start a group conversation. Splitting a workshop into two parts, with the first session explicitly focused on generating as many ideas and alternatives as possible, and the second part exploring, critiquing and combining them, can help enormously in removing the temptation to close things down too soon. And the parallel-working example from earlier – splitting the bigger group into small sub-teams to work on the same question – is another route to expanding the ideas and options.

There's no shortage of creative exercises like these, and more are being added to facilitation handbooks every year. These techniques aren't mutually exclusive; most are mutually supportive. The point is that they need to be deliberately introduced because without them the combination of silver bullet temptation and instant critique tendency will hugely constrain the potential of the endeavour.

Whether in everyday leadership decision-making, product and service design or commercial income development, creativity is an important muscle that needs regular exercise. Being able to look at a situation from different angles, to hold in one's head a variety of different solutions, to look for alternative paths even after a serviceable one has been found – these are things we seem to do naturally as children but steadily discard as we grow up, and yet they underpin our capacity for creative thinking and collective imagination, a capacity that fuels innovation and is essential for strategy development.

Every non-profit is different, every social challenge unique, and there is, quite literally, an infinite variety of possible solutions that non-profits could employ. Every day new social enterprises are springing up around the world, testing out new ways to fund and sustain change through innovative business models. It would be a quixotic venture to even attempt to cover all of them, and the examples I use throughout the book are by no means exhaustive. They are included simply to illustrate the potential from a particular approach, or of adopting a particular perspective.

Three of the most valuable perspectives for developing earned income and deploying commercial models for social impact are shown in Figure 2.1. The central section where all three circles overlap, labelled with the number 1, includes those opportunities that fit well with the mission, play to the organization's unique capabilities and meet a valuable need that customers will pay for.

FIGURE 2.1  Three perspectives for commercial opportunities

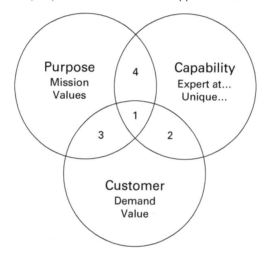

The concept of the three circles is not new, indeed it forms a central part of the thesis of Jim Collins's influential 2001 book, *Good to Great*.[1] Collins locates his 'sweet spot' for business success within the overlap of three circles: what you're passionate about, what you can be best in the world at, and what 'drives your economic engine'. There are problems with Collins's model, which I'll return to later in Chapter 5, and the simpler, more generic version in Figure 2.1 is a far more useful and appropriate model for non-profits. In addition, Figure 2.1 embraces the reality that some of the best strategic opportunities might not sit in the sweet spot at all.

Not all earned income needs to be 'on-mission'; new capabilities can be bought-in or developed if the opportunity is good enough; and different business models, particularly multi-sided models, can offer solutions where there's no obvious paying customer. The fewer circles that an idea fits within, the harder it will be to realize, and ideas that only fit into one circle are probably best left untouched. But that doesn't mean that all ideas that fall outside of the centre shouldn't be pursued. Many of the most innovative and value-creating ideas can be found in sections 2, 3 and 4 of the chart.

Over the next two chapters we will explore ways to work in all four of the labelled areas, but any earned income a non-profit is already generating is most likely to sit in sections 1 or 2, and when seeking new opportunities, looking at what you already have is a good place to begin.

## Expanding from a successful base

In 1957 Igor Ansoff had a paper called 'Strategies for Diversification' published in *Harvard Business Review*.[2] In the opening paragraphs of his article, citing the prior four decades of US corporate performance, Ansoff observed: 'Just to retain its relative position, a business firm must go through continuous growth and change.' Based on his research, he then argued that: 'There are four basic growth alternatives open to a business. It can grow through increased market penetration, through market development, through product development, or through diversification.'

Those alternatives became the four quadrants of what's now known as Ansoff's Matrix, and it's a useful conversation starter because it outlines a few simple generic routes to growth.

To illustrate by example: consumer goods business Colgate could grow its sales to a single household by getting more of the family using its tooth-paste, or getting them to brush their teeth more frequently, both of which might be easier than winning the custom of a household that's happily buying Crest, or launching into a new country that's never heard of Colgate. It could develop new products: floss, mouthwash, breath spray, to sell to the customers it already has; or it could move into a whole new category, as it did when it acquired Hill's Pet Nutrition in 1976. Colgate grew Hill's dog and cat food business to a turnover of over $2 billion a year and continues to own and operate it today.

The ease of expansion, into new customers, markets and geographies, or into new products, categories or industries, obviously varies by degree. Launching a new flavour of toothpaste is easier than an entirely new cate-gory of oral care products; and expanding into a new city in the same country will be easier than targeting a new type of consumer in a new country. Distance matters, and the further a business moves away from what it knows, the greater the challenge and risk, but potentially the greater the opportunity from both a money and a mission perspective.

The Scout Association, for example, is going through a golden period of expansion, driven by a strong sense of mission, which includes, as a priority, the desire to increase diversity within the movement. In an era when children and teenagers are becoming increasingly hard to disengage from electronic games, the number of young people within the UK Scouting movement has grown every year for the past 13 years. Between 2014 and 2018, membership of young people (6–18 years old) increased from 445,000 to 475,000, and a great deal of that growth has come from deliberate expansion into new demographics pursuant to their diversity aims, specifically: girls, different religious groups, and deprived communities. Over that same four-year period their market expansion strategy saw the number of Scout sections in areas of deprivation grow from less than 170 to over 830, while overall revenue grew from £28 million to £34 million.[3]

Market expansion is just one of Ansoff's routes to growth, and a non-profit example that illustrates all four might be a charity that works within a prison to help rehabilitate a particular type of offender. If its reach is limited to one segment of one prison's population, it can increase penetration by making a pitch to extend its service to more offenders within the prison, or it can expand its market by pitching its service to other offender management institutions. Alternatively, it might aim to expand from a product perspective, by building a broader portfolio of support services around the offender before and after release. Or it could diversify into the education system, using its knowledge to help reduce the likelihood of at-risk teenagers offending.

None of those growth opportunities is mutually exclusive, but each brings its own risks and demands different capabilities to be honed or developed: from relationship development and sales expertise, to new services and skills within its delivery teams. For the education opportunity, it might even make more sense to partner, merge with or acquire another non-profit that's already operating in the target market and has some of the skills and relationships that will be needed.

Partnership can be a lower-risk way to explore areas that are further away from core business, and working with another organization that already has the presence, market knowledge and expertise can offer a strong foothold from which to begin; one which, if the opportunity proves real, can develop into a longer-term alliance or merger.

As many leaders and commentators have observed, there are a great many charities, and plenty of them have big overlaps in their operations. It's often assumed that the sector would be far more efficient if it were consolidated through more mergers and acquisitions (M&A), and that may be the case. It's also assumed that it would be more effective, but that's less likely to be true. Often, it's the smaller charities that have the freedom to innovate, the bravery to go for the game-changing ideas, and the intimate local knowledge required to flex and adapt their work to the needs, not just of a community, but to the individuals within it.

The business world would be immeasurably poorer without the continual wave of start-ups and the myriad small businesses that make up a vibrant, creative and growing economy, and the third sector is no different. Parts of the non-profit sector are undoubtedly inefficient and would probably benefit from mergers, but efficiency alone is not a good enough reason.

Alex Skailes is Director at the Centre for Charity Effectiveness at Cass Business School, part of City University of London, and lectures on M&A in the sector. As she explains:

> We all know that the charity sector is widely diverse, and some non-profits can be more effective by keeping their independence. But when you look at other areas, like medical charities for example, there are many different charities all working in a similar area to find a cure and all struggling to get funding, to attract skilled trustees, and to get the best talent. It's therefore hard to see why they wouldn't create more value within a shorter timeframe for their beneficiaries by joining together.

Increased value for beneficiaries is the non-profit equivalent of increased value for shareholders, which should be the driver of M&A in the sector. But as the Good Mergers Index, produced annually by the Eastside Primetimers consultancy, shows most years, third-sector M&A activity tends to be driven more out of financial distress than the opportunity to grow impact. There are notable exceptions: Breast Cancer Now was formed through what's considered to be one of the sector's most successful recent mergers, predominantly because both of its predecessors recognized that delivering the key steps required to eliminate breast cancer would benefit greatly from one single voice with a wider reach, one single organization working with pharmaceutical companies, one centre of excellence within the UK. Consolidation for greater impact was similarly a key driver in the merger of Age Concern and Help the Aged, which formed Age UK in 2009 and, again, has been widely judged a success.

Other mergers have added beneficiary value by integrating pathways to enable a joined-up journey. Skailes shared with me the example of the Prince's Trust's 2011 acquisition of Fairbridge. The Prince's Trust works to help young people sometimes in difficult, often complex circumstances to access education and employment. Fairbridge offered outward-bound experiences to build self-confidence and self-awareness, which is often an important developmental step on the journey. Bringing the capabilities of both organizations together, vertically integrating through the supply chain, creates far more flexibility and provides a broader, more seamless and cost-effective approach, which serves to increase beneficiary value. As Skailes explained, 'For organizations such as Fairbridge, it was about putting the needs of their beneficiaries ahead of the continuing existence of the organization.'

An analysis of charity sector M&A, to support or challenge the view that value creation is a far more successful basis for a merger than cost reduction, has never been done, but within the commercial sphere, plenty of research has been carried out. Most M&A fail to deliver the anticipated gains, and almost never generate the expected efficiencies. The *Harvard Business Review* (HBR) has been publishing articles with tools and techniques to help improve the success rate of M&A for decades. Most of them begin with statistics from recent studies showing that between 70 and 90 per cent of M&A fail. And despite all of those articles, the numbers have barely moved since HBR began quoting them. Other assessments range between 50 and 85 per cent failure rates, and most conclude that the aggregate shareholder return from all of this M&A activity is negative overall.

On the flipside, the fact that 70 per cent or so of mergers fail means that the other 30 per cent succeed. In general, that's because they're aiming for far more than efficiency gains. One of those comparatively successful M&A ventures began in 2012 as a strategic alliance between US drugstore chain Walgreens and UK-based Boots. This followed many years and many attempts by Boots to break into the United States. By the time the final transaction went through in December 2014, the value of their combined shares had almost doubled.

Combining their supply chains did drive efficiencies, but it also dramatically extended their reach, particularly in the supply of pharmaceuticals through Alliance Boots' wholesale operations. The combination of their product and store portfolios also enriched both propositions and helped to drive top-line growth, particularly the rollout of Boots' premium brands across the Walgreen estate. It's undoubtedly helpful when the combined costs are lower after a merger, but it's even more helpful when the combined customer offer is far greater than the sum of its parts.

A strategic partnership is often a good route towards a merger, allowing both parties to explore the opportunities before they commit. And the merger with Walgreen did, indeed, enable Boots to successfully break into the United States – not an easy task for a retailer to accomplish on their own, even one with a strong track record of entering new markets.

In the early 1990s, Tesco developed plans to enter a new customer market: time-poor metropolitan urbanites, living and working in high-rent areas that had been, until then, unbridgeable gaps in its Superstore map. The two small-store formats they developed were Tesco Metro, for cities, and Tesco Express, designed for petrol station forecourts. For six years, Tesco worked on testing, refining and rethinking the models. By 1999, they had opened just 40 more Metros and 16 more Expresses, but that slow, thoughtful process paid dividends over the longer run. Once Tesco had proven the model, they picked up the pace dramatically, and in 2006 Tesco opened its 650th Express store.

On the back of that success, in 2007 Tesco announced it would be launching another new format in another new market, this time on the other side of the Atlantic. Tesco had spent two years researching the US market, including posting an entire research team to live and shop on the West Coast for a year. The result of that research would be 'Fresh and Easy', a new type of Tesco with a much fresher, healthier product offer, and in November 2007 they opened the doors of their first six stores in California.

Despite the first stores losing money, by April 2008, just six months later, Tesco had expanded that portfolio tenfold. By April 2010, Fresh and Easy had grown to 145 stores and lost £165 million in the year, yet CEO Terry Leahy announced another 50 store openings. Two months later he quit the business. In 2012, with spiralling losses, Fresh and Easy halted its rollout. The following year, Tesco closed 50 of the stores and paid an estimated £150 million to offload the rest of the estate. In all, Fresh and Easy cost Tesco over £1 billion in less time than it had taken to develop the Express format.[4]

It might have been easier had Tesco partnered or merged its way across the Atlantic, but the biggest misstep was not in deciding to go it alone. Other retailers have made it across successfully, and Tesco certainly had the capability. The biggest mistake was in ignoring the approach that had succeeded before, one that challenged their market research with real-life experience, that tested their hypotheses to destruction, and that developed and proved the proposition before throwing money at it. The financial impact of that hubris brought one of the UK's most successful businesses to its knees. Nobody gets it right every time, but this was an incredibly expensive way to get it wrong.

There is no value whatsoever in growing a business that's losing money, and the greater the scale, the more difficult it will be to fix. This is true whether targeting a merger, developing a brand-new venture or simply growing an existing one. For a non-profit, the growth opportunities that are closest to its current activities, whether winning new customers or adding new services, may seem as if they're lower risk. But that's only the case if the organization can deliver them efficiently and make enough profit to reinvest in its scale and its people. In Chapter 5 I will talk in more detail about how to improve business performance.

The point here, and one of the key lessons from the Tesco example, is that if the business isn't working well, it needs fixing first before it can be scaled up. Similarly, merging two organizations that are in financial distress won't magically solve their inability to make money.

The other lesson is that, however tempting it may be to rush into a new market opportunity, the further it is away from the core business, the more numerous the assumptions and the greater the need to test and validate them at the outset. Risks can't be avoided on the way to success; in fact, the greatest successes often come from the riskiest endeavours. In 2018, the world's six highest-valued companies were Apple, Amazon, Alphabet (Google), Microsoft, Facebook and Alibaba. All six started out by bringing new products and services to markets that were either entirely new to them or had previously not existed. Every one of them succeeded by taking risks.

Throughout the rest of this chapter and the next, we will look at opportunities that come from each of the three perspectives – the three circles in Figure 2.1, from commercializing capabilities and assets to developing business models for free and subsidized services, from the customer and beneficiary perspectives to the mission and social change. Each of these perspectives should provoke new ideas, and few of those ideas will come without risk. Risks are inevitable in any worthwhile endeavour, but they can be managed, and in Chapter 6 I will outline a process for managing those risks and developing the big opportunities, no matter how risky or how far they are from the core.

## Commercializing capabilities

There are so many ways that charities can earn income that it's often hard to know where to start. The simplest perspective to begin with is to look at the capabilities, assets and resources that a charity has, whether that's a physical building, a network of relationships, a rare expertise and so forth, and to look at how those assets could be used to earn money.

The question, from this 'capability' perspective, is therefore: 'We know we have these assets; we need to think of ways that we can package them up such that somebody will want to pay for them.' And that 'somebody' can often be a very broad church.

A charity that specializes in providing counselling, for example, might sell that service as a block contract to a local health provider, or as a short programme to an individual or a family. The marketing, pricing and administration might be different depending on the paying audience, but it's the same core service.

If some of the service users or beneficiaries are of working age, the charity could develop a case for employers to fund programmes for their staff; a case built on the fact that coping alone with a difficult and distracting personal situation will inevitably impact an employee's work performance. The value to the HR team might be improved employee wellbeing or staff satisfaction, but the value to the operations director might be a million-pound increase in productivity and a six-figure saving on recruitment costs.

Finding the right buyer and building the right investment case can have a huge impact on profitability, even though it's the same service being bought by the same company to deliver the same outcomes for those who receive it. The individual customer is different, their value equation is different, and if the marketing and the language of the sale are changed to suit them, the price can be dramatically different as well. The charity could commercialize its expertise further by training HR professionals in particularly high-risk businesses, documenting and licensing their unique counselling approach, providing audits and assessments, certifying the company's counsellors, providing a 'badge' for the business to recognize and publicize its commitment to the mental health of its people and so on.

If their counselling is sufficiently different from their competitors, maybe uses a different model or has dramatically better outcomes, they could protect their intellectual property and franchise the model to other non-profits or commercial providers. They could build a network of practitioners across public and private sectors, run events and conferences, partner with industry associations and establish themselves as the unequivocal experts in their niche.

Any of those things could bring in revenue, providing funds to subsidize counselling for those in no position to pay, and combined they would attract other experts and collaborators to carry out further research and capacity building. The more seriously the charity invests in developing its expertise in its niche and improving its outcomes, the greater the potential. The only constraints are the charity's confidence in that expertise, and its ambition to improve lives beyond its own immediate reach.

The NSPCC operates one example of this model. Having invested in research around child protection and safeguarding for many years, in 2009 the NSPCC formally launched its training and consultancy services to proactively share that learning with as wide a range as possible of other organizations working with children. Under the NSPCC Learning banner, the commercial model is both tiered (some things are free and others available for a fee) and flexible (the NSPCC has a ring-fenced fund to subsidize organizations that can't afford to pay). It's a model that allows the NSPCC to choose how profitable or otherwise it wants the service to be, and it generally chooses to run it at a net loss. In the 2016/17 financial year, for example, the Society invested £4.2 million in the service and recovered around £3.6 million in fees.

Skills for Care occupies a similar position with their social-care expertise, but unlike NSPCC they make a profit on their training and consultancy. However, both organizations share the same underlying philosophy, that their distinct capabilities provide tangible value to the organizations they work with, and by teaching others, they can extend their impact indirectly, far beyond their own footprint. And for both, it's the commercial, revenue-generating model that allows them to fund and scale that impact far further than they could afford to, if the cost rested solely on the charity itself.

Many charities maintain strong connections with professionals in their fields, or with the organizations that employ them, but few have invested in turning those networks into active communities with a desire to collaborate, learn and invest in their own development. NAS, for example, supports and moderates a vast online forum, hosting threads and conversations between thousands of autism professionals, from academia, education, health and social care, and many other sectors. They have turned their network into a valuable and distinctive asset, which gives them the capability to hear the ongoing conversations, to understand the gaps and needs of the community and to create and market conferences, training and events that will add genuine value and be well worth paying for.

Expertise is not the only non-profit capability that can be commercialized, but it's one that can offer a great deal of value, and it's often the one that's entirely overlooked. The single biggest barrier, in my experience, to building this type of commercial income is confidence. Confidence that there is genuine value in their expertise; confidence that they can deliver an event or a service of a professional standard; confidence that others will not just pay a fee, but will generate their own financial return; and above all, the confidence to set a price and stick to it.

Charging a fee is the ultimate test of the value delivered, and it's invariably the case that the more people pay for advice or education, the more likely they are to implement what they have learned. Probably the most consistent feedback I get from non-profits with whom I've worked in this area is the appreciation they gain about the value of what they have to offer.

Beyond the professional expertise that comes from their work with beneficiaries, non-profits may have 'functional' expertise they can rent out to other organizations. That might be providing HR or accounting services, managing financial transactions or looking after IT infrastructure. This isn't easy income for many charities – it requires a high degree of professionalism and the ability to deliver a consistently good level of service – but for larger organizations that already have formal service agreements between their central functions and their operational teams, this can be a relatively straightforward next step.

Some non-profits combine those head office services with renting out spare space in their buildings. Some have gone as far creating local charity and social enterprise hubs, providing flexible office solutions complete with IT and telecoms infrastructure. Others simply rent out spare desks, meeting rooms and larger spaces for events, with add-ons ranging from catering and AV equipment to professional conference services.

The deafblind charity Sense has taken that model a step further, developing an asset specifically to offer shared services. Touchbase Pears is a multi-purpose centre set up by Sense in Selly Oak, Birmingham, which opened in 2017. The aim was to combine Sense's West Midlands presence with a broader local community hub, and to attract other similar charities and social enterprises to co-locate within the building to increase collaboration and joint working. Tenants include Action on Hearing Loss, Forward Carers, RNIB, Adage Dance School and the NHS.

Sense has relocated its regional offices to the site and uses it as a base to deliver a wide variety of services and draw in a broad mix of income types. Social care and college services attract local authority funding. Its arts and sports programmes are funded in a variety of different ways and involve collaborations with the other tenants, and with organizations outside the building ranging from local care homes, theatres and arts venues to the Warwickshire Cricket Board and the Royal Birmingham Society of Artists.

Touchbase has a clear social purpose: it continues to strengthen local provision and deepen relationships with Sense's local partners, but at its heart it is a sustainable business. The café, conference and events facilities operate a fully commercial model, and their income, combined with the rent from other tenants, underpins the enterprise. Right from the outset, Sense built links with the regional Chambers of Commerce, involved KPMG in developing the model and the marketing, and installed a director-level finance professional to work on-site and manage the overall commercial performance.

## Leveraging a charity brand

One of the most valuable assets for many charities is the brand itself, and it's one that many charities have successfully used to generate earned income. That can be through developing branded products, licensing the brand, or commercializing it for cause-related marketing.

The Scout Association's branded clothing and accessories, which range from casual trousers to watches and cufflinks, is one example of commercializing a logo, but using a charity brand to differentiate goods for resale is a concept as old as the hills, and the strength of the brand is always the key to its success. When the Lance Armstrong Foundation pioneered the branded rubber bracelet, Armstrong's personal brand value was enormous, as was the revenue generated by bracelet sales. When his career and reputation spectacularly crashed, unsurprisingly, so did sales of the bracelets.

Licensing a non-profit brand can be more contentious, because of the obvious risk to brand reputation if a licensing partner screws up or has dark skeletons in the closet, but this is largely a question of doing the right due diligence and agreeing the right contracts. Indeed, when a charity licenses its brand as part of a qualification process, as a certification of service quality or building accessibility, for example, not only is the risk reduced, but there is a potential mission benefit from the licensing process itself. The Fairtrade Foundation generates over 80 per cent of its income, more than £10 million a year, from brand licensing, entirely based on that philosophy, and many other environmental organizations have successfully commercialized their brands in similar ways, to influence corporate behaviour, raise awareness and further their missions.

Brand partnerships and licensing can also help to bridge gaps in capability, whether a charity's capability gap around products and marketing, or a commercial organization's capability gap around social impact. When bottled-water business Belu was set up in 2004, its founder, film-maker Reed Paget, wanted to create an environmentally friendly bottled-water business, and in 2006 it was the first bottled-water firm to become 100 per cent carbon neutral. The problem was, it was losing money hand over fist, and while it did generate around £30,000 for charitable purposes each year, that was far below the implied promise to consumers and, indeed, to investors.

When Karen Lynch took over as CEO in 2009, she changed the strategy and radically refocused the organization. Belu switched from selling to consumers to selling into wholesale, targeting hotels and restaurants before expanding into supermarkets. She also tore up its approach to delivering social impact directly, and reached out to a charity, WaterAid, to take that whole side of the business model off Belu's hands.

As Lynch explained a few years later in an interview with the *Telegraph*:[5] 'I was managing the due diligence to build a dam in Rajasthan. It's great to say we did that, but for every £1 spent, WaterAid has the bigger impact. And it takes away the worry about how we were being charitable – they're the country's best-known water charity.'

WaterAid is now mentioned in every piece of Belu's marketing, its logo is on every pack, and every year, every penny of Belu's profits gets donated to WaterAid. In 2018 alone, that amounted to £1 million, bringing the running total to over £4 million since 2011.

Cause-related marketing partnerships are another way to raise the profile of a brand and its mission, while earning income along the way. For many charities, this is about getting a place within a business's corporate social responsibility (CSR) programme. CSR teams might open opportunities for corporate volunteering or donations, charity days or fundraising drives. But extending those relationships beyond the HR department, into the marketing and product teams or across the entire executive, can unlock far bigger opportunities.

At Paris Fashion Week in 2018, Lacoste launched a three-year partnership with the International Union for Conservation of Nature (IUCN), with the release of a limited edition Save Our Species collection, replacing the iconic Lacoste crocodile logo with a portfolio of 10 different designs, each representing a high-profile endangered species. The limited run of 1,775 polo shirts sold out within 24 hours, having garnered 600,000 social media shares and double that number of impressions. All sale proceeds went to the IUCN Save Our Species fund, and regular IUCN donations quadrupled during the operation.

In an announcement[6] sharing the results, IUCN highlighted the campaign's success as illustrative of the untapped potential of business and non-profit collaborations. Their statement recognized that 'Solutions that encourage businesses to engage in species conservation beyond philanthropic support are critical to scaling up actions and results beyond 2020', at the same time emphasizing the need for shared values and asking any interested businesses to contact them.

Later that same year, Diabetes UK launched[7] a three-year partnership with soft drink manufacturer Britvic, with two aims: to raise £500,000 in corporate donations and to work directly with Britvic's employees, raising their awareness about diabetes, obesity and the responsibility of manufacturers. Their hope for the latter was to try to change the industry from the inside. In stark contrast to the IUCN, the response to Diabetes UK's announcement, in both printed and social media, was immediate and predominantly negative.[8]

Where Lacoste had been seen as a positive engagement with an ethically neutral but very attractive brand, Britvic was viewed as a questionable tie-up with an enemy of healthy lifestyles. Had Diabetes UK set a standard for Britvic to achieve, had they worked with Britvic to draw up a commitment that would underpin their relationship, perhaps they could have created a more compelling narrative to deal with the public reaction. Had they proven their ability to influence, developed a working model with smaller, less polarizing drinks brands before stepping out with Britvic, perhaps they could have made a stronger case. Whatever the reality, the public perception was that they'd sold the brand and received nothing but money in return.

It remains to be seen whether the potential hit on fundraising will be offset by the corporate income, and equally whether the partnership and education will have any lasting influence on the direction of Britvic or the wider soft drinks industry. If it fails on either count, however, what it shouldn't do is put others off corporate partnerships or cause-based marketing. What it should do is inform their choices around the risks of different partners. It should also encourage them to look at the more established models that could help secure their aims with less risk to their reputation.

Organizations like Fairtrade and Rainforest Alliance accept money from commercial partners in exchange for the use of their brand, but only after they've achieved the specific standards and criteria required for certification.

In the opening chapter I mentioned how Greenpeace worked with corporates who wanted to change practices, but only as long as they were meeting their commitments as set out in policy documents that Greenpeace helped them to write.

Across the non-profit sector there are countless examples of charities providing badges for organizations that are either working towards or have achieved some standard in line with the certifier's mission. For many earned income opportunities, but particularly those that involve leveraging the brand or working with commercial businesses, clear aims, a transparent framework, strong ethical policies and good contracts are all essential ingredients for avoiding the downside risks.

What all these examples illustrate is that there is a vast spectrum of opportunities available to non-profits based around the expertise, resources and assets that they already have. But what they also illustrate is that to commercialize those opportunities, and particularly to achieve their full potential, new skills and capabilities will invariably be required. Hence, the capability-based approach to developing earned income can only ever be a starting point. At some point, one must step outside of the comfort zone.

## Beyond capability's comfort zone

Ideas that sit outside of current capability, in section 3 of the three perspectives chart (Figure 2.1), may be harder in the short term, but they can represent the greatest strategic opportunities. Capability offers a head-start, but being constrained by, or worse, intellectually shackled to the current ones, is a limitation that can prove fatal for non-profits and businesses alike.

Throughout the 1980s and 1990s, video rental giant Blockbuster had been focusing on developing its own core capabilities, primarily its store portfolio and supply chain. In 2000, when a financially distressed Netflix offered itself to Blockbuster for sale, CEO John Antico quickly turned them down. In his mind Netflix, which was a mail-order DVD rental firm at the time, was niche, it was losing money and it didn't fit with the core capabilities underpinning Blockbuster. Without a buyer, the financial challenges drove Netflix to innovate an online streaming service, something nobody in the industry had the capability to do at the time. Meanwhile Blockbuster profitably sweated its assets, confidently building its scale and retail capabilities. The rest is history.

At the time, Netflix lacked the capabilities that would lead to its success, just as the counselling charity from earlier might lack many of the capabilities it would ultimately need to deliver its own ambitious vision. The big, strategic opportunity for the charity, as for Netflix, would sit squarely in section 3 on the chart and may take years to fully realize. That doesn't mean it's a bad idea; in fact it could be transformational, not just for the charity, but for anyone needing counselling.

The elements of a vision don't all happen overnight; indeed many of them may never happen. A vision can be shaped, steps sketched out, and building blocks of capability and enterprise developed and tested. Experience and opportunity will reshape the vision over time, but progress would be made, and revenue and impact would almost certainly grow along the way. Achieving only a fraction of the initial vision would be a significant step on from where the charity is now.

Partnerships to bring in innovation capabilities can be particularly valuable. The growth in hubs, hot-houses and incubators across all sectors is testament, not just to the rising interest in these models, but to their potential value as well. From the venture capitalists of Silicon Valley to the consumer goods giants of Wall Street, more and more businesses are providing intensive support for entrepreneurs, from idea to innovation to scale-up, in return for an interest. Often that's in the form of equity, but it could just as easily be intellectual property rights, an option to acquire in future, and so forth.

Various charities have adopted a similar philosophy, sometimes collectively, sometimes individually, although usually less formally. For example, in preparation for the Care Act of 2014, a partnership of various disability and special education charities collectively invested in setting up SENDirect, a social enterprise working under the umbrella of one of the consortium's member organizations, Contact a Family (since renamed Contact).

The aim was to develop an online platform to curate the 'Local Offer' for communities, somewhere local authorities and independent providers could advertise their services, and where users could find them, compare reviews, and book whatever they required. The commercial model was primarily based on listing fees and would stand or fall on its ability to drive traffic. This 'partnership-for-enterprise' approach reduced each of the participants' individual financial risk and removed the temptation to develop competing platforms. At the same time, the partnership funded and empowered a dedicated team to work autonomously and entrepreneurially on a solution, which successfully launched in early 2015.

Other non-profits have developed their own enterprise incubators. In February 2019, Catch22 launched a social entrepreneurship programme using just under half a million pounds of funding secured from the National Lottery Community Fund. The aim of the 'Incubate, Accelerate, Amplify' programme was to identify up to five social entrepreneurs whose early-stage ideas could fit with any of Catch22's four strategic areas of focus, and to provide them with the funding and support they would need to succeed.

As the CEO, Chris Wright, said at the launch: 'We can't change things for the better standing alone. We need new ideas, new leaders and new ways of working together. Our support doesn't have to be financial. There are lots of other assets we can share: infrastructure, scale, networks, contracts, credibility. It just takes imagination.'

Unlike in the commercial world, Catch22 has no stake in the enterprises, which may be appropriate considering the programme is largely grant-funded. But as a general principle, the more expert support an enterprise receives, the more likely it is to succeed rapidly, and that support costs money and resources.

It's not atypical for charities in the medical research space to develop joint investments with academics or businesses to help fund and commercialize research, and most of those involve some mechanism to pay back the charity for their investment and risk. In May 2019, the UK medical research charity LifeArc received $1.3 billion from the sale of a portion of its royalty interest in Keytruda, the trading name for the immunotherapy drug pembrolizumab.[9]

Whether it's tiered commissions or a joint intellectual property (IP) licence, milestone payments or a formal equity stake, finding a form of commercial agreement that works for all parties within an incubator-style environment can make the concept far easier to justify and much more sustainable to maintain. These types of partnerships can be a very useful approach in the short term, particularly as a way to test new ideas, but they can also create risks over the longer term, especially where a partner's expertise comes to underpin a prominent service or income stream, and the organization itself becomes over-dependent on that capability.

Age UK has developed a wide range of services for older people. The charity has a relatively broad mission and a large customer base who are, in the main, also its beneficiaries. Because of that close affinity, its commercial developments have been informed by its deep insights into the things they most need, often things that have been outside its capability to deliver. As a result, it has often brought in those capabilities via third-sector and commercial partners and, for the most part, this model works well for all involved, but occasionally that reliance on partners has caused problems, most notably with its energy tariffs.

On 4 February 2016, *The Sun* newspaper led with the headline: 'Revealed: How Age UK pocketed £6 million bung from E.ON and pushed expensive power deals to OAPs'.[10] *The Sun*'s story outlined the price disparities between Age UK's two-year fixed-term deal and the lower rates that had been more recently introduced, stepped into two short hit-pieces on the 'fat-cat' CEOs of both Age UK and E.ON, and seamlessly concluded with a campaign for readers to sign up for its own energy deal, claiming an average saving of £268 per family.

As the rest of the media picked up the story, some also observed that not only had Age UK Enterprises received £6.3 million commission from E.ON for the energy tie-up, but also £22 million from Ageas for insurance and £9 million from Dignity for funeral plans, collectively converting to an £8.2 million pre-tax profit which had been passed to the charity. Each of these deals had been developed to save money for Age UK's beneficiaries and most had been running without issue for years, but those few months of highly volatile energy prices opened the charity up to a barrage of hostile fire. It didn't help that, in the prior two years, E.ON had been fined £7.75 million for incorrectly charging customers and £12 million for mis-selling energy contracts. Reputational damage can be contagious.

Age UK immediately suspended the energy service, and the regulator, Ofgem, was tasked by the government with an investigation. Ofgem's report[11] concluded that Age UK had no case to answer, but the Charity Commission also took a close look, and while its report[12] also cleared the charity, it made a series of recommendations.

In response, Age UK created a separate subsidiary for financial services and independent living products, introduced much tighter ethical trading principles and renegotiated contracts accordingly, at the cost of a significant slice of commission. Financial services remain a valuable part of the Age UK enterprise, but they also offer a salutary lesson on the risks of operating in volatile markets, particularly where internal capability is lacking. And just as with Diabetes UK's partnership with Britvic, they further underscore the importance of having strong ethical criteria, choosing the right partners to work with, and negotiating the right contracts with them.

So far, we've looked through the capability lens at some of the opportunities it can offer and the constraints it can introduce. In the next chapter we will add further ideas from the customer perspective, which, as we will see, can often be more of a kaleidoscope than a single lens.

# Endnotes

**1** Collins, J (2001) *Good to Great: Why some companies make the leap and others don't*, Random House Business, London

**2** Ansoff, H I (1957) Strategies for diversification, *Harvard Business Review*, 35 (5), pp 113–24

**3** The Scout Association (2018) Annual Report and Accounts 17/18, *The Scout Association*, https://scouts.org.uk/media/974857/The-Scouts-Annual-Report-2017-18.pdf (archived at https://perma.cc/FC9J-9QAR)

**4** The final disposal cost was widely reported in UK media; for example: Butler, S (2013) Tesco pays out to rid itself of US chain Fresh & Easy, 10 September 2013, *The Guardian*, www.theguardian.com/business/2013/sep/10/tesco-strikes-deal-fresh-and-easy (archived at https://perma.cc/E9HQ-U8AS). All other statistics within this story were drawn from Tesco annual reports filed at Companies House from 1993 to 2013 inclusive.

**5** Hurley, J (2012) Belu Boss Shows Bottle for a Turnaround, 28 February 2012, *The Telegraph*, www.telegraph.co.uk/finance/businessclub/9109449/Belu-boss-shows-bottle-for-a-turnaround.html (archived at https://perma.cc/V75C-EAGY)

**6** IUCN (2018) From Awareness to Action – Lacoste's Support for Species Conservation Gets Real, 28 September 2018, *IUCN*, www.saveourspecies.org/news/awareness-action-lacostes-support-species-conservation-gets-real (archived at https://perma.cc/DE54-VPKF)

**7** Diabetes UK (2018) We've Joined Forces with Britvic in a Three-Year Partnership, 21 November 2018, *Diabetes UK*, www.saveourspecies.org/news/awareness-action-lacostes-support-species-conservation-gets-real (archived at https://perma.cc/DE54-VPKF)

**8** Spencer, B (2018) Diabetes UK Charity Is Slammed for Signing £500,000 'Blood Money' Deal with the Maker of Fizzy Drinks Tango and Pepsi, 25 November 2018, *Daily Mail,* www.dailymail.co.uk/news/article-6427819/Diabetes-UK-charity-slammed-signing-500-000-blood-money-deal-Pepsi-producers.html (archived at https://perma.cc/4FPJ-HV2E)

**9** Civil Society (2019) LifeArc Charity Raises £1 Billion from Sale of Royalty Interest in Immunotherapy Drug, 20 May 2019, *Civil Society*, www.civilsociety.co.uk/news/lifearc-charity-sells-portion-of-royalty-interest-in-immunotherapy-drug-for-1bn.html (archived at https://perma.cc/4ZQE-UQ3N)

**10** Jones, D (2016) Revealed: How Age UK Pocketed £6 Million Bung from E.ON and Pushed Expensive Power Deals to OAPs, 4 February 2016, *The Sun,* www.thesun.co.uk/archives/news/34227/revealed-how-age-uk-pocketed-6m-bung-from-e-on-and-pushed-expensive-power-deals-to-oaps/ (archived at https://perma.cc/B6AL-3WDZ)

11  Ofgem (2016) Statement on E.ON's Age UK Tariff, 19 April 2016, Ofgem, www.ofgem.gov.uk/publications-and-updates/statement-e-ons-age-uk-tariff (archived at https://perma.cc/J3UG-LPU5)

12  UK Charity Commission (2016) Case Report Age UK (1128267), 19 April 2016, *UK Charity Commission*, https://assets.publishing.service.gov.uk/government/uploads/system/uploads/attachment_data/file/517523/Age_UK.pdf (archived at https://perma.cc/TXQ2-QW6R)

# 03

# Customer-centred models

## Multi-sided business models

The most common model in the business world is where a buyer pays a seller and the seller provides something in return. Many service delivery charities, however, operate an indirect model, where the charity provides the service, the beneficiary receives it, and a third party, usually a local authority or government agency, pays for it. The third party also gets a service in return for the fee, in the form of expertise, reports, and the outcomes that contribute to its own aims and targets. SENDirect, the partnership-enterprise I described earlier, is a different example of this same 'two-sided' business model, with providers paying for listings and service users getting access to those listings for free.

Two-sided models aren't unique to charities. Many news organizations, both offline and online, are funded almost entirely by advertisers who pay for those adverts based primarily on the size of the readership. Games console manufacturers also operate a two-sided model. They charge customers for the console and charge licence fees or royalties to games designers for the ability to sell games to their customers. Microsoft traditionally takes a loss on its Xbox console business to drive uptake, making its profit on developer fees. Nintendo, in contrast, puts more focus on console innovation and sets its pricing to make a profit on both sides of the model.

Marketing and selling consoles to the end user is critical, not just for the direct income but for the revenue from games – the more consoles out there, the more people will buy games, the greater the potential market for games designers and therefore the more those designers will invest in developing top titles for the console, increasing its attractiveness to the consumer. Marketing and selling that opportunity to games designers is every bit as critical as marketing the console to end users. Without a strong portfolio of games at launch, nobody will buy the console. Thus, two-sided models demand a pragmatic balance. Both sides of the equation need focus, attention and care if the model is to remain sustainable.

There is a similar balance to be struck with non-profit models. A service delivery charity has to promote and sell its provision to the service's commissioner, but it often also needs to market and 'sell' the service to the beneficiaries, or, in some cases, to the intermediaries and referral sources that will drive the service's uptake.

If the charity can't reach and engage the people it needs to serve, it won't deliver the outcomes it's aiming to produce, and it will fail in its mission. On the other side of the model, if it can't reach and engage the commissioners with a compelling value case for the project, or if it fails to keep the relationship on track between contract cycles, it will not get the support, the flexibility and the funding when it needs it most, and it will similarly fail in its mission. If Nintendo only engaged with games developers when it was ready to launch a new console, its business model wouldn't last more than six months.

This is perhaps the single biggest opportunity for service delivery charities, and for any other non-profit operating a multi-sided model.

In the overwhelming majority of charities that I've worked with, the focus on understanding and building a relationship with the beneficiary is unquestionable – they know that hooking into *the beneficiary's* priorities, *the beneficiary's* ambitions, *the beneficiary's* situation is critical for achieving a desired outcome. And yet, it's rare to find anything like that level of focus on understanding and relationship building with the other parties involved in the business model, such as commissioners and referral sources.

More often, those interactions are reactive, perfunctory, and in many cases almost entirely transactional, and there are plenty of voices in the sector arguing that's exactly how it should be; that to put any emphasis on commissioners' needs will inevitably compromise the non-profit's focus on the beneficiary and lead to it simply chasing money. It is a view predicated on the belief that a non-profit organization has so little influence that it will bend to the commissioner's will, throwing its moral compass out of the window at the first hint of losing a contract. It implies the non-profit can't be a peer but must always be a supplicant in the relationship; that it could never have the skills and self-confidence to make the relationship work for the organization and its beneficiaries. It is a myth entirely based on fear and inferiority.

A strong peer relationship does not mean blindly doing what commissioners say in pursuit of income; it means the opposite. Relationship is influence, and the quality of a relationship with commissioners defines a non-profit's ability to influence direction and decisions, to raise the profile of needs and issues, to develop a shared vision while assuming the welcomed role of trusted adviser and critical friend. Another myth is that developing close relationships to influence commissioners will break EU procurement guidelines. It doesn't, as *The Art of the Possible in Public Procurement*,[1] by Frank Villeneuve-Smith and Julian Blake, very ably explains.

A deep, trusting and influential relationship, built with ethics, integrity and the mission in mind, will neither undermine independence nor distract a charity from its work with beneficiaries; it will actively enable both. Poor commissioning practices aside, this fear and misconception is one of the main reasons so many service charities are now in such financial difficulty. In a multi-sided business, each side needs quality attention if the model is to succeed.

World Jewish Relief began life in 1933 as the Central British Fund for German Jewry and was instrumental in the Kindertransport programme that evacuated thousands of Jewish children from Germany and Austria when the Nazis came to power. Following the war, it worked with refugees and Holocaust survivors, and when the Soviet Union began to break up at the start of the 1990s, it refocused its efforts towards the two million Jews living in the now former Soviet states, such as Ukraine, Belarus and Moldova. Changing its name to World Jewish Relief in 1994, it worked with marginalized and impoverished Jewish communities, providing straightforward relief to begin with before developing, in line with the evolving approach across the international development community, towards livelihoods, economic inclusion and more sustainable development.

Its initial livelihoods programmes aimed to develop skills and find employment within local Jewish businesses for single Jewish mothers living in poverty, but over time that expanded to working with the wider unemployed or underemployed Jewish community, to engaging with non-Jewish employers and, eventually, to tackling a broader swathe of unemployed non-Jews in its areas of operation. With very little, if any, state support for people looking for employment, World Jewish Relief's efforts were transformational: over 75 per cent of programme participants not only found jobs but were still in them 18 months later. Its results were so impressive that in 2015, it was approached by the UK government to provide similar support to resettled Syrian refugees arriving into the UK – an entirely non-Jewish group.

World Jewish Relief's CEO, Paul Anticoni, talked me through what he thought they'd brought to the UK context:

> The main thing, and this was a tough lesson that we'd learned the hard way in Eastern Europe, is that getting people ready for employment is only half of the job. The other half is building relationships with potential employers and ensuring you are putting candidates in front of them that meet their recruitment requirements.
>
> We need to understand what each employer is looking for, what makes a great employee from their perspective, and select and develop our beneficiaries to meet those needs. If you build the relationship, treat employers as clients and not as donors, there's lots of demand and lots of engagement. We've been pleasantly surprised at the interest shown by big businesses to recruit from among our refugee participants. Timpson have been outstanding but so have Tesco, Casual Dining Group, Waitrose and Marks & Spencer. All of them have reached out to provide training, work experience and ultimately employment to refugees.

In some ways, World Jewish Relief have returned to their roots, offering a new life in the UK for those displaced by war, and enabling the continuation of the long tradition of refugee communities making valuable and lasting contributions to British society.

The reason for World Jewish Relief's success is their overt recognition of the multi-sided model, of which the beneficiaries are just one side. The programmes aim to get refugees into employment within 18–22 months, providing the government with a rapid return on investment through employment instead of benefits. But the return that underpins their entire ability to deliver, for refugees and funders alike, is the one they offer to employers in the form of a pipeline of diverse, engaged and capable new recruits.

The House of St Barnabas I mentioned earlier operates a four-sided business model: the beneficiaries, the referral sources, the future employers, and the club members who pay for it all through membership fees, attending its regular events and performances, and frequenting its bars and restaurant.

The organizations that refer homeless people who are ready to join the cohorts are customers. For them, the House of St Barnabas offers a service that they need as part of the journey for their beneficiary. They want good outcomes, they want positive results, or they won't refer their clients in future, and without a carefully selected cohort of trainees, each of whom is ready to make the transition, the House's model will fail.

The trainees themselves are customers, requiring personalized support and education to pass through the programme. And the future employers are customers. Many of them are connected with the club through membership, but as employers, they're looking to the club to prepare and train good-quality recruits who are ready, willing and able to step straight into the ranks of their teams. The fact that only one side of the business model generates income is irrelevant – all four customer groups need to get tangible value from their relationship with the club, to be engaged with, understood and nurtured, if the model is to remain successful.

These cross-subsidized, multi-sided models aren't unique to non-profits. Historically, airline passengers paid for tickets and the airline flew them where they wanted to go. Over recent decades, however, budget airlines have transformed the market using multi-sided models to subsidize ultra-low prices. Most budget airlines would be bankrupt if they relied solely on ticket revenue as they make a significant operating loss on passenger fares, but other income streams and other sides of the model make the financials work. Baggage fees, priority boarding and seat allocation charges are the most noticeable, but other income streams come from things like in-flight advertising and commissions on linked bookings for taxis, parking and hotels.

These are business relationships that provide value by converting the airline's access to one customer group into a packaged service it can sell to other groups. They represent new sides built onto the traditional model, where new services are being provided to new customer groups to cross-fund the airline's core audience. In 2016, these 'ancillary revenue' streams generated £1.5 billion for Ryanair, subsidizing ticket prices to the tune of over £160 million.[2] Later in this chapter I'll look at three examples within the Indian healthcare system that take a similar approach, using tiered pricing, add-on services, ancillary products and so forth, to maximize profit from affluent customers in order to cross-subsidize those who can't afford to pay, thereby providing free health services to the poor and uninsured.

Whether the primary customer, or beneficiary, is receiving their service at a lower cost or entirely for free, none of these models can be sustained, let alone achieve their full potential, unless the customers on each of the other sides are properly looked after. Whether they're a client, a customer or a commissioner, the service they're paying for, the value they expect to receive and, above all, the relationships that underpin them need to be nurtured. This is not rocket science, which makes it all the more surprising that so few non-profits do it really well.

## The untapped retail opportunity

In 2018, there were an estimated 11,200 charity shops in the UK, collectively turning over around £1.3 billion a year, and generating almost £300 million of annual profit for the sector.[3] While those numbers were relatively static from 2016 to 2018, over the preceding eight years, charity store numbers grew by almost 25 per cent. Retail can be a lucrative business, and for some charities it's a major contributor of income.

Charity retail is very different from its commercial counterpart in many ways, but there are also big similarities, particularly when it comes to future opportunities and the potential direction of travel. They also share the same business fundamentals.

Prior to the shifts created by the advent of technology, the general rule of thumb for any form of retail, whether charity or commercial, was that there were five key drivers of performance: place, product, price, promotion and people. For charities, the impact of getting the right place, or store location, is the same as for any retailer, but the drivers of product, price and promotion work very differently in the two domains.

Most commercial retailers have extraordinarily sophisticated analytics to understand and tweak pricing, to manage product selection, store layouts and brand adjacencies, and to develop and optimize promotional campaigns. They can do that because they sell the same products in every store, and they collect vast amounts of transaction and customer data every day. Charity shops don't have that luxury: every store's merchandise is different and comparatively little data is collected, so most of the decisions come down to the individual store manager's judgement and skill. That is why the fifth driver, people, is paramount for charity retailers.

Because of those powerful analytics, commercial retailers place a great deal of emphasis on store compliance. Charity retailers still need standards, from financial control and health and safety to customer service and the in-store environment, but the prevailing culture is, by necessity, less about compliance and much more about empowerment and responsibility. Whether attracting high-quality donated goods or highly committed volunteers, whether pricing unusual items or promoting them on niche websites, it's largely the leadership and entrepreneurial qualities of the individual store manager and their team that ultimately determine success.

That complex remit belies a second, more fundamental difference between the two. Unlike their counterparts, charity retailers are operating a multi-sided business model. On one side are the shoppers: the customers who pay in cash and get goods in return. On another side are the people and businesses who donate them in the first place. They are paying, in the form of goods, for the service of taking stuff off their hands, enabling it to be reused, repurposed or recycled rather than thrown away or paid to go into landfill.

There are plenty of reasons people choose to give the goods to charity rather than the alternatives: there's the emotional connection, the opportunity to support the charity, the desire to do something good or sometimes simply the convenience. And all of those are valuable differentiators for the charity, but none of them detracts from the essential fact that goods-donors are 'paying' customers, accessing a different side of the business model, without whom the entire enterprise couldn't succeed.

Recognizing this multi-sided nature is critical when looking at the bigger opportunities a charity can derive from a retail presence, particularly in the context of its other operations. Many retailing charities also provide services to beneficiaries, or run information and awareness campaigns, but the crossover with stores rarely comprises more than a window poster and a leaflet rack. Most charities have activities for fundraising, building the supporter network and attracting volunteers, but the potential role of retail in recruitment is often underplayed. Integrating all these different sides of the model into a sophisticated and seamless customer-supporter journey has enormous potential for charities with aspirations to take a lead in the sector.

Charities are always in competition, not just with each other for income and donations. They're competing against other messages for share of attention, against other priorities for political influence, against other commitments for volunteers' time. In any competition, some will innovate, and their performance will raise the bar for everyone else. The rest will inevitably need to change if they want to stay in the game, but the opportunity that they've missed in the meantime is lost forever. A changing market creates leaders and losers, and it is vision and ambition that distinguish the two.

Commercial retail is a prime example. In 1996, Boots the Chemist had an online store before most other retailers had even thought about it. It was one of the first to launch an electronic loyalty card, to go mobile, to put iPads in the hands of its staff. Boots didn't wait until it needed to change, it changed because it wanted to lead. The leaders, like Boots, continually raised the bar on customer expectations. The others, the ones who took slower, smaller steps as the leaders pulled away, are either playing catch-up or have gone out of business.

Yet throughout that revolution, the charity retail sector has barely changed, remaining almost untouched by the technological transformation.

Less than 2 per cent of charity retail trade happens online, and few have systems that recognize or track individual stock items, let alone individual customers. Even fewer dare to dream of a system that combines a person's purchasing patterns, donated goods history, online, social, campaign and service interactions to gently nudge occasional shoppers into a committed, valuable and lifelong supporter or volunteer relationship.

The shift to online, and the resulting footfall decline in high streets and retail destinations, has created a powerful incentive for commercial retailers to change how they work. Physical stores remain a valuable part of the mix, as evidenced by Amazon's expansion into bricks and mortar, but they're increasingly being used by customers to click-and-collect, to drop off returns and occasionally to browse for ideas, while the transaction itself often happens online. In-store purchases are increasingly likely to be urgent or on impulse, with considered purchases more likely to happen at home, in the office, on the train.

Apple stores have shown one possible future template. There are no shelves full of stock; instead there are examples of items to test, to play and interact with, experts to provide advice and service specialists for after-care and repair. Walls aren't covered with racks of boxes, but with imagery that exemplifies the brand at its best. Elsewhere, some fashion stores are introducing screens that act as mirrors, allowing shoppers to virtually try on clothes and cosmetics, making intelligent suggestions on colours and shapes to suit the individual customer.

Replacing piles of stock with samples and service is also becoming an increasingly effective way to deal with the rapid expansion of their online inventories – for many retailers, that online range now extends far beyond the store's physical capacity to accommodate it all. It also helps to clear the environment for more visual displays, stories and artefacts that illustrate the broader range, the brand and its core purpose. Thus, the role of the store is increasingly becoming one of marketing and customer service, projecting the brand, connecting the customer to its story and heritage, building and deepening the relationship: the 'halo' of value it creates, in other channels and over the longer term, is every bit as important as the money it takes through the till.

Those specific technology examples might not suit a charity store, but the underlying philosophy of personalization, connection and brand engagement couldn't be more relevant. It might be projecting a much more overt image of brand and purpose, opening a window on where and how the charity operates, its investments in logistics or safeguarding, showing a shopper how their spend has been used or tracking how the items they donated have been refurbished, sold and turned into aid packages, subtly drawing them into campaigns, community events and out-reach, in a person-alized, step-by-step journey of education and engagement.

Or, it could simply be telling them the Oxford store has just got some lovely jeans in their size, a bag that would go perfectly with the dress they bought, or an old vinyl recording of a band they've been searching for. The technology is there for all the above; the halo of lifetime loyalty and support is waiting to be captured.

Lifetime relationship value is the big opportunity for all retail brands, and because charities have multiple sides to their operation, that value has the potential to multiply across all its sides and audiences. Individuals are one example; another could be businesses that donate excess stock. The three biggest challenges for charity retailers are: getting volunteers, getting quality donations, and covering the ever-escalating costs of doing business. Building deeper relationships with those corporate customers can help with all three and could potentially open the door to a broader partnership.

One of the big trade-offs for charity retailers is moving stock between stores. Most have a process for passing on items that haven't sold within a couple of weeks to a different store nearby. It works well where local clus-ters of stores sit in different demographic areas, but getting the right products in the right place over longer distances can be an expensive challenge.

Some of the bigger charity retailers have developed specific formats and fascias for different types of products: Oxfam has specialist books, music and homeware stores along with a number of boutiques and emporia; Sue Ryder has vintage and retro stores and its own 'Saved' range of upcycled products; British Heart Foundation has furniture and electrical stores offer-ing free collection and interior-design inspiration; Mind also has a furniture format, and has recently begun rolling out '£5 or less' discount stores. All of these are great formats, but to maximize the potential of specialist outlets, to get the right products in the best place across the estate, requires scale, storage and, above all, logistics.

Corporate customers could, with a strong enough partnership, offer support with all three – some of them will have fleets of vehicles, picking up and dropping off in towns and cities the length and breadth of the country. For some charities, that logistics challenge extends far beyond the store network. International non-profits need to ship aid, supplies, people and equipment, sometimes with extreme urgency, often to distant locations. But many of those locations aren't too distant from the fast-moving and efficient supply chains of large global corporations – sometimes the very same corporations that donate excess stock to a charity's stores back home. Whether corporate or individual, relationships that begin in stores can open up a world of opportunities.

The question is not whether all of these opportunities exist, or how large they could be, nor is it even how they could be achieved. The technology is already there. I can donate an item to Oxfam and get told when it's sold, how much it has made, and even collect Nectar points on the sale if I want to. There are dozens of retailers out there who probably know more about my interests and preferences than my wife of 20 years. The question is: does charity retail have the vision and ambition to pursue the opportunities? What is the incentive to change and invest? How strong is the desire to reap the rewards of sector leadership? In the context of charity store performance, these are critical questions.

The single most striking thing about charity retail is its resilience. In the past 50 years, charity shops have weathered no shortage of competitive storms: the emergence of giant supermarket chains, the explosion of the car boot sale, the rise of online second-hand specialists like e-Bay, the growth of the 99p stores, the boom in discount clothing retailers like Matalan and Primark and, to a remarkable extent, the ongoing decline in high street shopping. They have a dedicated and increasingly skilled workforce, and they continue to appeal to young and old alike, with university towns often among the best performers in a charity's estate. And it's that very success that makes it hard to justify and embrace radical change, just like it did with Blockbuster.

Pressures may emerge to force the pace. At the time of writing, the looming threat of under-funded local authorities looking to increase their revenue through rates is a key concern in the sector. Alongside it sit the chronic increases in costs, from utilities and salaries to training and regulations, and the perennial challenges of recruiting volunteers and getting enough good-quality stock.

My guess, though, is that charity shops will somehow cope with them all, just as they've always done. Those big strategic opportunities will only be realized through vision and ambition: one charity on its own, or a small group of partners, taking the initiative and investing to develop the next-generation operating model for their retail divisions. The subsequent dilemma, of whether to keep those systems to themselves, or to license them across the wider sector, would make for a very nice problem to have.

## Evolving an earned income ecosystem

At the far end of the multi-sided business spectrum are businesses like Apple, which pioneered the concept of the 'business ecosystem'. Once upon a time, Apple was a small, struggling niche player in the home computer market. The launch of the Mac in 1998 and the iPod in 2001 got great headlines, but it wasn't until the 2003 release of the iTunes platform that Apple's growth began to take off.

From a consumer perspective, the simplicity of being able to listen to music, catch up on podcasts and seamlessly sync them to an iPod was a breakthrough, and parcelling all that into the iPhone was a game-changer. From a business perspective, it opened a whole new revenue side to the business while making customers far more inclined to stick with Apple products so they could access their music purchases. The app store launch in 2008 added a new dimension to the customer offer, yet more 'stickiness' for the Apple platform, and opened another new side to the business model, this time targeting third-party developers and businesses.

Apple's evolution into services, from credit cards to video streaming, continues today, and collectively contributes one-eighth of Apple's total revenue: almost $40 billion a year. All of it is built on the strength of the iPhone and iPad business, and it's all designed with stickiness in mind: to bring customers into the Apple ecosystem and to keep them there.

Likewise, Amazon has achieved its own extraordinary success, by developing a broad ecosystem of interrelated services and products, tied together under its super-sticky Amazon Prime membership model, and all built on the foundation of its strongest assets: in Amazon's case, its retail platform and IT capabilities. These two tech-giant examples might seem a world away from non-profits, but there are big parallels.

The aspirational vision for the counselling charity discussed in Chapter 2 was based on the same principle: a broad ecosystem of different services aimed at different but overlapping customer groups, from contracts and personal services to training, certification and conferences, linked together with a sticky, community-based subscription model, all based on developing and commercializing their core assets: in their case, their unique expertise.

Some charities, like the National Autistic Society, already operate across many of those facets. The NAS's commissioned services support around 2,000 autistic children and adults, while also providing a testing and development environment for practices, which can then be shared with the sector. Their autism network numbers over 15,000 professionals and academics around the world, and their training, consultancy and conferences businesses operate nationally and internationally to share their expertise through a range of trademarked education programmes.

They've developed internationally recognized diagnosis expertise through their Lorna Wing Centres in Essex and Kent, and they run a global accreditation business with a register of almost 500 different services in the UK and Ireland, and in countries as far afield as Malta, Kuwait and Singapore. All of this is underpinned by their autism expertise, cultivated and codified within their Centre for Autism division.

Like most multi-sided businesses, not all the sides of the NAS model are profitable, but each side of the model contributes to the others. The scale of its services income gives it a national profile and generates a surplus that contributes to The Centre for Autism, research and IP development, and the autism professional network. The network generates valuable insights and connections, provides a global marketing platform for events and conferences, underpins its accreditation, consulting and training, and supports its brand positioning as *the* global expert. That positioning adds credibility to its policy and campaigning, which in turn helps to highlight its charity fundraising, which helps pay for its national helpline, charitable activities and so forth. All of this strengthens its position when bidding for services. This integrated ecosystem, built on a strong foundation of autism expertise, has enabled NAS to become a globally recognized brand that leads in most of its chosen niches.

The complex, multi-sided models of Amazon and Apple weren't born on day one; they were built, steadily and incrementally, through trial and error, with plenty of aborted ideas and missteps along the way. What they both have, however, is an unwavering focus on the customer.

In April 1999, shortly before the first 'dot-com bubble' started to burst, Jeff Bezos, Amazon's founder, gave a prescient interview to CNBC, which is still available to watch online.[4] The interviewer was interested in whether investors should continue to pick dot-coms for investment, but for Bezos, online or offline was irrelevant. For him, the customer experience was the sole deciding factor for success.

Bezos predicted that many dot-com businesses would probably fail, and the winners might be almost impossible to pick, but: 'I believe if you can focus obsessively enough on customer experience: selection, ease of use, low prices, more information to make purchase decisions... plus great customer service, I think you have a good chance.'

When pushed on the attractiveness of online retail to investors, Bezos undercut the question with incisive precision: 'They should be investing in a company that invests in the customer experience.' For Bezos, retail or wholesale, digital or bricks and mortar, it made no difference. The customer is all that counts.

A year later, in March 2000, the dot-com bubble burst and technology stocks, including Amazon, saw an average of 75 per cent wiped off their share price. It was a rough ride, but while countless others fell by the wayside, Amazon's relentless focus on customer experience paid off over the long term, just as Bezos had said it would.

Two years earlier, in 1997, Steve Jobs made a very similar case. He had just returned to Apple, having been fired as CEO seven years prior, when he appeared at Apple's Worldwide Developers Conference in May of that year. During his Q&A, he was aggressively challenged by an audience member about his views on some of the emerging technologies Apple had failed to adopt. His response to the question was a paean to the customer perspective:

> One of the things I've always found is that you've got to start with the customer experience and work backwards for the technology. You can't start with the technology and try to figure out where you're going to try to sell it. And I made this mistake probably more than anybody else in this room. And I got the scar tissue to prove it.
>
> And as we have tried to come up with a strategy and a vision for Apple, it started with 'What incredible benefits can we give to the customer? Where can we take the customer?' Not starting with 'Let's sit down with the engineers and figure out what awesome technology we have and then how are we going to market that?' And I think that's the right path to take.[5]

For Blockbuster, capabilities became a mental straitjacket, just as they had for Kodak a decade before and for others before them. For Jobs and Bezos, founders of two of the world's most successful organizations, capabilities were merely enablers, things to be developed or abandoned in the service of customers.

It's no different for non-profits. Developing commercial ideas from a capability perspective is a pragmatic place to start in the pursuit of new earned income, but it's not a perspective to stick with for long-term success. Looking from the 'customer' perspective, and in particular, the most important customer: the beneficiary or 'mission' perspective, is critical for creating an aspirational and sustainable vision for enterprise.

## The customer-centric strategy

Overlooking the Thames from its vantage point at the north end of Waterloo Bridge, Somerset House is a vast and magnificent Georgian edifice with a long and impressive history. It was built by the Duke of Somerset in the mid-16th century, it was the childhood home of Queen Elizabeth I, the residence of subsequent queens, and, later, the headquarters of the Parliamentary Army in London. It was redesigned by Inigo Jones, renovated by Christopher Wren, then completely demolished and rebuilt at the end of the 18th century.

Since then, it has been home to the Royal Society and the Navy Board, it's housed Royal Academy Exhibitions, the Admiralty, the General Register Office and Board of Taxes, and, for 150 years, the Inland Revenue. In 1997 the Somerset House Trust was established to manage and preserve the building. A decade later, when the Inland Revenue began its relocation to Parliament Street, it left the Trust with a lot of empty space and the need to replace a major income stream.

The initial estimates for commercial rent were disappointingly low and the Trust's recently appointed Commercial Director, Mark Hislop, thought it might do better if it could focus on a specific group of customers and craft a proposition that offered more than just office-space for market-rent. By carefully restructuring the environment and the financial terms, Hislop aimed to attract a range of complementary businesses and charities, for whom co-location with each other and the Trust would add significant value in itself.

For many of these small and often very young organizations, traditional rental agreements with big deposits and long break-clauses carried far too much risk, so the Trust offered agreements that dramatically reduced those risks and combined all the co-location benefits, in return for a higher rent. The approach proved a great success, not just for the Trust, but also for its army of new tenants.

The Trust had a valuable asset, but only by taking a customer-centric perspective, by understanding the needs and challenges faced by the specific customers it wanted to attract and by adapting its offer to add distinct and tangible value to that group was it able to maximize the potential value of the asset and develop the relationships it now enjoys with those customers. This is just one example of the value of a customer-centric approach.

Throughout this section, where I refer to the customer, it means any person paying for or using the product or service a charity provides. That includes beneficiaries, individuals or buyers within other organizations, irrespective of whether they are using paid or free sides of the business model. The 'individual' nature of the customer is important. Buyers within an organization will be buying on behalf of that organization, but they are still individuals, whether they have complete autonomy or are part of a committee. They have aims and aspirations, not just for the organization they represent, but for their departments, their professional roles and for themselves as human beings, and the better those goals and aspirations are understood, the greater the opportunity to provide value for them, to offer a better service and experience, and to earn income in the process. But those aspirations often take time and effort to uncover.

There's an apocryphal anecdote, often misattributed to Henry Ford: 'If I had asked people what they wanted, they would have said faster horses.' What customers say they want is very often coloured by what they have come to expect. Their imagination is directed towards extending what's already available, rather than considering very different ways to meet their underlying need. In Ford's case, he interpreted that need as the ability to move people and goods more quickly, hence the value proposition of motorized transport.

It's possible that, had he probed further into their desires and aspirations, seeking to uncover why that ability was so important rather than simply meeting the need, he may have drawn out deeper aspirations: greater efficiency, faster communication, the ability to instantly satisfy a customer, to spend less time travelling and more time at home – the same ambitions, in fact, that are still driving many of the commercial, technological and social changes we see today (Figure 3.1).

In 1998 Steve Jobs was quoted in *Business Week*[6] saying: 'A lot of times, people don't know what they want until you show it to them.' Some people have taken those words as an attack on the value of market research – to be fair, most of those people have been market researchers – but 'a lot of times' what Jobs said is true. We may know where we aspire to go on holiday next year, we may have specific ambitions for our careers or our children, but we rarely sit down and think: 'How could my life be immeasurably easier? How could we work differently to achieve far, far more? How could I get rid of the innumerable niggles and small pains in my working day that have been there so long I barely notice them?' And even when we do ask those questions, few people have the expertise to translate those ambitions into ideas for change, and to take that further into new products and services that could address them.

FIGURE 3.1  Getting beyond wants, to needs and aspirations

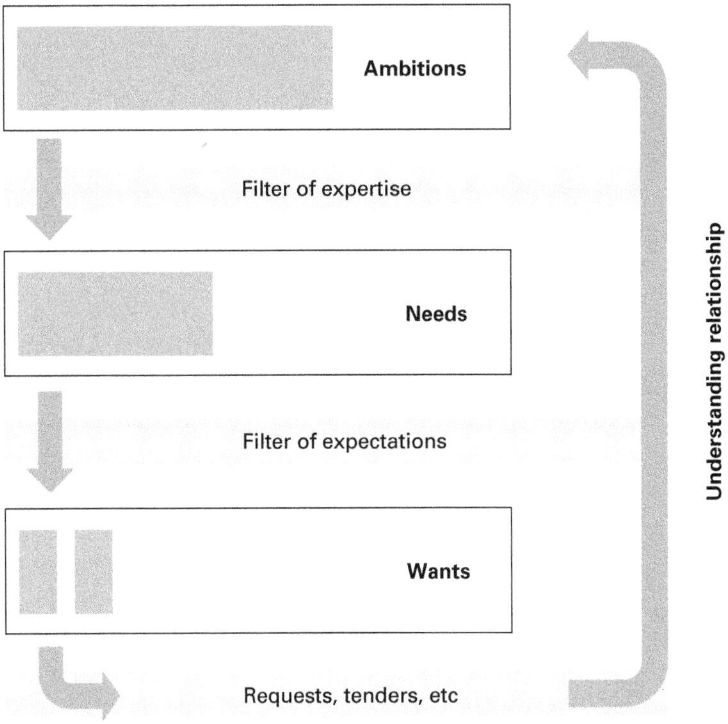

Without an external stimulus, like a dramatic change in circumstances, a trusted and enquiring friend, or a session with a coach or a counsellor, few of us make the time to even go there. And yet, those are the places that marketers and salespeople who want to develop commercial ideas need to get to with their customers. Those are the trusting relationships they need to foster if they're to uncover ways to provide more value. A broad understanding can help create some ideas, but it's those deeper conversations that draw out the real opportunities (Figure 3.2).

Developing ideas within the customer landscape is therefore an iterative process and, ideally, it's an ongoing one that will continue to provide new insights and ideas for years to come. The best customers to approach are usually the ones with the strongest relationships who are most likely to be comfortable opening up this type of dialogue. Their needs and aspirations will stimulate ideas for new propositions, which in turn may be relevant for other groups of customers who may, in turn, have other needs that stimulate other ideas and, thus, the landscape of opportunity expands ever wider.

FIGURE 3.2  Iterating new product and customer opportunities

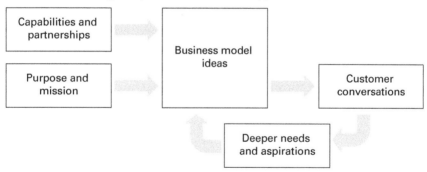

A large non-profit might decide to rent out some of the underused space above its retail premises, for example, targeting other non-profits working in similar fields. A deeper conversation might uncover the need for local IT hosting or the ability to deal with transactions, handle cash and banking. That might stimulate a broader concept of providing physical or even virtual office services to a broader range of non-profits and social enterprises, and perhaps even for start-up businesses.

These iterations can be captured visually in an opportunity landscape chart, which lists out the various customer groups, alongside the respective products and services that could fit their needs (Figure 3.3).

Further conversations with those new customers might uncover an opportunity to help with extending their reach through introductions or advertising, which might open up the conversation towards working with trusted businesses that are looking to market their services to the same audience, or potentially even to sell their products through the non-profit's stores or online platform.

FIGURE 3.3  Developing a landscape of opportunity from excess space

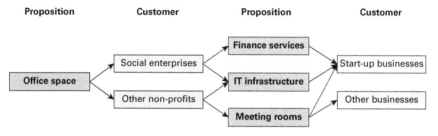

This iterative expansion, through different customer groups, their deeper needs and the potential solutions to satisfy them, extends the opportunity landscape, opening more sides to the model and more options for profitable lines of income. None of these ideas is mandatory, and there may be good reasons not to pursue them or to defer their decisions for future years, but not to include them for consideration at all would be naïve, particularly if they can help to form a sticky ecosystem around more valuable parts of the model.

The 'office space' chart in Figure 3.3 is purely illustrative, and obviously represents just a small slice of the broader opportunity. Through iteration, discussion and generating more ideas, the chart will expand much further. The 'medical research' chart in Figure 3.4, again purely illustrative, shows some of the concepts that have emerged in conversations with various charities in that space. It doesn't attempt to represent a comprehensive landscape of all the possible opportunities, merely to illustrate the approach.

In each of these charts, one proposition can be relevant to multiple customer groups, but might have a different level of appeal to each of them, and the same service can offer far greater value to some than it does to others. One medical non-profit I worked with had an abundance of data and insights about the condition it researched: its prevalence, different

FIGURE 3.4 Example opportunity landscape for a medical research charity

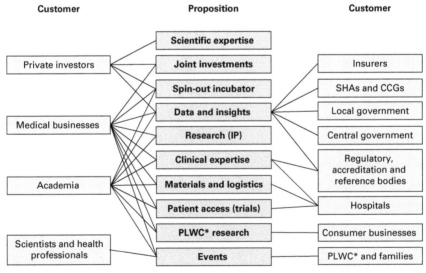

*PLWC people living with a condition within the charity's scope of expertise

presentations, impacts and associated needs. Its hypothesis that the data would be valuable for government policymaking and Strategic Health planning may have been true, but none of those organizations valued them enough to pay a great deal, so it chose to give them the data for free and to use it within policy campaigns. What it did discover, however, was that private medical businesses and investors did value the data and not only would they pay for it, but they were interested in commissioning further work with patient focus groups.

To access those opportunities, the non-profit needed to develop new ethical policies, step up its governance and work out how to craft contracts that would protect not only patients and beneficiaries but their own reputation as well. It turned out that they also needed to build their self-confidence to overcome the assumption within some of the businesses that a 'charity' would do this stuff at cost, or even for free, saving them a fortune on hiring professional researchers. It was quite a surprise for some of those businesses when they discovered the non-profit had become sufficiently astute to recognize the commercial value of what they were handing over. But the alternatives for them were patchy and ultimately more expensive, and the equation of supply and demand applies, irrespective of charitable status.

A landscape chart can also help uncover how a portfolio of services can be developed around the longer-term needs of a single customer type, even one that initially turns up with a very narrow 'want'. A different non-profit that I worked with had been approached by several independent research companies wanting specialist materials for their research: tissue, blood samples and so forth, of which the non-profit had an extensive bank. The non-profit team recognized that if their lab research was successful, those companies would inevitably need more materials, but they'd also need help to secure regulatory and ethical approvals, to recruit patients and carry out clinical trials, and to build a financial case for future investors, much of which they had experience in and could facilitate. By steering the conversation towards a more comprehensive, partnership approach, one that could last the lifetime of the project, the team developed a more integrated proposition. The value of their model goes far beyond providing a few samples, and it has since become a new and growing side to their business.

Customer-product landscapes are not mutually exclusive, and one organization might develop several. There's no reason a medical research charity with under-utilized space shouldn't explore different landscapes from both perspectives. It might well turn out that the biggest opportunity is in targeting the group of customers that fits the profile for both. Similarly, many

FIGURE 3.5 Example opportunity landscape for a large service delivery charity

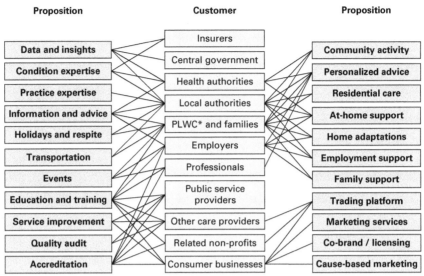

*PLWC people living with any of the conditions within the charity's areas of expertise

non-profits that carry out research also provide services for people living with that specific condition. In fact, their potential landscape for services can often be bigger and offer even more opportunities than the research side, like the example in Figure 3.5.

While the content of the boxes may vary, versions of this chart could apply to most service delivery charities and non-profits, and many of them will already operate many of the potential lines of business it includes. But few, if any, operate in all of them and there are undoubtedly more to be uncovered by continuing to deepen customer conversations and turn them into new ideas.

Customer perspective is the foundation of a good opportunity landscape. Whether the customer in question is a commissioner or a beneficiary, a big business or a small social enterprise, the greater the understanding of their needs and ultimate ambitions, the more opportunities that will emerge to meet them. The higher the value of those opportunities and the closer they fit the mission, the further towards the top right they will appear in the Profit/Impact Matrix from Chapter 1, and the stronger the case for their development.

The key to this entire process is going out, talking and listening to each of the potential customer groups, and then shaping and refining the propositions specifically for them, by 'starting with the customer and working back from there'. It's a timeless piece of sound advice, and one that should fit perfectly with the person-centric view most charities take to programme design. And yet, understanding the commercial customer can often be far harder for charities than it sounds.

Most charities find it easy to come up with new ideas for things they could sell, but not so easy to agree on the customers who will pay for them. Part of the reason is the 'more is less' paradox: most charity staff simply aren't used to thinking from the perspective of their commercial customers, so revert to the 'what else could we sell?' paradigm. But the other reason is that people working within charities can often develop strongly held biases that make the customer conversations very difficult. These biases are subtle and often don't emerge right away, but when they do, they can have a big impact.

## Resolving the customer conundrum

I recently worked with a charity whose income came almost entirely from fundraising and was looking at earned income for the first time. Together, we worked through and expanded the opportunity landscape, and identified 25 potential propositions that could be relevant to up to 19 different potential customer groups. All told, those combinations, of customers and propositions, ran to almost 100 different potential lines of business. The team-leaders took the most promising ideas away to develop further with their teams. Within a couple of weeks, however, the list had dwindled to a fraction of its former size because people within those various teams had sincere and deeply felt reservations about to whom it would be ethical to charge a fee.

There were concerns about taking money from beneficiaries and their families, as statistically they were likely to be financially harder-pressed than the average person. There were concerns about taking money from professionals in the field, because charging a fee might reduce their desire to access the research the charity wanted to share. There were concerns about taking money from businesses for customer and market research, as it might compromise the charity's independence, ethics or reputation. In fact, few of the potential target customers were free of reservations.

Each of these concerns was passionately and resolutely held by different groups of individuals within the organization, each of whom saw themselves as custodians of the charity's moral compass. Each belief undermined a discrete customer group, and, collectively, they reduced the indicative potential of earned income from over £10 million per year to around £2 million a year. As the pattern began to emerge, we reconvened the leadership team, and agreed that we needed to do much more work unpicking the biases within the organization, testing whether they were legitimate risks we would need to mitigate, or myths we would need to challenge. In the end, about half of the potential value made it back onto the agenda.

These barriers to charging different groups of potential customers are often well meant, but they're equally often misplaced and lacking in supporting evidence. In this case, the questions that went back to the various teams, to clarify the basis of their positions, included the following: had donors and supporters ever been asked whether they would see these types of activities as conflicts of interest? If it were positioned as consumer research, enabling the opportunity for them to inform and shape third-party developments, would they see it as a positive step? Would beneficiaries want to be offered a premium level of support at a price, or would they prefer a lower standard that could be sustained free of charge to everyone?

It transpired that none of the donors or beneficiaries had ever been spoken to about these questions, and had they been asked, may have had far fewer reservations than those within the organization. The views of internal teams, particularly those most entrenched in the status quo, are usually far more conservative than the people they support, and relying on their opinions alone risks patronizing external groups of stakeholders who may be far more open-minded than staff might think.

Richard Kramer, the CEO of Sense, recounted to me another, similar example, this time in the social-care sector. Sense was founded in 1955 by two mothers of children who were both deaf and blind. Over recent years the charity has extended from supporting purely deafblind people to supporting people living with a broader range of complex disabilities. In 2017/18 Sense's total revenue, including Sense Scotland and Sense International, was just over £88 million, £62 million of which came from commissioned care services, £11 million from retail and £9 million from fundraising. One of the strands within that fundraised income is a service that Sense has been consistently running for the last 40 years of its history: providing holidays for deafblind children.

Through a combination of fundraising and some historic grants, Sense was able to provide over 100 holidays each year for children, young people and adults, giving parents a much-needed break from caring. Over recent years, however, those historic grants had steadily declined, and while the holidays were increasingly oversubscribed, Sense's ability to fund them was becoming increasingly untenable. So, in 2018, Sense made the decision to ask families to contribute towards part of the costs.

'It was a very challenging decision internally,' Kramer explained to me, 'and there was certainly a great deal of reluctance to ask families for the money.' Having made the decision, though, I asked him how the families themselves had reacted. 'We actually encountered very little difficulty. We got a great deal of understanding from families, largely I think because we spent a lot of time preparing the ground: we worked together with them to get some of the cost funded by the local authorities, we looked at ways to help them use their direct payments, and I think families have understood the situation and the financial constraints we operate in.'

Of all the potential customer groups, the one that will always have the greatest immediate fit with any mission is the group that the organization was set up to serve: its beneficiaries. Direct services to beneficiaries benefit enormously from a non-profit's in-depth knowledge – it should already have a deep understanding of the things that will make the most positive difference to this audience. That knowledge, combined with the charity brand and its existing relationship with many beneficiaries, provides a powerful competitive advantage and the potential to develop a unique, highly valuable proposition. But the decision to charge beneficiaries is often one of the trickiest to manage within the sphere of earned income. For some charities, like Age UK, many of their beneficiaries have independent wealth or income from pensions and can afford to pay for elements of their services and support. Conversely, other non-profits will be working with beneficiaries who can't afford to pay, and for many, the truth will be somewhere in between. But commercial models are flexible things.

Some non-profits have purposefully extended the reach of their services to target a broader range of customers beyond their primary beneficiaries. By making their proposition attractive to those who can pay, creating tiered pricing and adding all manner of ancillary products and services, they have created sustainable commercial businesses that can cross-subsidize, reducing or entirely removing the cost for the most vulnerable and financially constrained.

Many healthcare providers, particularly in countries with widespread poverty, have successfully developed tiered pricing that enables them to charge only those who can afford to pay. The LV Prasad Eye Institute, a non-profit chain of eye clinics and specialist hospitals, operates over 200 sites in the south-eastern states of India, and since its foundation in 1987, has served over 26 million people. The institute operates a tiered pricing model. Core treatments are of the same standard and quality, irrespective of the patient's ability to pay, and over half of the group's customers in any given year get their treatment for free, cross-subsidized by those customers who can afford to buy the variety of 'deluxe' extras or ancillary retail products on offer.

Just a little further south, in Tamil Nadu, Aravind Eye Hospitals operates 13 separate hospitals with collectively over 4,000 beds and performs over a quarter of a million cataract operations a year. The treatment pricing is 'variable', whereby the majority of its operations are performed for free, paid for by the profit made on those patients who can afford the full price of the operation.

The group's core principles are that rich and poor receive exactly the same quality of service, and each hospital must be financially self-supporting. In both organizations, a ruthless focus on efficiency and productivity, for both paying and non-paying customers, underpins their ability to generate enough profit from paid work to cross-subsidize the unpaid work, without pricing themselves out of the paid market. Narayana Health, a private healthcare company founded in 2001, has developed a similar, highly efficient, cross-subsidized model in Bangalore for heart surgery and cardiac care.

Ziqitza Healthcare, a social enterprise founded in 2005, operates a fleet of over 3,000 ambulances across 16 Indian states, thanks to a $1.5 million impact investment in 2007. Ziqitza's objective is to provide ambulance services to all, irrespective of income, and so it charges a variable fee model. The rich pay more, the poor pay less, and very poor emergency victims are treated and transported free of charge. These four organizations represent a mix of for-profit and non-profit, using different models of tiered and flexible pricing, but the one thing they all have in common is that they have all scaled up their operations enormously since their inception, they have collectively saved and improved millions of lives, and they couldn't have done it without charging some of their beneficiaries.

A softer approach, with potentially broader applicability, is prompted donation. Before, during, or after a service is rendered, the approximate cost of its delivery is introduced, not to demand payment, but to share the fact that the service the customer is receiving has been paid for by another customer, and to offer the opportunity for the recipient to pay, should they feel able, for other customers like themselves to be similarly helped.

None of these models is mutually exclusive, nor do they negate the option to simply charge a fee for a rendered service, as many charities and non-profits choose to do. They're simply alternatives. The point is that pricing models can be adapted to suit the circumstance. Whether flat, tiered or flexible, whether mandatory or voluntary, a model can usually be developed that can mitigate ethical or moral concerns, while remaining financially sustainable. They can be tweaked and balanced over time to redress any unintended consequences, they can be loosened in times of greater need, or tightened to generate funds for investment and scaling up. The choices are there.

Clearly this market comes with moral and practical questions of afford-ability, the risk of creating a two-tier service and the reputational risks around being seen to profit from beneficiaries. The latter is often a major sticking point in engaging internal teams to consider these types of opportu-nity, not least because of the mauling Age UK took in the press over energy tariffs. But there are as many charities successfully selling to beneficiaries as there are different models to address those risks and concerns.

Charity professionals will always put beneficiaries first and opportunities for new commercial enterprises are invariably plentiful, but large swathes can evaporate extremely quickly when internal biases pull the shutters down before options can be properly explored. That the leadership remains as open-minded as possible during the exploration phase is critical. Concerns need to be aired, but they also need to be questioned, and it's the leadership's job to do that, accepting the challenge, but asking: 'How could we do this in an ethically sound way?'; 'What would need to be true for this to succeed *and* work for our beneficiaries?'; 'What do our beneficiaries *actually* think?'

At the heart of these discussions will be a balancing of the needs of the individual against the needs of the population. The more individuals can contribute financially, the more the organization can use that contribution to extend its reach to a wider population. This relates back to the impact discussions I mentioned in Chapter 1, around the extent to which the organ-ization is aiming to deliver a direct and profound impact for a small population, versus a potentially lower level of change for a larger popula-tion, or indeed, to focus their efforts on campaigning and influencing for much broader, systemic and structural change.

The breadth vs depth orientation of any non-profit is a major strategic choice, one that can polarize conversations with staff, trustees and donors alike. The right commercial model, one that is self-sustaining and scalable, has the potential to narrow that divide, enabling an organization to directly deliver a greater impact across a wider reach.

Scalable commercial models can not only be used to help individual beneficiaries, they can catalyse systemic change, addressing the context and challenges that sit around beneficiaries and alleviating the economic conditions that feed and sustain a raft of challenging social issues. Here too, business models and commercial ideas have a fundamental role to play in achieving the sustainable changes required to realize the greater vision of the non-profit.

## Endnotes

1  Villeneuve-Smith, F and Blake, J (2016) *The Art of the Possible in Public Procurement*, E3M Publications, London

2  Ryanair Investor Relations (2016) Annual Report 2016 (Page 7), *Ryanair Investor Relations*, https://investor.ryanair.com/wp-content/uploads/2016/07/Ryanair-Annual-Report-FY16.pdf (archived at https://perma.cc/D6K7-J95M)

3  Civil Society (2018) The Charity Shops Survey (2018), *Civil Society Media*, www.civilsociety.co.uk/product/charity-shops-survey-2018.html (archived at https://perma.cc/ERG8-WJK9)

4  Jeff Bezos 1999 interview on Amazon before the dot-com bubble burst (April 1999): Malter, J (1999) Jeff Bezos Has an Ambitious Vision for Amazon in 1999 Interview, *CNBC*, www.cnbc.com/2019/02/08/jeff-bezos-1999-interview-on-amazon-before-the-dotcom-bubble-burst.html (archived at https://perma.cc/ZEP4-B3LV)

5  Steve Jobs 'start with the customer' response at the Apple Worldwide Developer's Conference, May 1997, various recordings available on YouTube

6  Reinhardt, A (1998) There's Sanity Returning, 25 May, *BusinessWeek*

# 04

# The business of social change

## A theory of change

All charities and the vast majority of non-profits have a clear, stated purpose for their existence. In most cases it's formally enshrined in the registration documents and constitution, but it's usually more accurately described through their vision and mission statements. Commentators and academics continue to develop formal definitions and rules for both types of statement, while practitioners and organizations continue to bend and break them so they can create something useful. Definitions are a guide, so I will briefly step through them, but the bottom line is to do whatever works for you.

In the third sector, a vision statement tends to describe the world that the non-profit wants to see in the future: a world without suffering, poverty, pain or prejudice; a world in which beneficiaries enjoy greater freedoms, rights, quality of life and so forth. Within that context, a mission statement usually sets out the role that the organization intends to play in bringing that vision closer to reality: the areas upon which it will focus; the challenges on which it will lead; and often the disciplines, capabilities and values on which it intends to stand.

Underpinning the mission and values statements is usually a suite of strategic aims or priorities, often with associated targets or broad goals, which cascade into a variety of initiatives, programmes and actions to be pursued during the current strategy cycle.

Between each of those elements, between the vision and the mission, the mission and the aims, the aims and the initiatives, lies a set of assumptions and hypotheses: that these initiatives will deliver those aims, that those aims are the best way to achieve this mission, and that this mission is the right one for us to choose for realizing that vision. Most of those assumptions are implicit; many are inherited, often unconscious beliefs embedded within the

history and heritage of the organization. This is what we do because, well…
because this is what we do, and our beneficiaries tell us it works.

But times change, as do aspirations. It's one thing to provide a residential
care home for disabled people, to offer shelter for the homeless or food for
victims of disasters. It's another thing to provide pathways to independent
living, employment, social integration, long-term recovery and resilience,
sustainable social change. Over recent years, many non-profits have raised
their sights, stepped up their ambitions and elevated their missions, to such
an extent that 'what they've always done' is no longer a reliable guide to
what they should do next.

Theory of change is a process for drawing out those assumptions and
hypotheses between vision, mission and action, and making them explicit so
they can be tested, measured and adapted, based on objective evidence. It's
a way for non-profits to document and test their beliefs, to challenge themselves to unpick and properly understand all the components required to
bring about a specific change, whether at an individual, community or
global level. It's the philosophy that provoked and underpinned the radical
strategy (described earlier) that the NSPCC switched to in 2009.

The theory of change concept originated within the international development community as a way to improve their programmes, to collaborate
within a shared framework, and to unravel some of the seemingly most
intractable problems. A theory is developed, usually collaboratively with a
diverse group of experts sharing their experience, in order to create a visual
model for solving complex problems with many moving parts. A good
theory of change defines the combination of elements that all need to be
addressed, without which change either won't happen or won't last.

Theory of change isn't the only approach, nor is it without its critics, but
over recent years it's been adopted as a model by many other charities,
working across different sectors and disciplines, largely because it's useful
and, in general, because it works. But it is more than a tactical tool for
designing programmes. It's also a strategic tool that can help to unpick each
of the big, strategic challenges that need to be addressed for a non-profit to
realize its ultimate vision. A theory of change, therefore, should have a direct
influence on the organization's strategy, shaping its focus and investments,
and increasing its ability to engineer the changes that it needs to see happen.

In tourist spots around the developing world, teams of donkeys and
mules are often used to carry visitors around sites of interest, remote pyra-
mids, ancient ruins and so forth. In some cases, the animals are badly

handled, kept in poor conditions, receive little if any medical care and suffer with severe health problems as a result. Many animal welfare organizations will have come across situations like this and tried different approaches to change the animals' situation.

Their theories of change might include elements such as legislation, education and inspection; the provision of stables, amenities and quality local services – farriers, vets and the like. People who have experience of working in those communities might also point out other barriers to change that would need to be overcome, from culture and superstition to economics and environment. All those elements will likely need to be addressed if a programme is to maximize its impact and chances of success, and more elements might need to be considered if the change is to be self-sustaining once the programme ends.

Some of the elements might all sit within the capabilities of one organization, others might need partnerships to crack, and for some, there may be no answer as yet. The value of having an explicit theory for the required change is that it provides clarity about the issues and exposes the gaps that need to be filled. It's in these gaps, particularly those around sustaining a change over the long term, where opportunities to build commercial or market-based solutions can make the greatest difference.

Brooke, the working equine charity whose discussions around impact and reach I shared in Chapter 1, began life as the Old War Horse Memorial Hospital in Cairo, built in 1934 on the foundations of Dorothy Brooke's work, rescuing the war-horses that had been abandoned in Egypt following the First World War. Its purpose was to provide free treatment to needy horses, donkeys and mules working in and around the city, often in the very situations I mentioned earlier.

In the 1960s, recognizing the extreme needs in other parts of Egypt, Brooke opened clinics in Alexandria and Luxor, followed in the 1980s by a clinic at Aswan and another at Petra in Jordan. As the charity steadily raised its sights towards the vast number of equines working in similarly poor conditions around the globe, it was becoming apparent that the free-clinic model couldn't possibly scale to that degree, and so, drawing inspiration from the human side of the international development community, Brooke began developing its own theory of change.

The shift of emphasis in the years that followed, from purely providing free veterinary care to engineering a sustainable change within a community, was underpinned by simple observations. Healing an animal only to return it to the same situation is unsustainable. Animals can't change their situation, but people can. Those changes could be brought about through a combination of education, influencing, and building the quality and capacity of local service providers. In 2013 I began working with the team at Brooke to help redefine their strategy, based around their theory of change.

Since then, Brooke's theory of change has evolved to become much more detailed and sophisticated, and its strategy and activities have evolved along with it. For example, under its charitable objects, any treatment Brooke provides must be free, but providing free vet services in an area over the long term creates a permanent fundraising dependency and undercuts the ability of another, fee-charging vet to set up a practice. And so, Brooke has developed extensive partnerships with local organizations, service providers and training colleges, to help create sustainable economies around the animals that can embed a change in quality of life, while allowing Brooke to move on to a new location.

As the theory has expanded to encompass more learning, situational elements such as extreme poverty, the availability of clean water and the agency of women, who are often the animals' primary carers, have come into sharper focus. Through continually evolving the theory of change, the importance of these dependencies has become increasingly clear, and addressing them an increasingly important step in achieving Brooke's aspirations. In response to what it learns, Brooke continues to expand its partnerships, collaborations and policy and influencing work, including working more closely with humanitarian and relief organizations, whose beneficiaries often rely heavily on their working animals, and whose animals rely equally on them.

Thus, its evolving theory continues to shape its strategy, and its strategy continues to increase the reach and sustainability of Brooke's global impact.

## A shortcut to the insights

For organizations working with human beneficiaries, their lived experience can provide much of the raw material for a theory of change. In particular, it can quickly help to identify the major barriers they face in achieving their own ideal outcomes. During one project with a large social enterprise, we talked about the theory of change model and decided to develop one, not with great expectations, but just to see if it might tell us something useful. It did, surprisingly quickly.

Over several weeks I ran a series of workshops with their service users to draw out key moments from their personal stories. The conversations revolved primarily around the events that had made the most positive difference, and the frustrations that had held them back along the way. Obvious gaps in the wider landscape, particularly in the health and justice services, immediately rose into view, but the biggest barrier, by far, seemed to be the propensity for people to fall into the cracks between services, to be bounced like a hot potato between one service and another, or to be continually handed off to a service or department that never answered their phone.

On one level, this wasn't a huge surprise for those who'd worked for many years in the field, but the scale of the issue and its impact in comparison to other barriers brought it into a far sharper focus. It rapidly raised the profile and potential importance of some of the programmes the organization had been developing: programmes that combined continuity of support and advocacy with a capture-and-report system, feeding back to the key public-sector bodies on service experience, barriers and cracks in the system, and the often profound problems they were creating for service users that were leading to serious and far more expensive crises, further down the line.

Eventually the session insights were combined with other research and discussions and turned into a formal theory of change, but the point here is that a great deal of clarity and arguably a substantial part of the value emerged almost immediately and had a direct impact on the organization's view of how it needed to develop its commercial services.

A similar thing happened while working through a strategy development process with the National Autistic Society. Again, we began the process from the perspective of lived experience, and a sub-team went away to comb through their vast repository of research from people right across the autism spectrum, their families and carers, and to come up with a draft theory as a conversation starter. The team began their presentation by explaining why they'd not actually come back with a theory of change: situations were so different, the spectrum so broad and the life-stages of people they worked with so wide-ranging that they had chosen to use a different model, based loosely on the Hierarchy of Needs[1] pyramid developed by Abraham Maslow.

I should add that since then, the NAS team has developed extensive and detailed theories of change for individual aspects of its work with more discrete populations, for example in education and early years where it works much better. But as a first cut, the population-level insights from the hierarchy were extremely powerful.

At the base of the NAS pyramid were needs such as safeguarding and security, while the apex, Maslow's self-actualization section, talked more about the need for visible, aspirational role models for autistic people. The key elements from the research had been placed in the appropriate layer, and the team had coloured them according to how the data suggested the needs were being met (green), partially met (amber) or not met (red).

Certain elements, such as access to employment, were red, which was having a knock-on impact for many on the autism spectrum, because it undermined their ability to develop financial security, personal independence and achieve their aspirations. As with the previous example, this wasn't entirely revelatory for the team. Access to employment had long been a recognized barrier for autistic people, but the simple exercise of building and reviewing the hierarchy shone a spotlight on its relative importance, the distinct lack of historic progress, and the fact that the more ambitious goals for autistic individuals would be very difficult to achieve unless it was addressed.

In the years since that session, the NAS has significantly increased its work around access to employment, through partnerships and employer services, and collaborative campaigning and policy work with other large disability charities. In 2018 the NAS opened its first Enterprise Campus, in Essex. The Anderson School, named after a major benefactor, is located at the Enterprise Campus along with a NAS Lorna Wing Centre, providing various services to the school as well as to other public-sector and private customers, and an Enterprise Hub, specifically designed to provide a pathway for autistic students to progress from the school environment into employment.

The aim of the Enterprise Centre, as with the two other elements of the site, is to stand on its own commercial feet; to become financially self-sustaining by drawing in a wide mix of income streams. Those streams include social enterprises, specifically set up by NAS to provide work experience and training for students, both from the Anderson School and from other surrounding schools, but the centre is equally focused on building strong links with local and national businesses, to tap into apprenticeships, gain investment and, most importantly, find placements and jobs for its school leavers.

The NAS didn't need to develop a complete theory of change to gain the big insights, nor did it need to address the major gap it uncovered by trying to design a commercially self-sustaining solution. It could have stuck with more traditional, tried-and-tested charity techniques. It could have focused on influencing policy, educating employers, training teachers. It could have applied for grants or raised funds to support specific cohorts of autistic youths from school into work. But it chose the route it did because it wanted to find a model that was financially independent, one that it could scale, one that could be replicated anywhere it was required.

When CEO Mark Lever asked me to support them through the project, he shared with me his own personal aims for the site: that every single child in the school would leave into either further education or into employment, and that the financials would stack up well enough for every autism school and academy in the country to want to copy their approach. To achieve that, it was always going to need to develop a business model that didn't rely on fundraising and grants.

## Scalable and self-sustaining

Complex problems have many potential solutions. Analysis can identify a problem, but the process of developing the right solution is one of creative design. As the NAS example shows, bringing an overtly commercial perspective to that process right from the start can often uncover different, more sustainable solutions than traditional charity models. The Kenyan fishing industry offers more examples.

In Kenya, as in most sub-Saharan countries, the fishing industry splits along gender lines. Men own the boats and catch the fish; women buy the fish from them, process them and sell them, either locally or to male intermediaries who will take the fish to sell at the major markets. In many of these communities there exists a pervasive culture of 'jaboya', where sex is a prerequisite for the women to get the best fish from the fishermen and to get the best deals with intermediaries. This transactional sex trade has in turn led to high levels of HIV/AIDS, other sexually transmitted infections, depression, alcohol abuse and PTSD. Health and human rights campaigns have had little effect, as the behaviour is being fundamentally driven by economic necessity.

In 2012 the 'No Sex for Fish' programme was launched in the community of Nyamware beach on Kenya's Lake Victoria shoreline. The programme's plan was to provide boats, business skills and mentoring to women so they could integrate vertically; catching, processing and selling the fish without the need to trade sex. A women's cooperative was formed and around £3,000 of seed funding provided for the purchase of three boats. The boats were provided to members on a rent-to-buy basis, paying back their cost over two years, at which point the member took ownership of the boat and the repaid loan would then be used to build, or buy and repair, more boats for more women, perpetuating the shift towards economic empowerment.

The project was very successful.[2] Since then, the same programme has commenced in two other locations in Kenya, at Kusa in 2014 and at Nduru in 2016, both with increased amounts of seed funding and both showing signs of similar success.

In 2019, in association with the University of Reading, Paul Lindley, the founder of Ella's Kitchen, launched the inaugural 'just IMAGINE if...' competition. One of the finalists was Dave Okech, a Kenyan fisherman from Lake Victoria, mentored by social entrepreneur Iqbal Wahhab, OBE. Okech's pitch was a different solution that also aimed to accelerate the end of the practice of jaboya. His mobile app and online trading platform are designed to link traders, fish farmers and fish feed suppliers, to increase productivity and information flow throughout the supply chain, and to level the playing field for female buyers and sellers, allowing them to transact through their phones, rather than having to trade on the beach.

Two completely different solutions to the same social issue. Both approaches directly address the economic and structural barriers that have prevented the success of more traditional charity routes. Both have the potential to be entirely self-sustaining as they're built on sound, scalable commercial models. Both require seed funding, business skills and mentoring, but both have the capacity to repay that investment relatively quickly and generate a profit to fuel their expansion.

There are no silver bullets for delivering ambitious visions and complex missions, and just because an organization already has a model, a set of services or a theory of change, it doesn't mean there aren't better, more flexible, more sustainable alternatives based around a commercial business model. Sometimes all that's required is an infusion of childlike creativity and an open-minded response to the simple question: give me 10 other ways we could...

For any non-profit needing to rethink its activities or looking to address a social challenge in a more sustainable way, entrepreneurial and market-shaping business models should be the first port of call. There may not be a business solution to every problem, but an army of social entrepreneurs continues to demonstrate there's far more likelihood of finding one than any of us would have thought 20 years ago.

From environmentalism and animal rights to discrimination, gender equality and mental health awareness, the non-profit world has orchestrated many outstanding examples of social change. But when we look across society, at the extraordinary transformation in how people live, how they work, how they communicate and raise their children, the most profound and far-reaching changes have invariably come about through innovations in science and technology, often developed in academia, but primarily delivered at scale by businesses.

The waves of change those businesses have created have reshaped entire societies and touched billions of lives, sometimes for the better, sometimes less so. Whatever your political views, whether you like the direction of travel or not, it's hard to deny that the combination of science, business and the global market economy is the single most effective force for change that humanity has ever seen.

For non-profits that want to sustainably change the world, the questions can't be confined to: how can we fundraise for this, or where could we get a grant?

They have to begin with questions such as: how could we solve this with a market-based model; how would a Kenyan social entrepreneur approach the problem; how would Amazon do it; how could a business, whether run by us or someone else, get around these barriers and bring about a permanent, economically embedded change?

## Raising investment for impact

Money makes the world go around, and the non-profit world is no different. Funds are required to develop an idea, to test it and scale it up. A commercial model that generates a profit can reinvest that profit in scale, but quite often the need is more urgent, the opportunity for change more pressing than can be satisfied by organic growth through profits alone.

One of the advantages of any idea that generates a return, whether it's a business model or a fundraising programme, is that it immediately becomes a good candidate for investment from people outside the organization. That investment can come from a multitude of different sources, from banks or venture capitalists, crowd-sourced from the public or put up by a philanthropist, or, increasingly, secured through the growing number of social finance routes. All of these can help to increase impact at a pace and with a reach that no non-profit could afford to fund on its own.

The British Asian Trust's Development Impact Bond (DIB) I mentioned in Chapter 1 is just one example of the many different forms social finance can take: it is a rapidly evolving area with new approaches being pioneered on a regular basis. In 2016 I co-authored a short handbook[3] on the subject with Mark Salway from Cass Business School's Centre for Charity Effectiveness and Geoff Burnand from Investing for Good. It provides a good overview of the topic and a free copy of the handbook can be downloaded from the publications section of my website, but there are many other great resources online, some of which I've highlighted in the further reading section at the end of this book.

Just as in business fundraising, where seed funders, business angels, venture capital and commercial loans all have different roles to play, within the non-profit sphere, different types of project at different stages in their evolution will suit different financing models. Those based on proven models with low risk and decent return potential would be equally as attractive to a mainstream commercial lender as to a social financier. Others that are more speculative or early-stage might be more attractive for impact investors or philanthropists. More complex models often combine a mixture of all the above.

The British Asian Trust's DIB used a two-layer approach. The mechanism is complex and took some time to develop, but simplistically, the working capital to fund the project was invested, at its own risk, by UBS Optimus Foundation. That investment was backed by a range of funders and philanthropists and defined around clear targets for impact over a clear timescale. If the target outcomes are achieved, those 'outcome funders' pay back the working capital with an upside to the investors for the risk they've borne, in this case of 6 per cent; if not, the 'risk funder' loses its money. The outcome funders are guaranteed impact or they don't pay, but the only risk to the non-profit leading the delivery is its reputation.

It might sound like an overly complex alternative to securing a straightforward grant from the funders, but it does have significant advantages. One is cultural: when I spoke with British Asian Trust's CEO, Richard Hawkes, he explained how the non-profit sector in India has become much more commercial than it was just 10 years previously, and proudly so – many non-profits wouldn't accept grants today because of the impact on their reputation. It makes them look like an old-fashioned 'charity-case'.

A second is investor appetite. Investment management firms have developed and launched ethical or impact funds to attract and cater for customers who want to see their investments being used for good, even if that means compromising on risk or return. In fact, one of the biggest historic challenges for the social finance industry has not been raising capital, it's been finding projects to invest it in.

A third, and probably the most valuable, benefit of the impact bond approach is the flexibility it can provide. British Asian Trust's DIB was not the first in its space, and its forerunner, the Educate Girls Development Impact Bond, exemplifies the value of that flexibility. Its three-year programme, commenced in 2015, was risk-funded by UBS Optimus Foundation, and outcome-funded by the Children's Investment Fund Foundation.

The first year of the programme, while not a complete disaster, was extremely challenging, and the programme was falling well behind the trajectory it would need to achieve its targets. But within the plethora of measures that were being independently tracked and monitored, there were many valuable insights. Throughout the second year, a great deal of work went on around reshaping the activities, yielding an outstanding third-year performance and achieving 116 per cent of its enrolment target and 160 per cent of its learning target, as measured against a control group that didn't receive the interventions.[4] Educate Girls could never have achieved those outcomes if it hadn't had the flexibility to reinvent its initiative midway through the funded programme, a flexibility that few, if any, traditional funding mechanisms could hope to provide.

Funders want guarantees that their money will be put to good use, which creates tension between the concept of a funder paying for a guaranteed set of activities versus paying for a guaranteed set of results, as per the oft-criticized 'payment by results' style of commissioning. Both have serious shortcomings.

Funding for a tightly defined, pre-planned programme of activities leaves the non-profit with no flexibility to adjust those activities if they aren't working. It provides neither the room nor the incentive for innovation and can lead to vast sums being wasted. Conversely, payment by results places a huge burden of risk on the non-profit, particularly if circumstances change beyond its control.

A non-profit being paid for successful rehabilitation outcomes could be completely undone by a change in Justice Department policy that led to a rapid decline, or a change in the profile of the people it was supposed to be working with. That financial risk can be existential, and it's a major reason why so few non-profits are willing, or able, to bid for that type of work. The power of social finance, particularly of impact bonds, is that they have the potential to bridge that gap.

The first-ever impact bond was launched in the UK, at HMP Peterborough in 2010, to address that very issue. Its aim was finding new ways to reduce reoffending, and to demonstrate a mechanism that had the potential to fund outcomes *and* cover risk. The non-profit organization, Social Finance, raised £5 million from a consortium of trusts and foundations who took on the risk funder role at a 3 per cent interest premium. The money was invested through seven delivery organizations, ranging from national charities such as Mind and YMCA to local non-profits and commercial training providers. The outcome funder was the UK government, and its payment was based on clear measures and targets that would demonstrate, against a control group, indicative savings within and beyond the justice system, and thereby provide the government's return on the investment.

The programme was successful: it reduced reoffending rates by 9 per cent versus the control group, exceeding the 7.5 per cent target, and the risk investors received their repayment with interest.[5] But the initiative was sadly cut short in 2015 with the rollout of Transforming Rehabilitation, the more direct payment-by-results initiative whose headline-grabbing problems I described in Chapter 1.

It's impossible to have a conversation with anyone in the social finance sphere without hearing the phrase, 'Social finance isn't the right solution for everyone', which is certainly true. It's still in its infancy, and for every great example there are plenty of bad ones, where risk investors have subtly shifted most of the risk to charities while charging an interest premium; where expensive social bond mechanisms have been introduced simply to access different funding pots for services that have been running for years.

Even so, social finance can be an extremely powerful funding option for developing and taking to scale any intervention that creates some form of economic benefit. Impact bonds are just one of many alternatives, and their range and application are expanding all the time, which is why online resources that are kept well up to date, like those of Big Society Capital, Good Finance and Social Enterprise UK, are the best source of further information.

## Turning ideas into income

This chapter began with examples of creative processes, and with a philosophy that, at least to begin with, there is value in creating a wide range of ideas before starting to narrow down on the best. Those ideas can come from many different sources, from existing assets and capabilities to insights drawn from beneficiaries and customers, and to the needs of the mission itself.

Sources for business ideas can most often be found where:

- Your organization has unique technical expertise.
- It has underused assets, property or internal capacity.
- A service requires continual charitable funding.
- There are ways to add extensions or new sides to the business.
- You could commercialize your brand, network or relationships.
- Your brand could stretch into new products, retail or hospitality.
- Other organizations serve, employ or interact with your beneficiaries.
- Paying customers have other needs you could meet.
- Ancillary products or services could be built around a relationship.
- There are other customer groups that could use your service.
- Expanding the customer base could subsidize the most in need.
- Beneficiaries have barriers to independence and finance.
- Economic challenges prevent longer-term solutions.
- Creativity or technology could offer a new, commercial approach.
- There are hard-to-solve problems within your theory of change.
- Another non-profit or social enterprise is finding success.

All of those ideas can lead to conversations with potential customers and, if they're allowed to, can stimulate yet more ideas to be added to the list. All told, that's a lot of potential opportunities, far too many for one non-profit to pursue. And it would be foolish to try.

The 'more is less' paradox shows how spreading an organization too thin, especially through over-proliferation of small opportunities, can be distracting and damaging. And yet, exploring a broad variety of ideas increases the potential for income and impact, not to mention increasing the chance of finding one that works. There is clearly a tension between the need for focus and the need to explore a range of options, and that's where the interrelationship between ideas becomes most important.

Mutually supporting ideas form a cluster of opportunities that combine to create a more cohesive and resilient proposition. They can be developed and tested with customers in parallel, often within the same conversation, and collectively they can form the basis of an integrated, strategic approach to developing a commercial ecosystem, as opposed to the potential distractions of pursuing an ever-expanding range of individual ideas. We will look in more detail at the process for narrowing down and clustering in Chapter 6, within the context of creating a commercial strategy to turn those ideas into programmes and initiatives and develop them into profitable enterprises.

Invariably, developing those ideas through the process, and building a business upon them, will require new capabilities. It might also represent a challenge to many within the organization, not just around the skills, but with the broader concept of commerce. I will talk through some of the key skills in Chapter 7, and how to manage the leadership challenges, particularly around culture and engagement, in Chapter 8.

Before we get to that, however, it's worth looking at one other area where the single biggest opportunity is often hidden in plain sight. Most non-profits already earn some income, whether for delivering services or through their own trading or enterprise arms. And while looking at new ideas and initiatives can be exciting, impactful and lucrative, in many organizations there's a great deal of value to be realized by simply doing what it already does, but with a sharper commercial focus.

## Endnotes

1   Maslow's Hierarchy of Needs, from Maslow, A H (1943) A theory of human motivation, *Psychological Review*, 50 (4), pp 370–96

2   Nathenson, P *et al* (2017) No sex for fish: empowering women to promote health and economic opportunity in a localized place in Kenya, *Health Promotion International*, 32 (5), pp 800–07

3   Salway, M *et al* (2016) Social investment. Tools for success: Doing the right things and doing them right, Cass Business School, City University London

4   Kitzmuller, L *et al* (2018) Educate Girls Development Impact Bond Final Evaluation Report, 10 June 2018, *IDinsight*, www.idinsight.org/reports-2/2018/8/22/evaluating-the-educate-girls-development-impact-bond (archived at https://perma.cc/G339-ZF7L)

5   Civil Society (2017) Peterborough Social Impact Bond Investors Repaid in Full, 27 July 2017, *Civil Society*, www.civilsociety.co.uk/news/peterborough-social-impact-bond-investors-repaid-in-full.html (archived at https://perma.cc/3M4X-GMMW)

# 05

# Improving business performance

## Finding the diamonds

There's an old story about a Persian farmer that was popularized in lectures and speeches by the 19th-century Baptist minister Russell Conwell[1] and it goes something like this: Many years ago, when diamond mining was just taking off in India, Ali Hafed, the farmer in the story, became infatuated with the idea of finding diamonds. So, he sold his farm and travelled throughout Africa, Asia and Europe in his search, eventually running out of funds and killing himself in a fit of despondency. (I didn't say it was a happy story.)

Meanwhile, the man who bought his farm found a curious-looking rock in a stream that turned out to be a diamond, the first of many to be found in what became the Golkonda Diamond Mine. The moral of the story is that those bright shiny things you're after may be right there under your nose, if you only know what to look for.

Back in 2015, I led a strategic review with a wonderful charity, most of whose income came historically from local authority contracts. The initial brief was to help them find new business directions: new types of customer for whom they could develop new services and thereby reduce their dependency on such a precarious market, particularly as the austerity policies of the day were biting down hard.

Having done this kind of thing a few times in the past, I suggested that while we were exploring new opportunities, we should also run the slide-rule over the core part of the organization and look at the opportunities there as well. Luckily, the wise and far-sighted CEO and trustees agreed.

The plan that emerged was 20 per cent new business directions and 80 per cent big opportunities within their core markets. Those opportunities were aimed at different budgets, owned by different buyers, but, nevertheless, they would still be ultimately dependent on the public purse. It wasn't an easy shift in expectations to manage, but the executive worked hard to keep the board engaged, the trustees listened, challenged and adjusted to what had emerged in the review, and the plan was agreed. Eighty per cent of the growth focus would be on core business, because it was the best, most pragmatic decision to make under the circumstances, and the income from that growth would fund the 20 per cent of higher-risk, longer-term development, outside of the current niche.

Like many of the similar projects I've done, it underscores the premise of the farmer's story. There are big opportunities out there. Diversification into new markets can reduce risk and might help secure the future of an organization. And without doubt, exploring new markets and new innovations, new ways to deliver impact and income, should be a key part of any strategic agenda. But quite often, the biggest and easiest opportunities for both income and impact are much, much closer to home. They're just not easy to see, unless you know what to look for.

## Reassessing the business

As I mentioned in Chapter 1, the expansion, investment and subsequent tightening in many of the service markets in which UK charities operate have led to intensified competition and reduced profitability across the board, in some cases dramatically. Many charities have found themselves increasingly competing for marginal contracts that barely break even, with overheads they can no longer afford and charitable commitments they are struggling to fund.

Clearly there is a need to examine the state of a market that has become so core to so many of our non-profits; to rethink why, where, how and even if charities should still be competing for this kind of work. And for each charity within the sector, that translates into a pressing need to take a hard look across the portfolio of contracts and activities, and make some strategic decisions about their role in this new, changed landscape: where they should participate, where they can have most impact, and what they need to bring to the table if they're going to not just survive, but succeed, and make a genuine difference, over the long term.

Reviewing that portfolio and looking for places an organization should stop, start or continue in its work is an activity that most charities would claim to do. But few, in my experience, ever do it to the degree they need to, with dispassionate objectivity and with a genuinely strategic mindset. For most, it's part of an annual planning exercise, a hard-fought attempt to balance the books in the face of another tough year – an exercise that may start to surface the bigger, strategic questions, but invariably parks them for later, focusing instead on trimming costs here, renegotiating there, capping pay, recruitment, investment, to make it through another tight budget year.

When it takes more and more time and effort every year to get a car through its MOT, at some point it's worth taking a closer look under the bonnet, picking up on those long-postponed bigger questions and properly considering the options. Any charity that is looking to make strategic decisions around new commercial ventures would be well advised to start making strategic decisions around its existing ones first, to look properly at the markets it's already in, its advantages versus the competition, its impact and financial outlook, at the alternative options for the future.

A simple comparison of the best versus the worst, whether across the industry or across the range of services and locales within a single organization, can highlight not just those that are struggling, but also those that are outperforming. Those that may well be innovating under the radar: finding new ways to work, new models for delivery, new angles to strengthen relationships and build more profitable income. Those who are tapping into a better market or doing something different from the others. The potential diamonds, right under your feet.

Portfolio analysis is a catch-all term. There are lots of ways to do it and often the picture only becomes clear after looking through a few different lenses. The chart in Figure 5.1 is a financial analysis of a charity with a £30 million turnover, almost £27 million of which comes through traded income. This particular charity had already concluded that it needed to be aiming for just under 8 per cent profit across its commercial activities if it was going to be able to continue delivering its free charitable services and start investing in the research that it desperately wanted to pursue.

The chart comprises one rectangle for each service area. The height of each rectangle is the percentage contribution that the service makes to the organization; that is, the gross margin after direct costs of delivery but before the indirect ones, such as support costs, cross-charges and other overheads. The width of each rectangle is its sales for the year, which also means that the area of each rectangle (sales multiplied by margin) represents its profit contribution, before overheads. The fat rectangles bring in the most revenue; the tall ones are the most profitable; and those with the biggest overall area make the biggest overall contribution. The two horizontal lines are also important.

FIGURE 5.1  An analysis of revenue, margin and profit, versus a required target

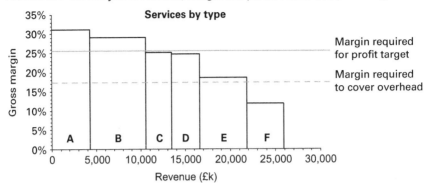

The dashed line is the current percentage overhead, essentially the break-even point after those indirect costs; and the solid line is the overall goal for margin. That solid line is around eight percentage points above the dotted line, because this particular organization is aiming to make an 8 per cent profit on its trading business.

What the chart illustrates is that E and F are where the problems lie. While they're both making a contribution, neither is profitable once the overheads, the central management team, the IT costs, building rents, insurance and the like are all taken into account. If they were spun out into standalone businesses, E might just about break even, but F would be under water from day one. It spotlights certain questions: why are E and F so much less profitable than A and B, what can be done about it, and what's their future? Based on their current margins, it wouldn't be one of expansion and growth.

The chart also shows that a slight increase or decrease in margins for services B and E would have a disproportionate effect on the overall profit, as together, they represent a big slice of the overall turnover. Together, all these observations draw towards a bigger question: what do we *want* this chart to look like? And realistically, what would need to happen, what would need to be true, for overall profitability to get where it needs to be? It's likely there will be various potential answers, various routes to reaching the goal, and each of them represents an opportunity that can be added into the mix of ideas.

A similar analysis based on regions, areas, customer types and segments can yield a fresh array of insights and questions. How come we do so well in Scotland, but we're losing our shirts in Kent? Why are we seeing so many more referrals from GPs, but not from emergency clinics? Why is there such a disparity between the volume of work we get from private prisons, and the volume we get from those that are state operated?

Likewise, a portfolio analysis based on reach or impact, rather than on financials, can shed light on a potentially mixed bag of performance highs and lows, highlighting areas that need turning around quickly and those that could show the way for future innovation. And it's the combination of both those lenses, looking at money and outcomes, that can give the clearest 20:20 vision, uncovering opportunities to turn the dial on profit and on impact, and demanding answers to the question: what do we *want* this picture to look like, and, realistically, how can we set about changing it?

The power of this kind of analysis, this forensic introspection, is in creating a shared picture that all the senior team can pull apart and discuss. In one of my early engagements within the non-profit world, as part of the preparation I asked the finance director for all of their performance analyses, hoping that I'd see some of these insights. I genuinely was stunned by the distance between the high-quality commercial reports I'd enjoyed throughout my business career and what I was provided with that day.

To be fair, up to that point, my work had been mostly within big, blue-chip businesses, with teams of commercial, financial and marketing analysts whose sole job was to produce this type of information. But even so, the gulf was spectacular.

Like a great many charities, their practice was to allocate all overheads across all departments, in a process called 'full cost recovery'. It's a financial management approach espoused by charity educators, associations and charity finance professionals, to ensure that when applying for grants or bidding for contracts, all of the costs, direct and indirect, are included in, and hopefully paid for by, the bid. It's a sensible approach for grant applications, but it's a terrible way to understand and manage organizational performance.

It's an enormous distraction within budgeting and management conversations, because it allocates to budget owners swathes of costs over which they have little understanding and absolutely no control. The 10 minutes I spent listening to a service delivery manager arguing that the increased IT cross-charge was the reason his region had missed budget was quite possibly the single most ridiculous waste of time I've ever experienced. The afternoon I spent trying to get a single, consolidated view of the total IT spend compared to the prior year, by piecing all of those same cross-charges back together, came a very close second.

As I talked the finance director through what I hoped to achieve by analysing the numbers in a different way, he was sceptical. 'This is what they're used to seeing. To be honest, I think if you show it any other way, it will only confuse them even more.'

Following the workshop, having completed and shared the portfolio analysis from a number of different perspectives, and discussed with the executives some of the things that had caught my eye, I received e-mails from over half of them. Their feedback ranged from 'That was a hell of an eye-opener' to 'That's the first time I've actually understood a finance presentation since I joined'.

Sophisticated financial analysis is invaluable to businesses, and whenever I've introduced any of these techniques into non-profits, that value has been recognized and the processes adopted from that point onwards. It can feel like a lot of work for finance teams the first time around, and it can take time to shift any deeply ingrained way of looking at the world. It will push people out of their comfort zones to prepare, and quite possibly to read, but after that first time, it will quickly become a way of life because of the powerful insights it can yield.

Alongside the internal view, there are two other views that are usually worth spending some time on while looking under the bonnet. They are the market: size, value, direction of travel and so forth; and the competition.

The market analysis in Figure 5.2 is from the same organization whose portfolio analysis appeared earlier in this section. In this chart, each service type is shown as a circle, the size of which represents the income it generates. The position on the horizontal axis shows how much my interviewees thought that the market for that particular service would grow over the next three years. The vertical position shows the margin of new business, based only on their most recent experience, so ignoring older, pre-existing contracts and just looking at the market as it appeared to be behaving at the time.

With each new perspective comes a deeper understanding. In this case, the combination of the portfolio view and the market view generated more useful insights, challenging some aspects of the previous thinking and reinforcing others. Service A looked to be steady, profitable, and would probably stay that way for a while, but Service B, the biggest single profit contributor, looked likely to become an issue in the not-too-distant future. It was bringing in good money, but the market looked set to shrink, and margins on new business were well below where they'd historically been. Service E, while still underperforming, started to look like a much better place to invest, as the market was growing and the margins on new business looked

FIGURE 5.2  An analysis of the potential growth and profitability of business lines

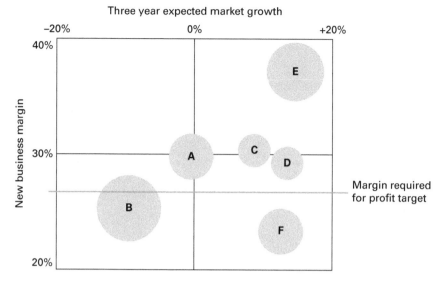

surprisingly strong, while service F, in contrast, looked increasingly like a problem that would only get worse unless a new, lower-cost model could be developed.

Each perspective raised new questions, and each of those gave rise to new potential actions: some that should be done anyway; others that should be investigated further. In this case, three of the main actions were: to investigate and understand what was driving the margin decline in service B, and what could be done about it; to develop a plan to dramatically accelerate the growth of service E; and to start exploring the marketplace and competition around service F.

The hypothesis for service F was that other providers appeared to be successfully delivering that type of service, to that same group of beneficiaries. If that were the case, it would be useful to understand what outcomes they were achieving and how they managed to remain financially viable. The follow-on questions would then be: whether their models could be replicated; whether they would be interested in a partnership or maybe even a merger; or whether they would consider running the services, either as a subcontractor, or by simply taking over the contracts and the staff.

Impact and quality of service were fundamental considerations. If an organization can have the same impact, or deliver a better quality of service or outcome, in a financially sustainable or even a more profitable way, what is the role of another charity in that market? It shouldn't be simply to make up the numbers on a commissioner's list of bidders, nor should it be to offer a cheaper, lower-quality alternative that will only serve to reduce the outcomes for beneficiaries. And nor should it be to imperil its own finances in order simply to win business and grow the top line. Sometimes exiting a service completely, yielding the field, passing the baton gracefully to other organizations, ones that are evidentially more fit for that purpose, is the most sensible, the most profitable, and indeed, the most charitable choice.

Analysis can help to understand how an organization got to where it is, but where it decides to go from there is about choices. For the charity in question, those choices emerged from further conversations looking at the major trends in its markets, building the future scenarios, creatively expanding the potential of what we had uncovered and how that potential might be realized.

By coming up with a few tactical plans to turn around areas that were underperforming, the charity might have delivered an incremental 1 or 2 per cent margin. But by taking a more strategic view, looking at the wider portfolio and longer-term market, the big opportunities became clearer and larger, and the collective value they offered, at least on paper, turned out to be significantly above that 8 per cent margin, giving them the confidence to kick-start the research programme.

Just as the analysis didn't define the opportunity, that 8 per cent aspiration didn't define the target. It catalysed the process, focused minds and supported the narrative, but the goals for each area that emerged were based on their full potential, which transpired to be much bigger than that original need. There were, indeed, great opportunities, right under their feet. The diamonds had been there all the time. As it turned out, they just needed the right lenses and a couple of fresh perspectives in order to find them.

## Redefining your role

Prior to 2017, Scope was one of the UK's largest charities with a £100 million annual turnover. I mentioned in Chapter 1 that the charity had been on a journey of evolution for over two decades, changing its name, expanding its remit to other disabilities and, in more recent years, steadily withdrawing from the residential-style services that it used to provide. In April 2017, Scope's CEO Mark Atkinson formalized that direction of travel, going public with their new strategy to fully exit service provision and instead to focus purely on advocacy, information and social change for people with disabilities.[2]

The strategy would see Scope's income reduce by 40 per cent and would cut staff numbers by two-thirds. Less than six months later, Scope announced the sale of its regulated and day services at 51 locations across England and Wales to the private provider Salutem Healthcare, and by May 2018, almost 1,600 staff had been transferred.[3]

It was a strategy that had been a long time in the making. In the spring of 2013, I interviewed Scope's then CEO, Richard Hawkes, about the journey that would culminate five years later, in that 2017 announcement. Hawkes explained to me how the world had changed around Scope, how people with disabilities needed very different kinds of services from those that were provided in the past. He went on to describe how the market had matured, how Scope was no longer especially advantaged or even particularly required in care provision, and how it could have far more impact by influencing, campaigning and collaborating with others. 'Many of the older services are still profitable,' he explained, 'but they're not what society should be providing for people anymore.' I asked him how long it had been since he'd come to that conclusion. 'Probably 20 years', he replied. 'It just took a while to bring everyone around to the same point of view.'

In May 2015, Hawkes left Scope to be succeeded by Atkinson. Six weeks after he'd left, I interviewed him again. Referring to our previous discussion, I explained how I could see that, from a mission perspective, killing off outdated services was the right thing to do, but I knew many other organizations in similar situations that were severely challenged by the idea of walking away from profitable services that were still in demand from commissioners.

His commitment was undimmed by the passage of time and events, and his response went straight to the heart of the matter. 'It's true of Scope, and it's true of a lot of charities and voluntary organizations… they never really ask themselves, why do we do the things that we do?' He related an example: 'I was once at a meeting with about 10 other disability organizations that all ran services. I asked them all why they ran services, and none of them were able to give a clear answer. I think a lot of organizations just do things because they always have.'

Later in the interview I predicted that social-care cuts would continue, that competition would intensify, that profitability across the entire sector would come under severe pressure, and asked what he thought the implications would be for service delivery charities. His answer went to the heart of the question of purpose and role that I touched on in Chapter 4: 'You can run services because they add credibility to what you do, to demonstrate to others how they can be done differently; you can innovate, run pioneering services; and for me, that's what the voluntary sector should be doing. We're never going to compete in the mass market, and I don't think that's what we should be trying to do.'

There is a strong case to be made that the mass market, even a booming one, isn't a good place for non-profits to be. Mass markets mature relatively quickly, and as they mature, they become characterized by commodity – products and services that are standardized, costs engineered to a minimum, the providers largely interchangeable. In those markets, the biggest, lowest-cost operators tend to take the majority of the share. Smaller, less cost-effective ones usually end up acquired and stripped of their customers, or slowly competed out of business. There are rarely more than one or two lowest-cost operators in any mature market, and it's unlikely any of them will be non-profits, because of three important factors: scale, finance and ethics.

Scale is a big factor in achieving lowest cost, and there are very few standalone charities that can match the scale of large businesses. Finance is another major constraint – businesses have far more flexibility than non-profits when it comes to raising debt, pouring money into advertising and sales, and running at a loss for long enough to shake out the competition. But ethics is usually the killer. The lowest-cost battleground is a quality tightrope, and for charities reliant on public support, often with trustees whose own family members may be service users, the lower end of the quality scale is neither an easy nor an attractive place to play.

That doesn't mean that charities shouldn't compete, but it does mean they need to have a compelling and distinct role that isn't predicated on low cost but is built on what they're bringing to the party that others aren't, what impact they can have that others can't. It means that charities need to clearly define what's special or unique about their proposition, what specifically gives them their competitive advantage. Whether it's raising standards and expectations, testing and developing innovative approaches, or delivering a niche specialism, unique local expertise or technical knowhow, it needs to be front-and-centre and crystal clear. The rational process of understanding those unique competitive advantages, of developing them, marketing them and finding the buyers and commissioners who value them enough to pay more than just commodity prices, is the key that can open opportunities in even the most competitive of mass markets.

The challenge for us, however, is that we aren't always rational. People are not naturally rational beings; people are naturally *rationalizing* beings.

As endless behavioural psychology studies have shown, most of the decisions we make every day are gut feel, instinctive, emotional. We rarely take the time to think our decisions through coldly and rationally; but we are excellent at rationalizing and justifying those decisions once we've made them, which explains the tendency of charities to rationalize why they stay in commoditized, marginal, service delivery markets, as opposed to rationally assessing whether they should. Or better still, creatively thinking how they might alter their position and proposition, to fundamentally rethink their role, to become financially more sustainable and to make a genuine, unique impact.

The ultimate impact question to ask is this: 'If we pulled out of the market or disappeared off the face of the earth, after a couple of months would anyone actually miss us?' If the true answer to that question is no, if commissioners and customers would simply find someone else, just as good, to fill the gap, it's time to rethink the charity's role in the market.

The question of role is central to any non-profit strategy. To achieve any strategic vision, any aspiration for a different future for beneficiaries, there are choices for the organization to make about the specific role it is best placed to play in bringing that change about. It is a strategic choice that is every bit as critical for fundraising-led charities as it is for those competing for earned income.

In 2009, the NSPCC developed a radical new strategy, driven out of the big challenges and structural issues it had identified as most affecting the lives of the children it aimed to support. The resulting strategy was focused around seven key areas that the research suggested were the most important to address in order to have the greatest impact on young lives.

Prior to that point, the organization had been delivering a huge range of services and interventions, most of which were paid for by its prodigious fundraised income and many of which were well received, but few had much, if any, evidence to show their effectiveness. The aim of the new strategy was to focus the organization on developing interventions that would measurably impact one or more of those seven focus areas: to identify new potential models and innovations, to refine and develop them, and to build a powerful evidence base that would encourage their adoption across the sector.

This involved not only a dramatic change in the activities NSPCC undertook, exiting hundreds of different services in scores of different locations, but changes to its processes, its culture and, more fundamentally, to the role it intended to play within the landscape. Its strategic choice was to fully embrace the role of innovator, expert and thought leader, rather than the role of long-term service provider. This was a role it recognized needed to exist to accelerate the breadth of change it wanted to see for its beneficiaries, and one that the NSPCC was uniquely positioned to deliver.

Over time, NSPCC began to recognize that even seven areas was spreading its resource and expertise too thinly, and that it could have far more impact within a narrower remit. By the end of 2018, that remit had tightened to just two critical areas: early years and child sexual abuse. The resulting focus has enabled the Society to test and develop a broad range of interventions in different contexts, to build a much better understanding of the processes and prerequisites for positive outcomes, to dramatically deepen its unique niche of expertise and offer it through an expanding array of partnerships, and to use its growing evidence and influence to start effecting broader structural change.

When Scope opened The Thomas Delarue School back in 1955, it wasn't because they wanted to compete with other schools for children with cerebral palsy. It was because there were no schools for children with cerebral palsy. Nobody was doing it, and it needed to be done. Go back to the roots of almost every major charity and you'll see a similar pattern. Charities are at their very best, not when they're competing to do things that others can do just as well, but when they're finding ways to do things that no one else can do, inventing the roles that will need to exist for a vision to be achieved.

The ideal opportunity for any organization, whether business or charity, is the problem that nobody else is addressing, the opportunity to build a new service or enterprise in that uncontested space and to deliver a profound impact that nobody was delivering before. The alternative is to find new ways to add something unique to an existing market. The key is to find a valuable niche, a way to do the job fundamentally better, with much better outcomes, or at much lower cost, to play the role in that market that nobody else is playing. A charity is never going to beat a global business at its own game. But it doesn't have to. It can win by being different; it can step out of their game, change the rules and start a completely new game on its own terms.

## Developing differentiation

The idea that a business should concentrate on those things that it can do better than anyone else is not new. It's one of the main points made by Michael Porter in his seminal 1985 book, *Competitive Advantage*,[4] in which he outlined two main business strategies: cost leadership and differentiation. While he did cover a third type of strategy that he called 'focus', he described it as a targeted-niche version of the other two. Essentially, Porter says that a business can succeed in one of two ways: being consistently the cheapest, or being the 'best' in some distinct, tangible way. Porter is not alone in that view. I share it, and so have most other observers of business.

In Chapter 2 I mentioned Jim Collins and his 2001 bestselling book that combined extensive research, analysis and insights from 11 'Good to Great' businesses. Collins explains differentiation using a fable about an encounter between a fox and a hedgehog: the fox may be good at many things, but the hedgehog only needs to be good at one thing in order to survive an encounter with a fox: turning into a spiked ball. He defines the hedgehog concept for a business as the overlap of his three circles: what you're passionate about; what you can be best in the world at, and what drives your economic engine. It is a good concept, but the big issue is its lack of objectivity. Business executives can have an extraordinary tendency to believe that what they do well is the same as what customers want, and there's a very fine line between confident marketing and believing one's own hype.

Collins illustrates the evolution of one of his Good to Great companies, Pitney Bowes, from manufacturing postage franking machines to becoming best in the world at 'messaging that requires sophisticated back-office equipment'. When the book was published, the Pitney Bowes share price was flying high at around $40 per share. By the end of 2018 that price had fallen to just below $7 per share. Between December 2005 and December 2018, Pitney Bowes' market capitalization fell by 80 per cent, from $5 billion to $1 billion. As it transpires, the market for 'messaging that requires sophisticated back-office equipment' is not nearly as big as the Pitney Bowes executives thought it might be.

Another of Collins's Good to Great businesses in 2001 was Fannie Mae, which aimed to be 'the best capital markets player in anything that pertains to mortgages', based on two best-in-the-world strengths: '(1) that it could be a full capital markets player as good as any on Wall Street and (2) that it could develop a unique capability to assess risk in mortgage-related securities'. Those strengths were brutally tested when the crash in value of mortgage-backed securities precipitated the 2008 financial crisis. Fannie Mae's ability to assess risk did indeed prove to have been unique, but not in a good way. The US government's only viable option was to take it into conservatorship (essentially, they bought almost 80 per cent of the stock); it required a $116 billion bail-out from the US treasury, and the CEO and board were summarily dismissed.

What these two examples show is not that differentiation leads to failure, but that simply being good at something, or in Fannie Mae's case, believing they were good at something that they weren't actually very good at, will not lead to success. Overconfidence in a capability is incredibly common, as is over-optimism in what the market might be willing to pay for. Collins' model is a useful touchstone, but it lacks the rigour and objectivity required to make sound choices.

Arguably the deepest look at the science of differentiation can be found in Kim and Mauborgne's 2015 bestseller, *Blue Ocean Strategy*.[5] In their book, the two INSEAD professors contend that extreme differentiation can help a business move out of a 'red ocean' (a highly competitive, bloody market) into a 'blue ocean'. Using examples such as Cirque du Soleil and Southwest Airlines, they illustrate how, by ignoring or cutting out specific parts of the mainstream offer, a business can invest in other aspects, creating a much more focused proposition that allows them to open their respective markets to a whole range of new customers.

According to Kim and Mauborgne, Southwest, the original budget airline, didn't set out to compete for other airlines' customers; they went after the blue ocean of customers who could never have previously afforded to fly. Similarly, Cirque du Soleil weren't after the traditional circus-going audience; in fact they targeted customers who wouldn't have been seen dead at Barnum and Bailey. Both of those businesses were extremely successful, and both created new markets for consumers who would never have considered using their pre-existing rivals.

These are insightful observations and great examples. Being academics, the authors then go on to outline a comprehensively analytical, one-size-fits-all process for finding these blue oceans. Unsurprisingly, each of their example businesses appears to have found their blue ocean through inspiration rather than analysis, but academia has an irresistible bias towards analytics – it might not be effective, but it's eminently teachable.

Methodologies aside, the concept of differentiation, of standing out from the competition by being distinctly better at certain things, at the direct expense of other things, including at the expense of no longer being the lowest priced, is a sound one. It's been around since the invention of the village market, and the reason for its longevity is simple: do it right and it works. But there are two problems: overconfidence in capability and over-optimism in market potential. Everyone likes to think they're better than the competition, and all passionate entrepreneurs and leaders are desperate to believe the market wants, and will continue to want, what they have to offer.

Kodak was genuinely the best in the world at what it did, the ideal Collins hedgehog concept. The market simply decided that it no longer wanted to use photographic film, just as movie fans decided they no longer wanted to schlep down to the high street to rent a cassette. Biases can cost dearly, and Kodak's over-optimism ultimately proved even more expensive than Tesco's overconfidence in their extensive Fresh and Easy research.

Tackling those biases can be relatively straightforward – one simple technique is the business card exercise. I'd just facilitated an away-day for the board of a large charity and in the wash-up afterwards, the CEO and I got talking about a question raised in one of the final sessions. The question was whether the services that the charity provided were genuinely differentiated. She was confident that the answer should have been a clear yes, and was disappointed others weren't so convinced. And so, I walked her through an exercise that I'd used with a group of business leaders the previous afternoon.

'Imagine,' I said, 'that on the train home tonight, you get talking to the person next to you and, just as you pull into the station, you happen to ask her what she does. It turns out that she is a big potential buyer of your services. You ask if you can meet up with her over a coffee, and she gives the "I'm really busy" look, but eventually she relents and asks you to write on the back of your business card what makes your services so special. She says she'll look at it back at the office, and if she thinks it's worth a coffee, she'll give you a call.'

Within 30 seconds, the CEO had reeled off about six great points that she would write on her card. I then explained the next part of the exercise. 'Once the group has written on their business cards, I ask them to visit the websites of their main competitors and, being completely objective, based purely on what they've read, to write down what they think the competitor's executives would put on the back of their business cards.'

The CEO paused, smiled ruefully, and said, 'They'd probably write pretty much the same as me'. She didn't even need to do the exercise to get the point. Differentiation is not shouting about what you're good at; it's knowing what makes you genuinely different and distinctly desirable.

The business card exercise is a good way to burst any overconfidence bubbles, and a great prelude to any serious discussion around developing more from the core trading business. The concept of differentiation, of finding and building a business around a niche position or a unique advantage, is the basis for sustainable profitability in any competitive market, which is why conversations about growth, about differentiation or new innovations need to be based on an objective understanding of how an organization, whether business or charity, *actually* compares against its competitors.

That comparison is only useful if it's made from the perspective of potential customers, not simply from the team's own, perhaps insular preconceptions. Whether it's deep market research, immersion with focus groups, competitor visits or something as simple as the business card exercise, objectivity is essential for the comparison to be worthwhile. Indeed, if it's not objective, there's a good chance it will do more harm than good, fostering complacency and reinforcing a false sense of security.

Kim and Mauborgne's blue ocean philosophy is right. It's impossible for an organization to be the best at everything – it will simply end up being average at them all. Instead, an organization needs to aim to be the best at just a few, interrelated things – things that really matter. The place to start, therefore, is with understanding what matters, unpicking the reasons that people do or don't buy, the things they consider most important when making their decision. This is a critical step in bursting that second bias bubble: the belief that the things you are good at are the things that customers most value.

A charity providing high-quality social-care services will naturally want to believe that commissioners should make decisions primarily on outcomes, on quality, on results. They are likely to have an inherent bias, an over-optimism about the value of the high-quality end of the market. But whether they like it or not, quality may not only prove to be just one of many considerations, it might be a long way down the list in the mind of the paying customer. Wishing that weren't the case will not solve the problem if it is.

Considerations for a commissioner will probably include some measure of outcomes, but will invariably include price, and most likely a variety of other things: the speed at which results can be seen; the visibility and PR value of a service; their previous experience with a provider; confidence in delivery, accessibility, transparency and so on. Compounding this, as any pollster will attest, people don't always vote how they say they will vote. They have a tendency not to do what they say they will do; they don't always make decisions how they think they make them; and they don't always behave how they like to believe they behave. When researchers ask people their opinions, they constantly have to bear in mind that people don't just lie to researchers, they often lie to themselves, and commissioners are people too. The information pack around an upcoming contract might say that quality is worth 80 per cent of the score for a particular bid, but the buyer's track record will tell you to what extent that 80 per cent is real, aspirational or self-delusional.

Drawing out and prioritizing decision criteria will always be a blend of experience and evidence, particularly evidence of actual behaviour – there's a huge difference between someone saying that they would buy a particular thing if it existed, and them actually stumping up the cash. The criteria will also be different for different groups: individuals will prioritize different things to commissioners; for them it might be most important that they can remain anonymous; that they can earn a living while they go through a programme; that it's at a convenient time, in a convenient place; that they can register without filling in a 10-page form. Nevertheless, getting beyond the optimism bias to that list of criteria for each group, prioritized objectively and collectively, is essential for developing a strong, differentiated and compelling proposition.

The key to successful differentiation is to define a target market, whether an existing market or a new one that's large and underserved, and to understand objectively what is most important to them in their decisions; to take those elements, and to choose at which of them your organization will excel, and which, if any, will need to be sacrificed to pay for that excellence. Irrespective of the process or methodology, there are two critical ingredients: objectivity in the assessment and creativity in the development. Here's an end-to-end case example of the process I use.

In 2015, one of my clients, whose business installed and maintained industrial equipment, introduced me to their biggest supplier. Both were family businesses, successful and growing in challenging markets, and had a long relationship built on mutual trust and respect. That supplier provided them with almost all their spare parts for the maintenance side of their business, and over its 20-year history it had risen to become the dominant player in the spares market, with over 25 per cent of the national market share.

Following up on the introduction I visited the site, where our initial one-hour meeting lasted almost three hours. The CEO was one of the nicest people I've ever met, cared deeply about his customers and his employees, and had a lifelong passion for motor racing. He'd built and raced off-road motorcycles as a kid and made his pocket money by letting school friends race around the nearby woods and fields on his bike at weekends. As his business had grown and eventually started to make him good money, he'd bought his own single-seater track car in kit form, built it himself in his garage, and started signing up for amateur races.

As he walked me around the entire operation, he showed me trophies from his races at Silverstone, Brands Hatch and Spa, introduced me to colleagues from almost every department, and talked me through the history of the business. The original idea had been a simple one. He and a colleague had been working in the sales function of one of the industry's biggest brand names, and regularly despaired about its customer service. The process, not just within that brand but across the industry, for repairing equipment, replacing worn and broken parts, managing and meeting the expectations of customers who'd paid good money for and heavily relied on the kit they'd bought, was atrocious.

It was a far cry from his experience of buying replacement parts for his racing car through the automotive industry. And it was a short step from that observation to imagine the potential that an automotive-style supply chain could offer to customers within his own industry. Twenty years ago, that innovative idea had not only driven their rapid early growth, it had started a mini-revolution. Over the next two decades, businesses across that industry either adopted the same approach or disappeared. By the time we met, that initial radical differentiation had all but evaporated. Only a few of their original competition remained, but those that had survived had adapted, consolidated and adopted similar practices: they were all essentially offering the same spares, at the same service levels, at a similar price, to the same customers. Growth was slowing, the competition was encroaching, and new thinking was needed.

The sales team believed that the business needed to increase stockholding and cut prices if it wanted to grow sales. They related various anecdotes of asking customers why they were buying elsewhere, only to get the reply: 'Because you didn't have the parts when I needed them.' And whenever they asked a prospective customer, 'What would it take to win your business?', the invariable answer was a very big discount.

The problem with getting feedback on price is that it's easy to take it at face value, and start cutting away. But price is never the whole story. What the prospect is often saying is that they can see no reason to switch from their current supplier except price. They're saying that there is no meaningful differentiation that appeals to them, so all other things being equal, the only thing that would attract them now would be a bigger discount.

To test their preconceptions, the team listened to a day's worth of customer phone calls, and a full week's worth of complaints. It turned out that calls followed a distinct pattern. The caller would describe a part or provide a code for one, ask if there was one in stock and how quickly it could be delivered, and finally, ask about the price. Customers would hang up if the phone wasn't answered quickly, or if the part couldn't get to them fast enough, before they ever got to the price question.

The single biggest cause of complaints and, as it transpired, of cancelled orders and customer defections was when promised delivery dates were missed. Most of their customers were engineers who needed those parts to fix equipment for their own customers. They were on urgent jobs with short lead-times, for customers who were losing money every hour their equipment was offline.

What those engineers needed above all from a parts-supplier was responsiveness, availability of parts, and delivery of those parts when they were promised, without fail. Turning up at a job without the requisite parts is not a good look for any engineer. So, in most situations, only if all three of those criteria were equal would price be the deciding factor.

The sales team themselves were heavily involved in the research, and to their enormous credit, they quickly got past their preconceptions and recognized the value of what they'd uncovered. Once those four criteria had been identified, we filled in a high-level grid, like the one in Figure 5.3, which helped us agree where the business was, and provided the framework for a deeper conversation around where we might dramatically improve, and how the business might position itself strategically to stand out much more clearly from the pack.

By comparing objectively against the competition, the team created a clear picture of the current situation (the grey circles). On one aspect they were ahead of the competition, on two others they were comparable, and on one, they were off the pace. The question then was: where could we be? What would it take to put clear blue water between us and the competition on any of these criteria?

FIGURE 5.3  The differentiation grid

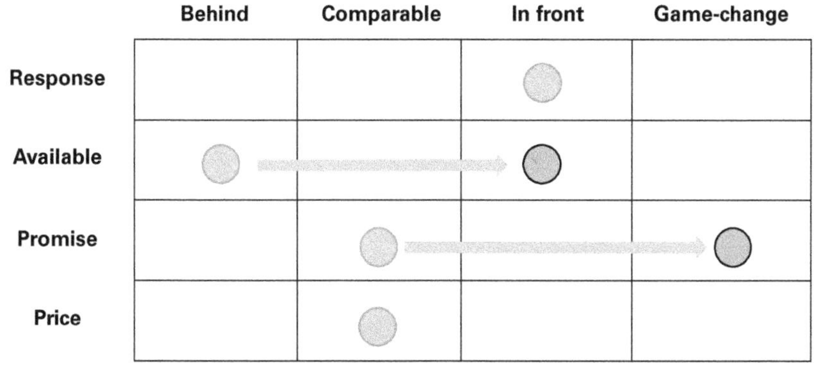

|  | Behind | Comparable | In front | Game-change |
|---|---|---|---|---|
| Response |  |  | ⬤ |  |
| Available | ⬤ → |  | ⬤ |  |
| Promise |  | ⬤ → |  | ⬤ |
| Price |  | ⬤ |  |  |

The model provided genuine insights and provoked extremely innovative ideas for their future strategic position, but it only did so because the team were open-minded and objective enough to be critical of their own response and delivery. They embraced the challenge that a business could only be described as ahead of the competition if what it provided set it apart strongly enough for customers to switch their loyalties. At the front of the pack is still in the pack. To be truly differentiated requires a bigger leap.

Different organizations will prioritize different criteria, aiming to be better than the competition at different things. It's why Aldi and Waitrose can happily coexist with their relatively extreme positions. Through recessions and economic booms alike, while the 'good at everything', middle-of-the-road, main pack of supermarkets – ASDA, Tesco, Sainsbury's – all saw their market shares slip away, the Aldis and Waitroses, those businesses clearly positioned away from the pack, continued to grow. In the words of Texan populist Jim Hightower, 'There's nothing in the middle of the road but yellow stripes and dead armadillos.'

Using some of those simple creative techniques from Chapter 2, and by looking at a range of businesses outside the industry, the spare parts team came up with ideas across all four of their criteria, and eventually worked up plans to invest in just two: collaborating in radically different ways with importers and manufacturers to transform availability, and using new technology to transform their ability to keep delivery promises. For the latter, the potential was there to go beyond mere differentiation, to set a new standard that could fundamentally change customer expectations and behaviour. Taking inspiration from the home shopping market, the question was raised: 'What would need to be true for us to offer next day delivery, on-site, guaranteed?'

The idea of guaranteed delivery, let alone within 24 hours, was something no competitor had ever gone near. Like their original automotive model, 'next-day delivery guaranteed' offered them a second potential game-changer for the industry. In the search for differentiation, game-changers are the holy grail.

## Changing the game

The genuine game-changer isn't simply better than what's out there already. It's something that will make everything out there obsolete. It will transform the current way of doing things to such an extent that everyone else will have to follow the lead; they will have to adopt the same innovation, whatever it costs, or they will die out. Game-changing innovations like the touch-screen phone, the bagless vacuum cleaner, the video-on-demand model – once someone has put it out there, there's no going back; the rest of the industry has to stop what it's doing and race to catch up.

Gillette changed the shaving game with one product: the safety razor, making their cutthroat razor competitors obsolete at a single stroke. Ford's Model T changed the game for personal transportation. People still own horses, just as some people still use cutthroat razors and phones with numbered keys, but the mass market for all of them has long since moved on.

ArtistShare started a crowdfunding model in 2003 and was swiftly followed by start-ups like IndieGoGo and KickStarter. Together they pioneered a new industry, bypassing banks and changing the game for start-ups seeking funding. By 2012, according to Statista, the global value of crowdfunding had exploded, to almost $2.7 billion. By 2014, that figure had grown to over $16 billion per year.[6] More and more start-ups and businesses are switching to crowdfunded or peer-lending models, and the banking industry is still struggling to respond.

In the non-profit sector, various international development organizations have collectively changed the game by shifting the focus from alleviating crises to enabling communities to sustainably develop their own prosperity and resilience. The Grameen Bank changed the game for community and entrepreneurial investment, kick-starting the whole micro-finance industry. Indeed, the Grameen Bank alone now provides funding equivalent to around 2 per cent of the total UK non-profit sector, and it's growing far more quickly.

Differentiation is essential but it's game-changers that change the world.

A game-changer is always a gamble. By definition it is an innovation, something that's not been tried before, at least in the context in which it's now going to be used. It's the single best way to open up a core market to a new wave of growth, and to create a material impact above and beyond what other providers are doing. A game-changer that transforms outcomes, the customer experience or business profitability, or that establishes a new model or market, will by definition be copied, so it needs to be developed, validated and scaled at pace if it's to provide a return, and for the team that gets to work on it, that's quite often the most exciting thing about it.

That notion of time-constraint, of a limited window in which to develop, test and roll out a game-changer, brings me to the final insight from the differentiation grid we saw in Figure 5.3, and it's probably the most important one of all. Everything on the grid will be continually and inexorably dragged to the left by the force of competition. Competitors compete. Innovations get copied or cloned. Game-changers, by definition, eventually become the industry norm. Differentiation is ephemeral. Any strategy that assumes a competitive advantage will not be chased down by the competition is doomed to failure. The only way to stay ahead of the pack is to keep moving.

Once an organization achieves a distinct advantage in some way, shape or form, they need to move quickly to capitalize on it, and keep innovating to retain it. The first digital cameras were a game-changer for the photographic industry, just as the first bagless cleaner was a game-changer for vacuums. The difference between those two examples is that nobody remembers the first digital camera. Kodak, which invented it, dismissed it, and, 36 years later, filed for bankruptcy because of it. Fuji, which was the first to launch, very quickly got caught by the pack, as a paranoid and fast-paced competitive set of technology companies immediately closed the gap.

Dyson, in contrast, stole a huge march in a slower, more conservative market with a bold launch and a continual stream of innovations, constantly enhancing and extending their line of products. Just as failure hasn't been fatal for Hoover, success hasn't been final for Dyson. The competitors are still there, adapting and adopting as much as they can, and the impact of Dyson's innovations will continue to spread well beyond the footprint of their own products.

In the same way, success for a charity game-changer is never final. There are always more innovations to find, other problems to solve, better outcomes to seek, and more ripples of improvement to send out across the market pond, steadily changing the sector by example, as only envied-leaders can.

## Endnotes

1  Several of Russell Conwell's speeches were subsequently turned into books, including *Acres of Diamonds*. Conwell, R H and Shackleton, R (2009) *Acres of Diamonds*, CreateSpace Independent Publishing Platform

2  Atkinson, M (2017) How We're Building a Greater Scope for Greater Impact, NPC, www.thinknpc.org/resource-hub/how-were-building-a-greater-scope-for-greater-impact/ (archived at https://perma.cc/JKT3-YPT3)

3  Scope completes transfer of frontline services and staff today (1 May 2018), Civil Society

4  Porter, M E (1985) *Competitive Advantage: Creating and sustaining superior performance*, Free Press, New York

5  Chan Kim, W and Mauborgne, R (2005) *Blue Ocean Strategy: How to create uncontested market space and make the competition irrelevant*, Harvard Business School Press, Brighton, MA

6  Statista (nd) Value of Funds Raised by Crowdfunding Platforms Worldwide from 2012 to 2014 (in Billion US Dollars), Statista, www.statista.com/statistics/269957/estimated-volume-of-funds-raised-by-crowdfunding-platforms-worldwide/ (archived at https://perma.cc/V23M-4BNX)

# 06

# A strategy for commerce

## The power of ambition

In 1989, Stephen Covey published a self-help book, which went on to sell over 25 million copies. Entitled *The 7 Habits of Highly Effective People,*[1] it's an impressive book, with principles that have stood the test of time. If you've not read it, let me recommend it now. Habit number two, which I will evoke here, is to 'Begin with the end in mind'; that is, to envisage a future which you can then work towards.

For an organizational strategy, that future begins with a vision of the change that the non-profit wants to see in the world, and choices about the role it intends to play in bringing that change about. Those choices define what the organization will need to become and where it will need to focus its efforts, which in turn, creates a strategic agenda of the big things that need to happen, some plans and initiatives, often some restructuring and capability development, annual budgets and so forth (Figure 6.1).

The process for developing commercial income is slightly more complex, in that there are two 'ends'. The first end is the strategy itself, specifically, the creation of a development agenda with a clear focus on a small number of big, distinct ideas. The second is the end of the broader undertaking, the development of sustainable, profitable income streams. Two distinct stages – the strategy stage and the development phase – which I briefly outlined at the end of Chapter 1. The strategy stage is broadly a process of opening up and narrowing down to land on a few big ideas that will form the development agenda. The development stage is a different, much more iterative process, of taking those ideas outside of the organization, talking to and working with customers, listening, designing and refining, to find and prove the best models for realizing the opportunities.

FIGURE 6.1  Outline process for developing an organizational strategy

| | | |
|---|---|---|
| **Change we want to see** | | Vision |
| **Role we choose to play** | Mission | Values |
| **What we must become** | Organization structure ⟷ Strategic agenda ⟷ Ethics and standards | |
| **Steps we need to take** | Activities and initiatives | |
| **Investment we need to make** | Budget | |

Because these opportunities are new and they've probably not been tried before, the development stage will inevitably be dynamic and unpredictable. Hence, the development agenda won't be a detailed set of plans, but an outline of each of the opportunities, the approach the team will take to develop them, some clear first steps along with required resources, and a way to manage their progress: measures, decision points and so forth. But the one thing they will also need is a clear vision of the potential scale and impact of the idea, to act as a guiding star for the work, and a powerful drive to bring that vision to life.

The potential for new commercial income is rarely constrained by lack of opportunity; more often it's defined by two things: the size of an organization's ambition and the quality of the people involved in bringing it about. The combination of those two elements will define the pace and the scale of success, and they both need to be there, right from the start.

The initial ambition, in particular, can have major consequences on the outcome. That's because the pressure to start looking at earned income growth is most often driven by pragmatic needs: a growing deficit in the accounts, services running at a loss, chronic concerns over financial sustainability. Those practical pressures are useful in galvanizing efforts and forming a narrative for the organization, but they're not a good way to define an ambition.

A couple of years ago I had lunch with the leader of a charity who described how his organization had previously been spending almost a million pounds a year providing training and information events. Historically they'd been unable to get funding and were reluctant to charge a fee, believing it might reduce attendance and limit their impact.

But they'd also been acutely aware that, unless they could find a way to offset at least some of their costs, they couldn't expand their coverage and reach any further. He told me their target had been to try to find ways to reduce or get sponsorship for 50 per cent of the costs while keeping delivery free, hoping it would enable them to double their reach. A goal that, as it turned out, was not far off what they achieved.

But what also became apparent during the research, and the reason for our conversation, it transpired, was that they'd found other charities who seemed able to charge for their training and events, apparently unconcerned about putting off attendees. Indeed, one charity seemed to have flipped, just two years before, from 'for free' to 'for a fee'.

I pointed to the assumption in the approach his charity had taken, that charging fees would reduce impact. Maybe, I suggested, the other charity thought differently. Perhaps they'd assumed that, while registrations could go down, so might last-minute drop-outs and no-shows. Their assumption could have been that with the right content and promotion, attendances wouldn't drop at all. It's often the case that those who've invested financially can be more committed to implementing what they've learned, more interested in collaborating and sharing their results afterwards. One hypothesis could be that impact will be increased by charging, and it's an easily testable theory.

I'm not sure this helped alleviate my fellow diner's concerns. If anything, it reinforced his worry that they might have hit their target but failed to achieve the bigger opportunity. It wasn't a failure of execution – they had succeeded in their plans. If anything, it was a failure to recognize and challenge their assumptions; a failure of strategic thinking, ambition and imagination (Figure 6.2).

There's a qualitative difference between strategy and long-range planning, one that can open up a world of opportunities when it's properly understood. Planning is incremental. It starts from where you are, with what you have, doing what you do, and works out how much further you can get. Strategy starts with a bold ambition, a vision of the future you want, and works back from there, to develop a sense of what your organization will need to become to succeed. The fundamental difference is one of mindset, of

FIGURE 6.2  The imagination gap between strategy and long-range planning

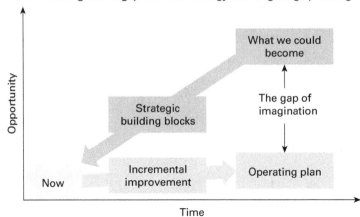

asking 'How could we...' instead of 'How do we...'. For example, 'How could we develop a training programme that our target audience would be queuing up to pay for?' instead of 'How do we fund more of the events that we currently deliver?' The answer requires a different way of thinking, one that doesn't always come naturally.

A CEO, with whom I'd been working for some time, once asked if I would have a coaching session with one of his team – apparently it was something she had specifically asked for in her review. It came as a bit of a surprise because the previous time we'd met, we'd had what some might call a fairly 'robust' dialogue. When we met, I asked her why she'd requested the session, and she explained: 'The last time we were together, I was sure it [the project we had been debating] couldn't be delivered for nine months, that's why I argued so hard. But then you asked me that question. You asked: "What would need to be true to deliver it in three?"

'When I thought about it afterwards, I realized I've got so used to working with a set amount of resource and balancing all the different priorities, that my mind has become a bit boxed in.' She continued, 'I think I need more conversations like this to just "un-stick" my thinking.'

She's not alone. Most senior people, in most organizations, got where they are by being good at three things: planning, managing and reacting; by becoming experts at using the resources available right now to solve today's problems today, to deliver what's needed this minute, this week, this month. Those skills are great for hitting a budget, but they're not helpful when developing a strategy. Defining a genuinely strategic ambition demands letting go of the constraints of today, the limiting assumptions about what capability the organization has and what it can do.

It means asking, 'What would need to be true…' to solve this social problem with a commercial model; 'How could we…' double traded income over the next two years; 'What would we need to become…' to be completely independent of grant funding. It may be that by the end of the process, some of those ambitions aren't achievable, but setting them out at the beginning is essential, because the one invaluable quality they have is that they won't be achieved by continuing with the current approach. They demand creative thinking and imagination.

Traditional models for strategy development rarely help to bridge that imagination gap. In most business education modules, strategy development is taught as a primarily analytical process: SWOT, market and competitor analysis; PESTL and Porter's forces; do enough slicing and dicing of business performance and a strategy will fall out the bottom. It's taught that way because analytical techniques are easy to teach, far easier than trying to teach vision and creativity. It would be fine if the past were a reliable guide to the future, but it's not.

Developing a strategy by simply analysing, by projecting from past performance or recent market intelligence, is like driving a car by looking in the rear-view mirror and assuming the road ahead will continue on the same path. Kodak, Nokia, Blockbuster, Carillion, all had strategies. Comprehensive, expensive strategies built on a wealth of analysis of past and present, in which they were extremely confident. So confident, in fact, that none of them even looked up to see the hairpin bends in the road just ahead.

Analysis plays an important role and good information is essential, but the future will be different from the past. Strategy is about starting with an ambitious end in mind, one that recognizes the future may not be like the present, and then working back to develop a plan. But it's also about recognizing that the future may not unfold as expected and new things will be learned and discovered along the way. That's why strategy needs to be regularly revisited, ambition needs to be free to evolve, and plans will need to be reshaped as circumstances change, insights emerge and hypotheses get punched in the mouth. A good commercial strategy is therefore based on four simple principles: begin with the future, think big, start small, and fail fast.

## Beginning with the future

In 1970, futurists Alvin and Heidi Toffler published a book called *Future Shock*.[2] Their central concern was the psychological impact on individuals of rapid societal change – in their words, of 'too much change in too short a period of time'. The title encapsulated the idea that if someone from a few hundred years ago suddenly arrived in the world of today, they might well die of shock.

Consider that, for much of human history, progress had been at such a pace that someone skipping forward a few thousand years might be surprised by the advances in cave art, the change from stone to bronze tools, or bronze to iron weapons, but would adapt fairly quickly; but someone from, say, the Iceni tribe of the first century, arriving in the court of Elizabeth I, would have one hell of a shock. A shock, but probably not as big a one as for an Elizabethan turning up in a post-industrialized Manchester factory in the 1840s, and certainly not as big as the shock that a Victorian would get if they landed in the middle of an airport, an ELO concert, a Skype meeting, or the Trafford Centre on a crazy Saturday afternoon the week before Christmas.

What this implies, and indeed history supports, is that the pace of change, socially, economically and especially technologically, has accelerated exponentially, over almost every period in history, to the point where change is now so rapid and continuous that our lives are almost unrecognizable to someone born just a century ago. And we're showing no sign yet that we're even close to 'peak change'. In 10 years' time, that bewildered look a teenager receives from a grandparent when trying to explain Bitcoin is probably the same look that a 55-year-old CEO will be giving to their 25-year-old Head of AI when being presented with a new marketing strategy.

Developing new ideas is not an overnight job, which is why anticipating the future is such a critical step in starting out on opportunities that might take months, or even years to fully develop. There's no point developing new services or products that are relevant to customers today, only to find that by the time they're ready to launch, the audience, the technology and the competition have all moved on. Conversely, an idea that's ahead of its time and beyond an organization's capability now might find a ready market by the time it comes to launch.

Canadian ice hockey player and occasional futurist genius, Wayne Gretzky, made a deceptively simple observation that deserves the longevity it's garnered: 'I skate to where the puck is going to be, not where it's been.' It was his ability to read the game, to anticipate how the next few seconds would unfold, that allowed him to be in the right place at the right time, so consistently, in fact, that he remains the only player in National Hockey League (NHL) history to have scored over 200 goals in a season; a feat he managed four times in his glittering career.

There were plenty of times when Gretsky anticipated a scenario that didn't pan out, but he played the percentages and his results speak for themselves. In the same way, looking at the future and extrapolating trends, to develop scenarios around how that future could unfold, is a critical stage in any strategy's development. Strategy needs to take you where the puck is going to be, not to where it has been. Your predictions will never be perfect, but they're a better yardstick than either the past or the present.

Scenario planning is a quick and insightful way to create a vision of the future and has just two simple steps. First, identify which trends and potential events to take seriously, and second, combine them into a scenario that can be useful in shaping the thinking.

A few years ago, I was working with a non-profit that operated schools for children with special educational needs (SEN), and there were various trends that we identified. More children were receiving a formal diagnosis; there was greater appetite for those with less complex needs to be included and supported within mainstream schools; the schools themselves were being strongly encouraged to move out of local authority control by becoming Academies and independent chains, and, as a result, were gaining increasing freedom and starting to more actively compete for students and reputation. These trends all pointed towards a future scenario that could be significantly different from the landscape of the past.

One problem this scenario raised for the charity was that historically their schools had generated a surplus, which had been used to support its overheads and charitable work. By changing to an Academy model, which appeared inevitable in the longer term, all the income received would need to stay within the educational trust; there would no longer be a surplus flowing into the charity. The trust would be trading off the charity's brand, using its years of expertise and likely recruiting from its cohort of trained staff, for free: a nice advantage for the trust, but a financial challenge for the charity.

The key insight from this was the potential need to create a formal, commercial service relationship between the charity and the educational trust, and to define services, training programmes, and advisory support much more clearly, so they could recover an appropriate fee. Knowing that the trust would be independent and therefore obliged to shop around for these services, they'd need to be of excellent quality and good value for money. The flipside was that once those services were formalized, they could also be offered to others. Indeed, the rapid growth of Academies and Free Schools with increased autonomy and flexibility, and with potentially more SEN-registered children, could be far more of a market opportunity than a competitive threat.

Scenario planning can be a powerful tool, particularly where the trends are clear and their implications easy to see. But there are other times when the important trends are more remote, and their implications need a bit more work to be drawn out.

In one scenario planning exercise with a research charity, we had identified a bunch of major trends on the scientific side: growing research areas, clinical practices, potential breakthroughs and so on. We were about halfway through the process when one of the attendees pointed out that we hadn't really talked about the technology trends, which turned out to be surprisingly important. Part of the charity's role was in global coordination: of patients, treatments and surgery, and all the data and logistics that went with it, from hospital visits to DNA screening.

Some big trends are difficult to grapple with, often because they're multifaceted, fast moving and comparatively hard to predict. The scenarios that emerge from combining vast and interconnected global datasets, virtual and augmented reality, and artificial intelligence (AI), for instance, are potentially so far-reaching that their possibilities border on science fiction. For these types of scenario, personification can be a very useful way in. Personifying a trend is simpler than it sounds and can quickly unlock the conversation and the imagination. In this case, I suggested we personify AI and Big Data as Google, and we picked out two augmented reality applications that we found online, which were being developed for healthcare and surgery. We then asked ourselves the preposterous but surprisingly effective question: 'If Google bought those two businesses, and decided to transform our entire market, how would they – how *could* they do it?'

For the next 30 minutes, the team broke into small groups, drew their thoughts on flip-chart pages, and played back their ideas in the form of a news article from five years in the future, describing a 'revolutionary new approach'. What they had created were scenarios, unlikely for sure, but provocative, inspiring and extremely useful nonetheless, particularly when looking at the follow-up question: 'Given that a fair portion of them are technically possible, and could revolutionize the effectiveness of what we do, what aspects of that future would have the most positive impact, and what is our role in bringing them about?'

This process, of extending trends into discrete scenarios, and personifying the ones that are harder to pin down, helps us to build pictures of the potential futures we could face. Some will be very likely, others will be more directional or illustrative of the possibilities, but each can be helpful in taking people out of the present and into a world of opportunity, and to imagine a future context for the organization that could be very different from its past.

Scenario planning can also galvanize actions that are strategically important but feel less pressing or urgent than the day-to-day. Developing provocative scenarios around the various threats and opportunities for charity retailers in Chapter 3, for example, could be one way to raise their internal profile and priority. Richard Williams, Director of Enterprise and Development at the National Council for Voluntary Organisations (NCVO), talked me through how one particular scenario had galvanized action within his organization.

In 2008, NCVO, whose Almanac data appeared at the very start of this book, started scenario planning around changes in government policy. Tony Blair had just left office, the banks had crashed, public finances were not in a good place, and meanwhile NCVO was getting around 45 per cent of its total income through government funding. One of the scenarios they envisaged was that a new government would slash that funding in half.

It was largely the implication of that scenario that triggered NCVO to invest around £2.5 million in developing its London home, creating rental space for two other organizations and a suite of meeting and conference rooms. By 2018, rent and conference income had grown to almost 30 per cent of NCVO's total income. Other initiatives to grow membership, events and various earned income streams were similarly triggered by the scenario plan, and it's as well that they were.

Between 2012 and 2015, NCVO's government funding was cut, not merely by half, but almost completely. By 2018 it had fallen from 45 per cent of the organization's income to just 2 per cent. And yet, NCVO found ways to entirely neutralize the impact on its financial position, while increasing its membership reach and surveyed engagement throughout the period. The scenario plan didn't get the future exactly right, but that's the nature of scenario planning. What it did do was give NCVO a two-year head-start and a powerful sense of urgency, both of which it used to outstanding effect to secure its own financial future and to significantly enhance its portfolio of services for members.

The benefits of this type of scenario planning are threefold. The first, as with NCVO, is that it can create a sense of urgency and catalyse critical actions. The second is that it will generate ideas, often big ones, radical ones, ones that could be genuinely transformational. The third is the future context it defines, in which other ideas, from other perspectives, will need to be able to work: to be attractive to beneficiaries, customers or commissioners, and to help position the organization in a unique space or niche where it can have incremental impact and escape from the competition.

FIGURE 6.3  The future-back strategy model

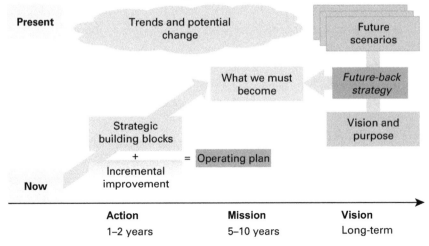

From a broader, organizational perspective, those same future scenarios can encourage better strategic thinking about the organization and the people it supports. They can inform the conversation about the role that the non-profit will need to play, and what it will need to become, in order to fulfil that role and achieve its ultimate purpose.

The diagram in Figure 6.3 shows the how all those elements come together to develop a future-back strategy, one that sets out the vision that the organization wants to achieve, within the context of the future that is likely to emerge based on current trends. The choices the organization then makes, about the role it will need to play and what it will need to become, can then be broken down into big, strategic building blocks, one of which will hopefully be a commercial development agenda.

## Creating a focused agenda

Alan George Lafley, known by most as 'A G', led global consumer goods giant Procter and Gamble (P&G) for two stints, the first from 2000 to 2010, and the second from 2013 to 2015. For most of that time he and his team worked with a strategy consultant, Roger L Martin, and between those two stints, Lafley and Martin collaborated on a book that encapsulated their approach to strategy at P&G. The book was called *Playing to Win*,[3] and their entire approach was based on answering two questions: where should the business play, and how will it win?

For a business, where to play will be defined by the market dynamics, growth potential, profitability and so forth, but also by the organization's ability to win in that market, based on its unique innovations and capabilities. For mission-driven non-profits, where to play will largely be defined by what needs to be done for the vision to be realized, the role it needs to perform, the unmet need, the theory of change and so on, but equally, by where the organization can succeed, where it can do a better job than anyone else, where it can 'win'. The aim of Lafley and Martin's approach was to create pin-sharp focus on the choice of market and the development of a winning business model in that market. For Lafley, there was no prize for second place, no purpose in making up the numbers. If a brand couldn't become number one in its market, it had no future in the P&G portfolio. It was that strategic philosophy that enabled P&G to more than double in size and value over the first 10 years of Lafley's tenure.

In September 1997, while Lafley was being groomed for CEO success in Cincinnati, Steve Jobs was in Cupertino, watching the company he had founded, and been unceremoniously sacked by, approach bankruptcy. By the time Jobs agreed to return and take the reins, Apple had just two months of cash left to burn. One of the first things he did was to slash 80 per cent of the product inventory and cut 70 per cent of the innovation projects from the product roadmap. Into the bin went Apple's previous strategy of entering more and more categories, along with a plethora of 'quick-win' product extensions, to be replaced with Steve's vision of a very small number of 'insanely great' products, backed by great marketing and great execution.

Instead of diversifying into lots of things, the renewed Apple focused on just a few potentially huge opportunities, and then scaled them beyond what anyone thought was possible. Apple, consistently named as one of the world's most innovative[4] and financially successful organizations, makes most of its money from just five products: Macs, iPods, iPads, iPhones and watches. And four of them are essentially the same thing in a different-sized case. Compared to P&G, Apple plays in a tiny number of markets, but that focus has given it an extraordinary capacity to win in all of them.

Focus is a huge factor in the success of non-profits as well, as the earlier examples from RNIB and Skills for Care should attest. That's why a commercial development agenda should focus on no more than three or four opportunities at most, maybe even fewer, otherwise they simply won't get the investment, focus and support they will need to fulfil their true potential. But getting down to a few, big opportunities means putting aside a great many that don't make the cut, some of which will appear to be very attractive quick wins that really feel like they ought to be pursued. But the thing about quick wins is that they're rarely quick, they never deliver as much of a win as they promise, and they invariably steal time and focus away from the bigger ideas.

They're tempting because people can already see how they can be done, they'll have something to show for their efforts relatively soon and everyone will feel successful. But quick wins don't move the strategy forward nor, for all the brief sense of success, do they inspire the people within the organization towards greater things.

In 1962, JFK inspired a generation with these words: 'We choose to go to the moon and do the other things, not because they are easy, but because they are hard, because that goal will serve to organize and measure the best of our energies and skills.' At no point in his speech did JFK list a dozen quick wins that he intended to crack on with first to build some momentum and get a few runs on the board. Quick wins are a distraction. There will always be more where those first few came from, and those big, scary moon-shot opportunities will languish on the to-do pile for month after month.

The chart in Figure 6.4 is fast and easy to use and is one way to avoid the tyranny of quick wins taking over the selection process. A chart on the wall, a bunch of Post-its and a 20-minute exercise with the team can quickly draw out agreement on where the biggest opportunities are, and, starting top right

FIGURE 6.4  The value versus difficulty trade-off

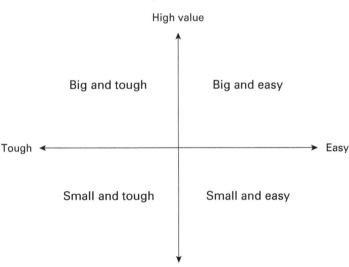

and moving top left, can shortcut a great deal of debate. Putting the remaining Post-its in a box marked 'for next year' can also be very helpful in getting people to let go of their favourites. The box might never see the light of day again, but it doesn't matter; the conversation has moved on and the opportunities have been narrowed down to the ones that can really make a difference.

There will be other criteria for choosing the final list of opportunities that will make it onto the development agenda, and there's no single right way to narrow down a long list to a short one. The Profit/Impact Matrix is a good tool, as is a test against the future scenarios, and the closer the fit with the organization's future role and mission the better, but the exact criteria will be different in each situation. Some non-profits may need to prioritize financial value, investment or speed of return; others will be influenced by risks or capacity constraints; some may be constrained by their values, constitution or articles of association. But whatever the basis for selection, there are four principles that should always be front of mind:

1  **Think big**
   Ideas that look small will only ever *be* small. Shortlist only those ideas that have the potential to create a transformational change.

2  **Play to your strengths**
   If you're going to compete, choose a game you can win. Prioritize those ideas for which you can develop a clear advantage.

3  **Take risks**
   The development process includes steps to test, adapt and prove each initiative before investing to scale anything up. There's no value in playing safe.

4  **Focus**
   More than one, less than six. Three is a good number to aim for.

## Maximizing opportunities

As we saw earlier, ambition is an essential aspect in maximizing the value of opportunities, but another is combination. Right from the start, before narrowing down the options, there can be enormous benefit from looking at how different ideas might fit together to become more than the sum of their parts. Often there are natural clusters or a broader ecosystem of opportunity that can be developed from ideas that may have emerged from completely different conversations and perspectives.

In one organization I worked with, one of the teams suggested increasing the scope and ambition of the charity's professional training service into higher-value tiers of content and support. Other ideas had previously come from a different group to educate professionals in other fields who had important interactions with their beneficiaries. And still more ideas had emerged from separate conversations about the quality of care services, and of independent living aids on the market, and how beneficiaries would benefit from some kind of focus-group testing, standards ratings or an independent badge of quality.

Each of these ideas had come from a different source, been proposed and championed by different people, and yet, as we worked back through that long initial list and started discussing how the different ideas related to each other, the concept of an integrated service across partner and related organizations, one that could pave the way for professional and product certification, emerged as one of the most interesting areas to explore.

To recognize these clusters and to build on them, to uncover the bigger opportunities they represent and to fully appreciate their potential, requires that same strategic mindset that I mentioned in the last section. Considering not: 'What can we do with what we have?' but instead: 'What could this be if we put everything behind it?' Maximizing the opportunities throughout this process requires a sustained emphasis on combining and expanding the potential of ideas – it's easy to underestimate how important that is, but without it, the opportunity value can evaporate surprisingly quickly.

The temptation is often very powerful, particularly for those closest to the relevant parts of the organization, to reframe what's being discussed as an extension of what's already being done, to switch to a tactical, planning mindset and revert to what is known, rather than to think afresh. It's hard for experts in any subject, who live it every day, not to limit the discussion with their experience and preconceptions; to allow their biases of what would or wouldn't be practical, viable or acceptable to curtail the conversation about what could be possible.

The customer biases I mentioned earlier, for example how charging might create a barrier for professionals, a two-tier system for beneficiaries, a reputational risk from corporates, are all likely to emerge. It's rarely a simple case of resistance to change, however much it may feel like it. These are often deeply held beliefs, embedded within and handed down through departmental cultures and advocated because they are honestly felt to be in the best interests of the organization. Some of those beliefs may be flawed, but none of them can be ignored, because they will come back to bite.

Strategy processes generally consist of a small number of discrete workshops, with time in between when most of the real work gets done. Figure 6.5 shows the overall process to create a commercial development agenda. Some organizations will be able to do this faster and more efficiently than others: for some it might be a couple of workshops over a few weeks, for others it might take half a dozen over as many months.

Ultimately, the quality and value of the end result: the agenda, opportunities and initiatives, will depend entirely on how well each of those workshops delivers on its aims, and the success of each of those workshops depends

FIGURE 6.5  Process to create a commercial development agenda

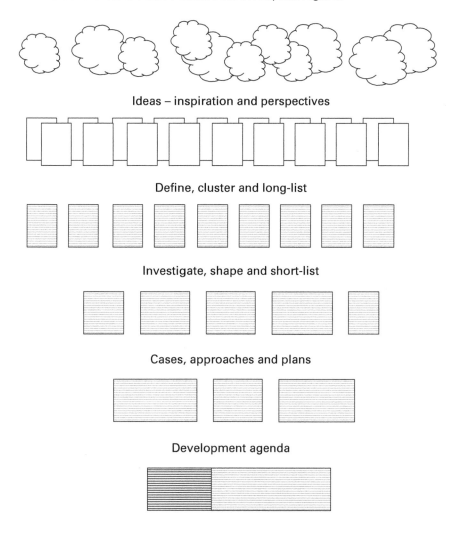

Ideas – inspiration and perspectives

Define, cluster and long-list

Investigate, shape and short-list

Cases, approaches and plans

Development agenda

entirely on the quality of the individual work that happens in between. That time, in between workshops, is where the process will flourish or fail, and its where those biases and beliefs will all come into play.

It is in between the workshops that ideas and opportunities get explored and defined, written up in documents that describe the potential value and impact, what's in and out of scope, who the paying customers would be, what the potential scale, risks and uncertainties might be. The people who do that work will invariably be the people who know the areas best, which means they are the same people who are most likely to have constraining assumptions, ethical concerns and unconscious biases. Thus, the opportunities envisaged in a workshop can sometimes be very different from the ones that come back in a scoping document a few weeks later.

The first step in avoiding this issue is to create an environment where those concerns are welcomed into the conversation, where assumptions and biases can be drawn out and discussed. Once they're out in the open, they can be articulated as risks that can be safely tested and potentially mitigated, and as hypotheses that can be validated or disproved long before anything gets rolled out. An approach that recognizes and accepts emotional reservations, and turns them into a rational, grown-up discussion, is not only reassuring for the individuals; it sets a cultural expectation that concerns will be heard, but they can also be overcome.

The second step is to proactively support people between the sessions. Exploring and researching commercial opportunities is often a new experience for people working in a non-profit. It can be daunting, and even if they appear confident, most will benefit from support or coaching to help them through the tasks. That support needs to echo the same emotional-rational approach to accepting and drawing out concerns, rationalizing them into hypotheses and accommodating them as tests or risks within a project. This is why choosing someone really good to manage the overall process can make a huge difference in the scale of opportunities that ultimately emerge. Someone who can coordinate the detail but also take the time to check in regularly, to listen and advise, understand the emotional context of the people and teams they're working with and gently nudge them back on track, can be worth their weight in gold.

To maximize the potential of the opportunities, therefore, the process will need three essential elements: it has to be led with an ambitious vision; set in an environment of trust and openness for ideas and concerns alike; and underpinned with a combination of emotional as well as practical support for the people doing the work.

I've yet to experience a process with all of those elements in place that hasn't found extensive opportunities and made a dramatic difference. Conversely, whenever a process has hit potholes or delays, where the size of opportunity has fallen short of the potential, it has invariably been due to the absence of one or more of them. Combining those three elements should lead to the opportunities increasing in potential at each stage of the process, resulting in an exciting, high-potential development agenda.

Each of the opportunities that makes it into the final development agenda will be big and ambitious, but at that point, each will still be based on a whole bunch of assumptions and hypotheses: the assumption that it's possible; that it will have the desired impact; that paying customers exist, can be found and will want what's on offer. The purpose of the second stage is to develop the idea into a real proposition, to engage with customers, test and refine it, and to validate or disprove each of those assumptions, without spending too much time and money on ideas that aren't going to work.

The approach will need to be flexible but the measurement needs to be rigorous in order to provide both the learning and the evidence that it works. As much as the service or product itself may change during its development, the outcomes that it's trying to achieve won't change, nor will the measures and performance indicators, the targets and decision points.

To accommodate that combination of flexibility and rigour, the development stage of the process has three high-level phases: getting an idea up and running, whether as a prototype or a small test with a couple of customers; validating and proving the model on a slightly larger scale; and finally investing in its expansion or rollout (Figure 6.6). The idea is to get through the first two of those phases as quickly and cheaply as possible, building and proving the investment case for phase three's expansion.

This approach embodies the 'fail fast and learn quickly' philosophy that's been instrumental in the success of many technology entrepreneurs, and is exemplified in Eric Reiss's 2011 book, *The Lean Startup*.[5] I've given more copies of that book to my charity clients than any other.

The plans for each of the opportunities within the development agenda will be based around that three-phase process. The owners will need to define who they're going to work with from the customer perspective, how they are going to work up and prototype a product or service, and the business model that will go along with it if it's going to be able to scale. They will also need to outline the key measures of success, and how they intend to test and validate each of their hypotheses and find ways to disprove or mitigate any big risks. Those measures will be required not just around the impact,

FIGURE 6.6  The development curve for commercial ideas

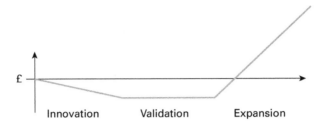

but also around the business model and its ability to be rapidly and cost-effectively scaled. Some non-profits are incredibly adept at the former: developing, testing and validating the impact of their interventions. Very few are adept at the latter: validating a model's capacity for commercial growth.

The NSPCC is an excellent example of the former. In Chapter 5 I described the strategic change in direction that the NSPCC undertook in 2009, where it shifted its focus from services to innovation. Critical to their success since then has been their innovation model. The NSPCC model comprises a six-stage process that includes prototyping, developing and refining on a small scale, before expanding to a slightly larger scale to formally validate against control groups. It's a more nuanced model than the one in Figure 6.6, and more tailored to the context in which the NSPCC works, but it follows the same three-phase approach, and on the impact side, it's extremely effective and robust.

The later stages of the NSPCC process, for actually scaling an intervention, are currently less well developed. The organization has a proud history of getting its funding primarily through public donation, and much of its success over the years has been facilitated by the flexibility that model provides. But research is an expensive business, scaling interventions through fundraising alone is not sustainable, and in any case, returning to service delivery is not part of NSPCC's vision.

It's probably fair to say that the organization is still working out its own internal view on the options, who to charge, what to charge for, how to leverage its research and brand, its expertise and intellectual property, and what its ambitions should be for commercially earned income. But it has recognized that the value its insights offer is potentially very high, and an income-generating approach to scaling could dramatically increase the reach of its work and build the capacity for further innovations.

The challenge for the NSPCC, as it is for most organizations in the non-profit sector, is that developing and proving a scalable business model is at least as big a task as developing and proving an intervention's impact. Both aspects need to run alongside each other, from prototype and testing through to validation, and each should influence the other. A service that delivers brilliant outcomes but is completely unaffordable for the target market will ultimately have far less impact than one that delivers 80 per cent of the outcomes for a fraction of the cost. Considering both aspects together rather than separately is likely to produce a far better model, with a much greater potential to successfully scale up.

It is this ability to grow and expand that ultimately defines the maximum potential of an opportunity. Working out how it can be expanded, what steps would need to be taken, what approach would be pursued, then testing that they work, is every bit as important as demonstrating the impact. Impact is clearly a prerequisite, but impact alone is not enough to rapidly scale up an innovation, as a great many non-profits have discovered.

## Seven commercial essentials

The purpose of the validation phase, in Figure 6.5, is to prove that the innovation can demonstrably do everything that will be required in order to successfully grow to scale. It is the culmination of a process of rapid learning and refinement, one that only ends when it succeeds in hitting all of its targets, or the plug is pulled because it's clear that it never will. It's what Educating Girls spent three years on and, as we saw in Chapter 2, it's what Tesco spent six years doing with their Express format, and what they singularly failed to do with Fresh and Easy.

For organizations like the NSPCC, validation is focused on measuring impact and outcomes. For others, like the Development Impact Bond examples, it also includes economic measures to understand whether the predicted savings or financial returns are emerging where they're supposed to, and to identify and unpick any unexpected issues preventing their realization. But for full-on commercial models, there are seven elements required for sustainable growth that are equally essential to validate.

The seven commercial essentials range from the ability to make customers aware of what you can do for them, and to provoke their interest, to being able to convert that interest, at least some of the time, into a profitable sale. In order to be ready for investment, a commercial model needs to have demonstrated that it:

- provides distinct, measurable value to the paying customer;
- can be effectively and efficiently delivered, time after time;
- can generate demand within a large potential market of customers;
- can cost-effectively create interest and attract those potential customers;
- can consistently convert a good proportion of that interest into sales;
- can retain customers, deepening their loyalty and increasing their value;
- makes enough money to cover every cost and fund new investment.

There is a tendency to assume, not just in charities, but in many small and mid-sized businesses as well, that if a product or service is good enough, it will sell itself. That's why most innovations fail to take off. The validation phase isn't just about getting the proposition worked out, it's about getting the whole package worked out: proving there is a large potential market out there; finding the most cost-effective channels for marketing; a viable model for sales; proving that a customer, who has cost time, money and effort to recruit, has a lifetime value beyond the first transaction.

None of these is difficult to explore, to find solutions for, and to demonstrate that those solutions work, but they have to be part of the plan or they won't happen. Which brings us to the development process itself: taking an idea on paper into a real-life proposition, getting it working and proving it can scale.

There are two generic approaches to innovation; both work well, but some situations will suit one better than the other. One approach is to test out lots of variations in parallel and rapidly work out which ones are best. The other is to pick one idea and refine it over and over with a small group of customers, until it works. It's like a chef developing a new curry recipe: she can cook up a dozen variations for customers to taste, she could even serve each one for a week in her restaurant to see which customers come back, or she could invite a few customers into the kitchen, put together a basic recipe, then keep tweaking, adding, getting them to taste, until they're delighted.

In practice, ideas aimed at a wide audience with a relatively low price can benefit most from the multi-variant approach. Higher-value services with a smaller potential audience tend to succeed better with the co-creation approach, but they're not mutually exclusive. Starting with a range of tests and then quickly narrowing onto one or two to iterate with customers is a perfectly good approach (Figure 6.7).

FIGURE 6.7 Two approaches to innovation

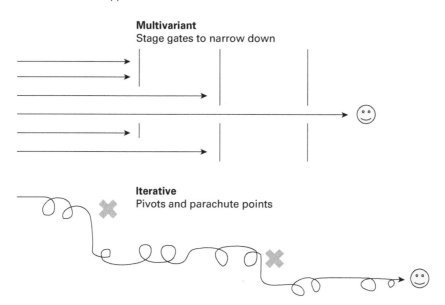

The key is to start with an outline plan that will work best for the particular type of opportunity in question, to set clear measures of success across all seven essentials, then to test, learn, change, and test again, as quickly and cheaply as possible. Most of the cost will likely be in the form of people: good people who have the skills to engage with customers, the flexibility to listen and adapt to what they hear, the confidence to iterate the offer and even to change the whole approach if they need to in order to find a solution that works.

That development process might take three months, or as with Educating Girls, it might take three years with a major 'pivot' being required halfway through, which is why a final, critical part of the strategy is the governance model. How often they will check in, how far they will be allowed to go, how much they can spend and, ultimately, at what point the plug will be pulled. Finding the fastest, cheapest way to fail, to prove that an idea isn't going to make it to scale, is every bit as important as finding the best way to succeed. Which is why the final part of the process in developing the agenda is defining not just the measures of success, but the indicators of failure and the milestones at which go, or no-go, decisions should be made.

Milestones and 'parachute points' (where a project can be cancelled at minimal cost), and the steering or reporting forum that will make those calls, all need to be part and parcel of the plans. Those, along with the financials: investment, value case and maximum downside if the plug has to be pulled, form the basis of approval for the strategy. If that strategy is successful, the initial ideas will be developed, tested and validated. Their impact and their value to customers will be proven, as will the approach for marketing and selling them.

That final point can't be overstated. You can have the best commercial ideas in the world, but if you can't market and sell them, they won't benefit anyone.

## Endnotes

**1** Covey, S R (1989) *The 7 Habits of Highly Effective People: Powerful lessons in personal change*, Simon & Schuster, New York

**2** Toffler, A (1970) *Future Shock*, Random House, New York

**3** Martin, R and Lafley, A G (2013) *Playing to Win: How strategy really works*, Harvard Business Review Press, Brighton, MA

**4** Ringel, M *et al* (2018) The Most Innovative Companies 2018: Innovators go all in on digital, 17 January, Boston Consulting Group

**5** Ries, E (2011) *The Lean Startup: How constant innovation creates radically successful businesses*, Penguin, Harmondsworth

# 07

# Keys to commercial success

## Marketing demystified

Marketing is not just an important skill for scaling innovations; it's a critical discipline that underpins the sustainability and profitability of just about any organization. Nor is it simply a tactical set of activities; it's a strategic way of thinking that's as relevant across the executive as it is within a small corner of the external communications team.

At a tactical level, commercial marketing is not the same as marketing for fundraising and campaigning. It's often directed at a different audience, based on a different premise, will use different channels and platforms, and carry a different message, often in a very different tone. At a strategic level, it's even more different. Many of the areas I've already covered are aspects of strategic marketing, from customer insights to brand positioning and product differentiation, and there are libraries of books and no shortage of business courses and consultants specializing in its myriad facets. But behind all that complexity, the purpose of commercial marketing is simple: to attract customers into the sales process.

That sales process might be a simple click on a 'buy now' button or an in-depth meeting about needs and potential solutions. Different sales models will inevitably require a different marketing approach to support them, and optimizing that approach will be a continual process of learning and evolution, remarkably similar to that of a theory of change. Ultimately, marketing is about prompting a desired change in the attitude and behaviour of a particular group of individuals. Changing human behaviour is at the heart of what many charities do and is something at which a great many of them excel. Rethinking marketing in terms of engaging a desired and beneficial behavioural change, and unpicking the key steps with a theory of change for marketing, can enable a charity to use the enormous advantages that its social change skills can offer to develop far more efficient and effective marketing for its commercial work. The main steps required for that behavioural change are reasonably well known; it's how to get customers to take those steps that each organization needs to learn for itself.

In 1908, Elias St. Elmo Lewis published a book called *Financial Advertising*,[1] which contained the first incarnation of what would go on to become the 'purchase funnel', a theory that has influenced advertisers and marketers ever since. Lewis's original three aspects of effective advertising were to attract attention, to awaken interest, and to persuade or convince the customer to buy. Subsequently a fourth was added, to get the customer to act, and the acronym AIDA adopted, to describe the steps in the purchase journey as: Awareness, Interest, Desire and Action. Later, the funnel metaphor was introduced, to recognize how the potential audience within the funnel inevitably narrows from one step to the next.

Almost every marketing team has their own conceptual version of the purchase funnel and what it takes to move customers through it, even if it only exists in their heads. Some have more steps, some fewer; some focus entirely what happens before a sale, others on what happens afterwards as well. Figure 7.1 shows mine. One of the biggest changes in marketing since Lewis's time is the advent of social media. Referral has always been a key factor in high-value sales and professional and personal service businesses, but Facebook, Instagram and a plethora of other platforms have extended that dynamic much further into consumer markets, reducing the public's reliance on adverts and increasing the role of advocates. The model in Figure 7.1 reflects that change.

The choice of stages and language will be context specific, but whether the focus is advocacy or advertising, knowing where customers sit in the funnel and tailoring activity to meet them and move them is fundamental to any marketing strategy. If the marketing team for a toothpaste brand knew that 90 per cent of their target market were aware of the brand, but only 20 per cent would consider buying it, they would realize very quickly that spending money raising awareness isn't going to drive sales.

Doing more research might tell them that most of those drop-outs buy toothpaste to freshen their breath, and because they associate the brand in question with whitening and other brands with freshness, the brand would need to reposition its marketing messages, and possibly redesign its product, if it wanted to engage their interest and thereby grow its sales. Thus, understanding customers, repositioning products and articulating them in a way

FIGURE 7.1  An example purchase funnel

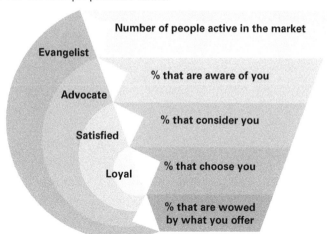

that 'resonates' with the target customers' perceived needs are prerequisites for effective marketing.

Moving customers further through the funnel, from considering to choosing, is aided enormously by differentiation: the distinctiveness of the proposition, the attractiveness of the brand and the impact of the message in getting those things across. The business card exercise in Chapter 5 is actually a marketing exercise, as is the strategic differentiation grid. These are both ways to sharpen a proposition in order to create a marketing message that will persuade potential customers to make the right choice, but crafting that message is an art – one that's far older than the advertising industry.

Probably compiled between 330 and 320 BCE from notes to support his lectures to the students at his Lyceum, Aristotle's *Rhetoric*[2] outlines the three modes of persuasion that are every bit as central to marketing today as they were to public speaking over two millennia ago: logos, pathos and ethos.

**Logos** is the logical, rational argument, of product functionality or a business case for investment. Logos is the articulation of value: this is what you get for your money, and why it's worth spending more to get it.

**Pathos** is emotion. While rational argument might influence choice, the desire to choose and to act on that choice is invariably emotional. I might say that I want to move to a new house for rational reasons: size, location and so forth, but I'll probably have put up with those practical inconveniences for some time, until I hit an emotional tipping point that moves me to action. I might want one that's the right size, has a nice garden, good schools and transport links, but the emotions I feel when I walk up the path and through the front door will have a huge influence on which house I choose to buy.

**Ethos** is credibility: the character, the ethics, the authenticity of the personality making the pitch. It's the essential third leg of the marketing stool and it's why we have celebrity endorsements, why we listen to people we believe are experts, why we value peer recommendations above all others.

All of these come together in the three Cs of marketing: customer, content and channel. The choice of customer that's being marketed to, and where they are likely to be within the purchasing funnel, will dictate the type of content that could move them to the next stage (eg from in need to aware, or from considering to choosing). Understanding what drives the customer will also inform how to balance the rational case and the emotional one to best effect, and will help to determine how best to convey credibility.

The combination of customer and content will also define which channels are most likely to be effective. The visual nature of Instagram lends itself to emotional content: inspiration, aspiration and desire, while an advertorial in a periodical might be a better place for the rational case, and a published journal paper better for credibility, but none of those will be effective unless the potential customer sees it, and most importantly, sees it while they're in buying-mode. An operations director for a major corporation isn't going to choose her next business-wide training programme by reading a Facebook post or a promoted tweet on a Sunday afternoon, nor is she going to spend six-figure sums based on a speculative e-mail and a slick website.

What might turn her head, though, would be a non-profit delivering a keynote or workshop at her industry conference, especially if it's a two-hander with a client who happens to be that operations director's peer in another organization, and listening to that peer talk about the experience and the benefits that came from working together. The credibility and emotional impact would be far more profound than if the non-profit were simply manning a stand in the break-out area, no matter how compelling the rational arguments on their posters and brochures might be. Furthermore, if that client up on the stage happens to be one of her competitors, or someone she knows and esteems, and the benefits he describes include personal ones – making his life easier, making the team more positive – the emotional and credibility modes will be even more impactful and may prove so persuasive that she will want to work with the non-profit irrespective of whether the business case stacks up. Customer advocacy and evangelism can create powerful marketing strategies.

Going back to the innovation process from Chapter 6, for any new development, the marketing strategy doesn't need to be fully worked out on day one. To begin with, the majority of customers and sales will probably come, not from marketing (or as 'inbound sales calls', to use the sales vernacular), but from outbound sales activity – from getting out and talking with people, tapping into pre-existing relationships, working through the network and gaining introductions, and that's as it should be. Outbound selling, particularly at the higher-value end, is invariably the fastest way to kick-start a trial. But this is where we come back to the question of scalability.

Outbound selling can be very time intensive, and the initial customers will, almost by definition, be easier to reach and engage than the wider audience that will be required to grow beyond the trial phase. Proving that an outbound sales model can acquire easy-to-reach customers is not the same as demonstrating the ability to cost-effectively grow a business. As onerous and challenging as it may sound, at some point during the validation process the team will need to draft out a marketing strategy and then go out and get some proof that it can work, that it can generate inbound sales leads, and that those leads can be converted into business.

The most effective marketing gets in front of the ideal prospective customer whenever they're most likely to be in a receptive mode, meeting them wherever they are in the purchase journey, with the right blend of ethos, pathos and logos, to nudge them through the stages of the funnel, to get them to want to engage with the sales process, whatever that happens to be. The right blend only comes through practice, through trial and error, which is why it's so important to include marketing as a distinct requirement in the innovation and validation process.

Listening to customers, getting as clear an understanding as possible of their different segments and archetypes, what they value, how they make choices, the language they use when describing their needs, are all invaluable at the outset, but marketing will always be a learning journey: of learning better ways of raising awareness and connecting it to need; of articulating unique value and establishing credibility; of engendering a powerful emotional appeal to act.

The more effective the marketing becomes, the easier the sales process that follows it will be. For some, that process will be as simple as a click on an online image, but for other, higher-value or more complex sales, it will be a conversation; a meeting; a process of relationship building and dialogue. That's why, as I mentioned at the start of the chapter, the aim of marketing, and therefore the strategies and plans, and even the measures within a validation phase, will depend entirely on the model that's going to be used for sales.

In a retail model, where relatively low-value products and services are being marketed to a wide audience, marketing needs to take the customer right through to the start of the transaction itself – to the store, the website or the telephone booking line. In contrast, marketing's end goal for a more complex or higher-value sale is much more likely to be a call or a meeting with a salesperson, which can often be a tougher sell to a prospective customer than an online click. Either way, if marketing doesn't link properly to the sales process, it will inevitably damage growth, but if the message is compelling enough, even that can be overcome.

The aim of retail marketing is to get the customer wanting to buy the product. The aim of the sales process is to make it as easy and intuitive as possible for them to buy, ideally without them even having to think about it. But there are many examples where, if the marketing is good enough and customers want it enough, they'll find a way to buy it, even if it means scouring the internet or queuing for hours outside a store.

Likewise, the aim of high-value marketing is not simply to articulate a rationale and some options, and offer a phone number or a 'contact us' webpage, it's to provoke a strong enough desire in the customer that they want to make contact, to prioritize time for that meeting, and to be open for that dialogue. Making that contact as easy as possible to achieve is, of course, a good thing to do, but if the desire is strong enough, customers will find a way to get in touch, and, ironically, sometimes the more effort a customer has to make to get into the sales process, the more committed they become to the relationship that ensues.

## Relationships built on value

For a business to be successful over the longer term, not only must it deliver great value to its customers, but its marketing must be able to articulate that value to new, prospective ones. It needs to create the perception of 'distinct value', that is, the additional level of value that its products or services deliver when compared to the available alternatives.

As we've seen, that additional value can come from a rational or an emotional perspective. Aston Martin cars, Louboutin shoes and Nike trainers might all claim some rational benefits over and above the alternatives, but they're each priced primarily on their emotional appeal. Time was that the big, branded products on supermarket shelves could be as well, but stores' own-label and the high-quality discount alternatives in chains such as Lidl and Aldi have steadily built their own levels of consumer trust, and the perceived additional value of many big consumer brands has steadily eroded as a result, as has the price premium they can now command.

Additional value, plus the scarcity of the proposition (per the laws of supply and demand), are two of the biggest factors in price. The rarer something is and the greater the additional rational and emotional value it offers, the higher it can be priced and the more margin it will deliver. That's why a consumer business with a strong, credible brand that has a powerful emotional appeal can sell products for far more than they cost to produce, and why people will always pay more for something that is customized or bespoke than they will for something they can get off the shelf at a dozen different places.

It can be true in product retail, it's almost always true in personal services, and it's invariably the case at the high-value end: relationships, conversations between individuals, rapport, trust and confidence are essential in turning a contact into a contract. The provision of value is the foundation of long-term commercial relationships, and it's that combination of financial and personal, emotional trust and connection, and unique distinctiveness, that will underpin a successful and sustainable enterprise.

The implications are relevant for any business. Pitching something that doesn't offer significant and compelling additional value, to customers with whom you have neither a strong relationship nor a deep emotional connection, means that the only way you can possibly win business is through a rock-bottom price. The converse is also true: developing a strong, dependent relationship, and offering a unique or highly bespoke proposition, can create plenty of headroom on price and deliver very attractive margins. This insight explains, for example, why so many non-profits struggle to make decent money when commercializing their knowledge and expertise (Figure 7.2).

The temptation for many organizations is to package their expertise into off-the-shelf courses, or days of consultant time. This commoditizes what they do, pushing prospective customers to make comparisons with what other types of consultant charge for a day, and the fees for other courses in the sector, irrespective of whether the value they provide is remotely

FIGURE 7.2 The value of expertise

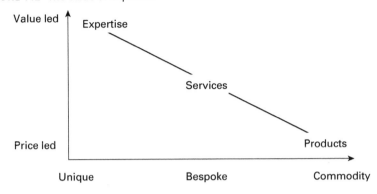

comparable. And it's not just customers who are influenced in this way; so are internal teams.

I've lost count of the number of times I've spoken with training teams about the outcomes people get from attending their courses, and the value it provides to them and their organizations, only to get to the pricing conversation and hear, 'But that's what most people charge for a one-day course...'. Something that could well be unique and of very high value is priced as a commodity, simply because of the way it's presented to customers. The fact that it's also usually offered as a transactional sale, rather than being developed through a relationship-based sales approach, is another issue and one that I'll return to shortly.

Alongside scarcity and perceived additional value, the third critical factor in securing good margins is the confidence it takes to put a high price out there and to stick with it, irrespective of psychological bias or the pressure to drive sales. Pricing is a statement that underscores a brand's perceived value. If Chanel dropped their prices because they were worried about Next, it would destroy that value, undermine scarcity and kill the brand. Non-profits have the same choices about positioning as anyone else and might choose a low price to better serve the mission, but nevertheless, it is a choice, and one that sends a powerful psychological signal about the value on offer. A high price implies a high value, a low price implies a commodity, and most customers expect to get what they pay for. There are more than enough external pressures pushing down on price and margin, without a non-profit adding its own internal ones through lack of confidence in the value it offers and the price that value should command.

The same principles apply to public-sector markets. The sole purpose of most tender and procurement processes is to commoditize what is being purchased: to define not only the requirement, but the specific details of the service being commissioned, in such a way that there's a level playing field to accommodate as many competitors as possible, in order that they can slug it out, primarily on price. Commissioners might be measured on social outcomes, but however much we may wish it weren't the case, their procurement teams are invariably measured purely on financials. That's why building a relationship with commissioners themselves, based on a much broader concept of value, engaging them with unique solutions and enabling them to manage the propensity of their procurement teams to specify, commoditize and manufacture competition, is critical in public services markets. Perceived value, whether rational or emotional, takes time and effort to build within the mind of any buyer, which is why there is a great deal of truth in the old adage: 'If the first you hear about an opportunity is when you read the tender document, you've already lost.'

Consistently building new layers of value into a relationship is essential for escaping commoditization, retaining customers and avoiding the low-price tender trap, but it's also important for attracting customers in the first place, and for developing more valuable, long-term relationships. This is the concept of the value gradient, an example of which is in Figure 7.3.

Charity umbrella organization, NCVO, has a training and consultancy model based on exactly those principles. It offers a great deal of information for free, from its Almanac data about the sector to 'how-to' information on governance, volunteering HR and so forth. Those free resources establish it as the first port of call for many of those topics. Toolkits, diagnostics, reports

FIGURE 7.3  Example value gradient

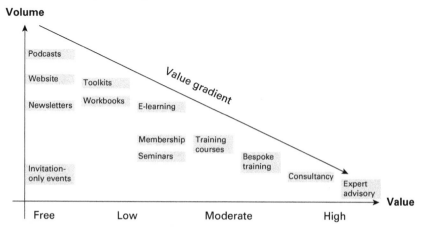

and workbooks that follow from those overviews are available for a fee with big, sometimes 100 per cent, member discounts.

Those tools are backed by training courses and programmes for a more substantial fee, with customized training and consultancy services at the far end of the value gradient. NCVO has 14,500 member organizations, whose membership fee is tiered by turnover. The smallest get free membership, the largest still pay less than £1,000 per year, although there are add-on tiers for access to exclusive events. Even so, NCVO's total membership income is around £1 million per year, versus around £2.1 million per year from the training, events and consulting offers for those same member organizations that sit further along the value gradient.

Organizations are more likely to join NCVO if they're able to get discounts on books and courses, but once they're members, they're also more likely to use NCVO for training and consultancy, because their membership has fostered a trusting relationship. NCVO's value gradient demonstrates the two qualities that can rapidly build and retain high-value customer relationships: it is simultaneously frictionless and sticky. Frictionless, in that for a customer it's a simple, almost natural, friction-free journey to engage with them, then to slide along the value gradient in line with the customer's needs. Every move to the right adds more value, makes a customer's life easier and helps them to solve more of their problems. It's also sticky, in that the more elements that the customer engages with, the less likely they are to consider going elsewhere for any of them, particularly if they've signed up to a membership or subscription. It is the same principle that makes the average Amazon Prime customer spend more than twice as much with Amazon as a non-Prime customer.

Frictionless and sticky are nakedly commercial concepts, and whether they are being used ethically or not depends entirely on the value gradient underneath them. To be ethical, the value at every step in the curve needs to be real, and it needs to serve the best interests of the customer. Just because a sticky relationship makes a customer less likely to look elsewhere, it doesn't provide an excuse to offer them less value for a higher price than they could get if they searched around. Relying on customers not finding out about a better option is not a recipe for sustainable success, it's a recipe for a brand disaster as soon as word gets out, as Age UK unintentionally discovered with utility tariffs.

If the proposition genuinely provides great value, if it genuinely helps customers improve their situation, then it is important to tell them about it and to encourage them to engage. Ethical marketing is not about persuading someone to do something that's in *your* best interests; it's about enabling them to make a choice that you believe could be in *their* best interests, one that will lead to better outcomes for *them*. It's about offering them value for which they will most likely be grateful.

A few years ago, a very old friend took me out for a drink and told me that he'd quit his corporate career and set up shop as a chimney sweep. This might sound apocryphal but it's a true story. When I'd finished asking the obvious questions about mid-life crises, we moved on to talk about his new business. The biggest challenge, as he'd learned during his training and had reinforced when speaking with his initial customers, is that people forget to get their chimneys swept. They might have it done when they first move in, but it rarely occurs to them to have it done again until it starts getting blocked or, God forbid, catches fire.

We kicked around some marketing ideas until, on the third beer, the 'Chimney Care Plan' was born – a unique and complimentary personal reminder service for loyal customers, with a frequency that could be set by them. I thought no more of it until about a year later, when we met up again for a beer. During the conversation, I asked him if he'd ever tried out the idea that we'd had.

'It's strange,' he replied, 'I reckon about 90 per cent of customers have signed up for it – it's really only the students that don't. I'm half booked up for this year already, and that's without any marketing.'

'That's brilliant', I said. 'Why do you say it's strange?' He put down his pint, and with a furrowed brow replied: 'They keep asking how much it costs. I don't think they can believe the reminder service is free.'

Great marketing shouldn't feel like marketing at all, it should feel like a service. NCVO doesn't attempt to channel or trick people into higher-value products through manipulative marketing, it makes them available because it knows members need them, and the more targeted and effective its marketing, the better it will be at enabling members to recognize and access what they need, and the more successful and sustainable their organizations should become as a result. If an organization can provide unique additional value to customers who need that value, it's not only appropriate to help customers understand and access it, it's an ethical obligation and potentially a highly valued service. And the same should be true, as we will see, for the sales process itself.

## Principles of ethical selling

Right at the start of the book, I touched on the language barriers that often arise when introducing commercial concepts into charity and non-profit cultures. It's a particular issue when it comes to sales skills, and the first time it comes up in conversation I usually get the same reaction: 'The idea of "selling" makes our people feel uncomfortable.' And it's not surprising.

The popular perception of sales sits somewhere between the pushy, manipulative egotists from *The Apprentice* and the original 'Wolf of Wall Street', Jordan Belfort.[3] Both reinforce the assumption that 'selling' is about finding ways to get punters to part with their money for something they neither need nor want; and that salespeople should 'Always Be Closing', to quote the iconic, caffeine-fuelled rant that Alec Baldwin delivers while hazing his new sales team in the film *Glengarry Glen Ross*.[4] And if that's what your people think, it's no wonder they feel uncomfortable. It's unethical, self-serving, and entirely the wrong mindset.

Nobody sets out to work in the third sector because they want a job in sales, but most people who work in sales didn't actually set out wanting a job in sales either. I don't think I've once heard a kid reply 'Sales' to the question 'What do you want to do when you grow up?' But the reality is that, for most of us, selling is an important skill, not just in business development, but in many aspects of our lives: selling our ideas to colleagues, selling a vision to stakeholders, selling the terrifying concept of green vegetables to our children. Those activities don't feel unethical or exploitative, and nor should any form of ethical selling.

When a personal coach works with a client to help her to set goals, to work through the barriers and clear away the obstacles, and to start and stay on the journey to achieving what she, herself, has defined as success, the coach is not selling her on that journey. He is helping her to understand what she needs, helping build confidence in the process and commitment to making it happen. *She* is selling *herself* on the actions and outcomes, because only then will she have the intrinsic motivation to follow through. The coach's expertise is in facilitating that process, bringing his experience to bear, to challenge goals, highlight common barriers, test whether the actions and steps the client intends to take will help her achieve her aims. It's hard to find a better parallel for the process of ethical selling.

Ethical selling is not about cold calling and persuading someone to buy from a list of products or services. It's the opposite. Ethical selling is about helping someone who trusts you enough to talk about a situation or a problem that they have, and working out what a solution might look like for them. If you can provide that solution, all the better. If not, simply through the conversation you've helped them clarify their needs, and at some point, when they have a different problem that you can help solve, they will almost certainly call you again.

Many years ago, in a time long before data protection laws, I was tasked with sourcing a contact list of 'ideal target' customers. Having spent the evening searching the internet for data providers, I e-mailed a couple of the most credible sites, to get a sense of what was available and how much it would cost. First thing in the morning my phone rang. It took me a bleary-eyed minute to work out my phone number had been in the signature on my e-mail, and my reaction was probably a little frosty. I just wanted an e-mail with a price, not a pushy salesman calling me halfway through my first coffee of the day. But that's not what I got. Instead, I got James.

James didn't call me to sell. He called to help me work things out. He began by saying they had over a million businesses on their database, and the more clearly we could specify exactly what we needed and precisely how we wanted to use it, the more cost-effective it would be. That simple statement made it immediately apparent that continuing with the conversation was going to serve my interests, and it gained James implicit permission to ask questions about what I wanted the data for, how we were intending to use it, and ultimately, the broader business problem we were trying to solve and the outcomes we hoped to achieve.

The questions he asked, and the suggestions he made, demonstrated a clear expertise around the subject. Not only was the data that I came away with far better suited to the purpose, my thoughts around how we would use it were immeasurably clearer. Was James the lowest price? I have no idea. I do know that he helped shape my thinking, gave me exactly what it turned out that I needed, he undoubtedly steered us towards a better outcome and he absolutely earned the business. Whenever the team needed data after that, his was the first number we would call.

Nobody likes being 'sold' to, and with an entire universe of information at our fingertips, none of us needs a salesperson to give us information – we can invariably get far better, more objective descriptions and comparisons online. What we do need, though, is expert advice to help us, and to test and challenge our preconceptions, particularly when making complex decisions in areas where we don't have a great deal of expertise. Someone we feel we can trust, who listens and understands, gets past our wants and into our needs and aspirations, and who can coach us through a decision process that will help us recognize and choose that which is in our best interests.

The 'pitch' might still have a place in showpiece events, for funding a film or getting in front of a panel of investors. But a pitch assumes that the person making it already understands, not just what the recipient says they want, but what they actually need. Even if the proposal is in response to a detailed brief, without a conversation it dramatically reduces the potential to use the expertise within the room to find a far better solution, and without establishing at least a basic level of trust, rapport and connection, it dramatically reduces the potential headroom on price.

Imagine the reaction of a Harley Street consultant if a new patient, having self-diagnosed their condition, turned up with a schedule of tests and treatments already prepared, and asked the consultant for a proposal and a price to carry them out. It is the consultant who has the expertise, who leads the patient through the diagnostic process and then prescribes the course of action. She is no more likely to pitch a solution before diagnosis than she is to assume the patient's diagnosis is the correct one. But that's precisely what many non-profits, which are equally expert in their own fields, do whenever they're approached by customers and commissioners who want their services or their expertise.

The process of ethical selling is diagnosis, followed by prescription. It operates by asking expert questions that get to the deeper needs and aspirations that we saw in Chapter 3, coaching through the decision process, defining a solution that's in the recipient's best interest, that will help them achieve the outcomes they need, and that will deliver an equitable return for the seller on the unique value they provide.

Developing the skills, the language and the behaviour to get that implicit permission to ask probing, sometimes challenging questions, and to quickly create the trust and rapport required for a potential customer to open up and answer them truthfully, is not something that can be easily learned from a book. Like riding a bike or learning to ski, it takes practice. One of the hardest behavioural shifts for many of my clients, when I teach them how to sell, is to simply ask a question and then shut up. The temptation is often to keep talking, to keep 'selling', until the prospective customer buckles under the sheer weight of words and says 'yes'. It never works. Usually the only reason they say yes is to get the meeting over with while they work out how they can follow up with a no and avoid having to meet that person again.

The skills required for ethical selling are ones of building rapport, creating trust, leading and shaping conversations by asking questions and active listening, and working out, on the fly, creative solutions to meet the deeper need. Even if the solution does end up being an off-the-shelf service or a combination of existing courses, it will still feel like a bespoke solution, the prospective customer will have gained from the conversation and a relationship will have begun to form. The more people who can develop those skills and model those behaviours, the more successful the organization will be, and anyone who meets with or speaks with potential customers, whatever their title, however junior or senior, should understand how to sell.

In the early spring of 2019, I met with an old friend and former colleague who had since become the CEO of a large, for-profit chain of care homes. He spoke about the challenges of looking after older people, particularly those whose mental health is in decline, describing the increasing prevalence of dementia and the investment they were having to find for staff training. 'We want to stay at the top of the quality table,' he explained, 'and if the team don't know their stuff, that's not going to happen, and the risk of things going wrong just spirals.'

Knowing a few non-profits in that space, I asked if he needed any introductions, but he'd already signed a six-figure training deal with a university. 'Their pitch was for an even bigger fee, but we got them down a bit on price. Interestingly, the one thing they wouldn't concede on was the time they needed to do the training. When you're pulling that many staff out of the homes, you want to cover as much as you can, but they wouldn't move on session length at all. It's good though. Shows integrity. Shows they're serious.'

'Why didn't you talk to any of the charities about it?' I asked. 'I'm sure most of them offer training.'

'I've met them all', he replied. 'I've offered them free space to run sessions in homes, but all they were interested in was getting more residents out to their own sessions, in church halls and things. I mean, if it was me or you, you'd take the space, save some money, then talk about what else you could do, build the relationship, build the business. I don't know… I just didn't get the impression they were interested, or maybe they just don't think that way.'

For higher-value products and services, the sole purpose of marketing is to open up a conversation with a buyer about the potential for doing business together. If the people having those conversations don't understand how to sell, or, worse, aren't even going to try to build a relationship based on the value they can provide, all the marketing in the world isn't going to help. The organization can fill the purchasing funnel and create as many contacts as it wants, but it's not going to have any impact or make any money.

The senior members of most non-profit organizations, from the executives and CEO to the trustees and Chair, are all fully aware of the role they can play in engaging with philanthropists and funders. Few recognize they have the same role to play in commercial marketing and sales, but they are the ones who ultimately set the priorities, sign off the investments, and judge the performance of the commercial parts of their enterprise.

They are often also the ones who can most easily access the highest-value customers, who get invited onto platforms to speak, who can open doors and initiate conversations that can lead to future business. Understanding the process and developing the ability to sell is not something that can be confined to a business development team buried in the bowels of the building. If the organization needs to sell, everyone needs to know how.

## Maximizing the value of the sale

In the opening chapter I talked about the importance of profit, and how maximizing the profit opportunity of a commercial income stream in an organization that will use that profit to fund greater impact is an ethical imperative. Nowhere is that opportunity more easily gained or lost than in the sales process, where the potential value that will be created, and how that value will be shared, are largely determined.

There is an art to creating value through a sales process, but underneath that art is an increasing amount of science. The concept of 'solution selling' had been around for several years before Neil Rackham formalized it into a defined methodology in his unfortunately titled book, SPIN Selling,[5] first published in 1988. Through his research with around 6,000 professional salespeople, Rackham objectively demonstrated the impact of the SPIN approach, and it has since gone on to shape the philosophy of most modern sales techniques.

The title could have been worse: Rackham initially named his four stages Situation, Problem, Implications, Value, but in a book that sets out to debunk the historic model of the fast-talking salesman, he wisely chose to avoid the resulting acronym, and replaced the fourth word with Need instead. The focus of Rackham's work is primarily on the conversation between buyer and seller, and for anyone who wants to explore the science behind modern sales techniques more deeply, SPIN Selling is the first book on the reading list. But that conversation is only one stage in the process, and it's important to see it in context before getting into the detail (Figure 7.4).

FIGURE 7.4  The good sales cycle

The first phase in the sales process is finding the right buyer. Inbound leads will come from effective marketing and outbound activity will usually find success by gaining personal referrals and introductions. Cold calling has never been a particularly effective approach for outbound sales, but reaching out to a target customer with an offer of value, whether that's some useful and relevant insights or an invitation to a private event, for instance, can increase the chance of engagement significantly.

The objectives of any first contact are, as E St Elmo Lewis described over a century ago: to engage attention, elicit interest, invoke desire (in this case, the desire to follow up with a conversation) and to provoke action. Unless an e-mail contains something of genuine, relevant interest that invokes a positive desire to find out more, the only action it's likely to provoke is to be moved to the junk folder.

Not everyone who responds to marketing is a buyer, and an essential step in any sales process is qualification: determining, subtly and politely, whether the person can talk about the deeper needs, or is simply following a brief from someone else; whether they actually hold the budget, or are merely making recommendations; and whether they have the authority to approve a proposal or need sign-off from someone above.

It's very easy, and very common, for those inexperienced or untrained in sales to waste inordinate amounts of time speaking to people who are easy to reach, engaged and responsive, but can't explore the broader need, don't control the budget and lack the authority to make the final decision. They may be nice people, they may be introducers and they may even have some influence, but they aren't buyers, and spending any more time than is absolutely necessary for a rapid introduction to the real buyer creates no value for anyone. Qualifying and categorizing contacts not only improves efficiency, it allows cohorts of customers to be tracked through the stages of the purchasing process, and it becomes a key measure of progress and a robust indicator of future business.

Reaching a qualified buyer is the first phase; the second is building a shared understanding of the value they could gain by becoming a customer. To maximize that value for both parties, the process must be one of diagnosis before prescription, and diagnosis can't be performed by reeling off a whole bunch of products and services, in the hope that one might hit the target.

This is the fundamental difference between selling and pitching. One of the first things a prospective customer will often say, for example, is: 'Tell me about what you do…' or even, 'How do you think you can help?' Good sales professionals don't feel pressured into giving long, comprehensive answers because they know it's not helpful at that stage. Instead, they usually have simple stock responses, like James in the data example, that give a very brief overview but then secure permission to ask questions. An organization might be able to do a wide variety of things, only a few of which might be relevant to the person in question, and it's not unreasonable to explain, after a short introduction, that by knowing a bit more about them and their situation, it would be easier to identify pertinent examples and make more useful suggestions.

It's that 'permission to ask' that enables the conversation to uncover much greater value opportunities, and it's where the techniques of *SPIN Selling* and its relatives, from 'solution selling'[6] to 'the challenger sales model',[7] and myriad proprietary variations in between, all come into their own. The main differences between the variants are the formality of the process and the style of the conversation. The sales approach I advocate for most non-profits is a form of 'consultative selling', which sits at the collaborative end of the style

FIGURE 7.5 Uncovering the full value case

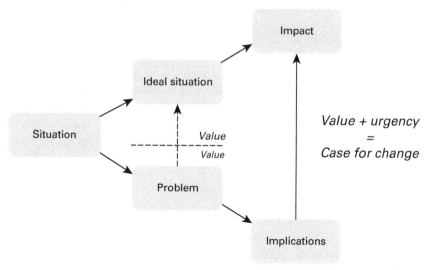

spectrum, because it usually fits best with the culture and capability of their teams (Figure 7.5).

The diagram in Figure 7.5 is broadly common to all SPIN-based sales models and illustrates how a seller and a potential customer can develop a broader appreciation of the full value of working together. By listening the customer's situation, an experienced seller will draw out the underlying problems that they could help to address. However, simply solving an immediate problem provides less value than helping the customer to achieve a more aspirational outcome. Plus, by asking them to define and talk about their idealized goal-state, the seller can help the customer to begin emotionally engaging with the potential benefit of finding a better solution. To further that customer engagement, the seller will then ask about the negative implications of not resolving the problem, and the wider positive impact that could result from attaining that ideal outcome. Let me offer an example.

Around 10 per cent of the UK population are carers. Some do it full-time, but most are juggling their caring duties with part-time or full-time jobs, sometimes with demanding careers. Without support and flexibility, balancing those duties can at times become incredibly stressful, and that leads to problems for the employer: absenteeism, lower productivity, early retirements and resignations, as their employees are forced to choose between their career, their loved ones and their sanity.

The implications for the employer, if the situation isn't addressed, include not only the financial cost, of lost productivity and constant recruitment, but the drain on expensively trained talent, the narrowing of their potential pool for new recruits, the loss of diversity and the cultural and morale implications for other employees from watching their colleagues burn out and quit. Conversely, the impact of creating an environment and a support system that enables carers to thrive within the workplace is the reverse of each of those implications, from cost savings to staff engagement and loyalty. That initial impact can translate into further benefits in customer service, brand marketing and employer reputation, to name but a few.

Few employers will join all of those dots; many would simply reach out for help because of a rise in staff complaints, looking for simple, low-cost ways to address them. But simply mitigating those symptoms doesn't offer the best outcome for the employer. The greater prize is the value of that complete transition: from the downward spiral in talent, morale and performance to the rapid benefits of dramatically improved engagement, reputation and revenue. It is the role of the salesperson to help the employer to make that mental shift, to recognize the much greater value opportunity hidden beneath those uncomfortable symptoms, and to appreciate the potential they have to get a far greater return from a more substantial investment.

A low-level administrator sent out to find a 'cure for staff complaints' will be unable to grasp or engage with the bigger opportunity – their remit having been entirely defined by 'what the boss wants'. Thus, getting directly to the *right* buyer, in this case, someone who has the budgetary responsibility for large numbers of employees, who is having to pay for the implications and would be rewarded with the benefits, is fundamental for uncovering and realizing the full potential value for both parties. Similar cases could equally be made for gender diversity, disability inclusion in the workforce and so on.

The aim of consultative selling is not simply to pitch that value to potential customers, but to enable them, by guiding the conversation, to uncover and articulate the implications and benefits for themselves, in direct relation to their own situations. It is an essential part of ensuring not only the relevance of the solution, but also the emotional engagement of the customer, particularly when questions are asked about them as an individual, such as: 'What difference would this make to you and the team? If we got this right, how would it affect you personally?'

Engagement comes from conversation, which means questions can't be formulaic but must flow from what's been said. It must never feel like an interrogation, but like an open discussion between peers with complementary expertise, fluid and enjoyable, yet continually directed by the seller's curiosity. The enjoyment most people get from a conversation is in direct proportion to the share of the time they spend speaking. Thus, an effective sales conversation is enjoyed by the buyer and directed by the seller: the seller asks most of the questions, and the buyer spends most of the time talking.

Returning to Aristotle, the rational value case that emerges from the discussion is the first of his modes of persuasion, but logic alone is rarely enough to engage commitment and never enough to maximize the potential value of the sale. The second mode, emotional engagement, is essential for both, and that's what is added through a consultative selling approach. The third mode, as we saw earlier, is credibility; in this case, building the customer's confidence that the person in front of them is the best choice of partner to help them realize their newly defined goals. Asking thought-provoking questions, identifying and articulating the underlying problems, using examples of other customers' implications and subsequent outcomes as fuel for the discussion, all of these demonstrate a far deeper level of insight and build real trust, rapport and credibility. And all of them help to clearly differentiate the seller's organization as the experts, not only in their technical field, but in being uniquely able to understand and deliver the broader outcomes the buyer now wants.

By the end of the conversation, buyer and seller should be able to summarize a verbal agreement, not on the details of the service being provided, that comes later, but on the ideal situation, the outcomes desired, how success might be measured and the full value case for investment, quantified financially and richly described non-financially. A final question, around when the buyer would want to have realized those benefits, will establish a timeline, relative urgency and some agreed next steps, which will include a more detailed proposal.

The seller's job is then to go away and work out how that ideal situation can be realized and what their organization can contribute, whether that's a combination of existing services or something more bespoke. The more bespoke, the higher the price, irrespective of whether it costs any more to deliver.

Value, scarcity and the seller's own confidence are the three drivers of price, which means that, for a unique proposition that offers a high level of value, the cost of delivery has no bearing whatever on price, other than as an internal baseline that needs to be exceeded. The consultative sales process is designed to dramatically enhance value and scarcity, but self-confidence is often the downfall of non-profits, particularly when it comes to challenging poor procurement practices.

If the seller has managed the process effectively, they will avoid being thrown into an open tender, but it's possible the buyer will share the agreed objectives to try to solicit other competitors; it's not particularly ethical, but it's hard to prevent. The design of the solution, however, is the intellectual property of the seller, and that ownership should be confidently asserted through a confidentiality clause in any proposal.

Far too many non-profits (and businesses as well for that matter) allow themselves to be slaves to an arbitrary procurement process: effectively giving free consultancy only to have their ideas taken and shared with the competition at bid-stage; pricing in terms of commodities, of days and courses, rather than the value they provide, because that's what the procurement team have specified they need to do. It takes real self-confidence to push back on those requirements, to test the relationship with the buyer, to assert a more equitable approach, with the alternative that the customer's best potential solution will otherwise walk away. Without that self-confidence, all the value uncovered through the process will end up with the customer. But with that self-confidence will also come an equitable and profitable share of the value.

## The four-fold return on investment

Considering the investment that it takes, in both time and money, to recruit a new customer, it should come as little surprise that retaining customers and building the value of established relationships is far more efficient than continually burning cash to replace ones that leave. Subscription, membership and recurring revenue models are increasingly being adopted in businesses for exactly those reasons. The revenue that Netflix gains from a subscription is far more valuable than the same income would be from rentals or pay-per-view, because it provides far greater predictability and resilience, and it virtually guarantees a repeat purchase at the end of each year, as subscribers become increasingly habituated to using its service.

A subscription-based business model increases the likelihood of repeat purchase, but as we saw earlier, there is a range of ways to achieve the same 'sticky' propositions to help retain customers. The fundamental requirement for all of them, though, is that the customer is getting, and recognizes that they're getting, something valuable from the ongoing relationship.

So, understanding and reinforcing that sense of value is a key part of retention, and, therefore, repeat purchasing. Netflix can get a proxy measure of the degree to which customers feel they're getting value by the volume of content they watch and the time they spend using the service. Those engagement analytics are so central to their decisions on what content they buy, commission and promote that they refuse to even disclose what's popular, let alone viewing figures, because of the commercial value of the information.

For most businesses, getting a read on the customer perception of value, where it sits, how it's changing and why, is an altogether more manual affair, but it's no less commercially valuable, and of course, the same is true for non-profits. It's the ability to gather that information and the capacity to act on it, to address any declines and to keep growing that perceived value, that increases the customer's propensity to return, and dramatically increases the return on the investment it took to get that first sale.

Repeat business is by far the most obvious way to increase the return on sales and marketing investment, but there are three others which can be equally valuable, and which collectively can multiply that return many times over. The second route is to go beyond simple repeat business, and build new, additional lines of business with the same customer. That might be by expanding the relationship to be able to offer a broader portfolio of products and services, add-ons and upgrades. For corporate customers it can also be through finding other potential buyers in the same organization.

Trees for Cities is a non-profit founded as Trees for London in 1993 by a group of four friends. They are the only UK charity working at a national and international scale to improve lives by planting trees in cities, and they have three main earned-income streams, all of which are aimed at corporate customers. Corporates can pay for a volunteering day of planting and team-building, they can pay for trees to be planted to offset their carbon emissions or, if they meet the ethical criteria, they can engage Trees for Cities for partnership marketing, lending an environmental aspect to marketing campaigns, such as: 'For every new account we open, or for every 100 units we sell, we plant a tree'.

Many corporates could potentially become customers for all three services, and with small businesses, engaging those conversations is relatively straightforward, as most of the decisions will probably be made by the same person. For larger businesses, however, HR might engage with volunteering; corporate finance or the CSR team with carbon offsetting; and the marketing division with partnership marketing; each of whom may be in different business units, possibly even different countries. Some customers might also be subsidiaries within a global group structure, providing a potential route into a far more valuable relationship if the right connections can be made. For Trees for Cities to maximize the value of these customers and develop a deeper, stickier relationship, gaining internal referrals and introductions is essential. And prerequisite for those introductions will be delivering a high level of perceived value, and a conscious focus on relationship development.

A third way to gain more value from a customer relationship is through introductions and peer referral beyond the customer's organization, and for this, the same two prerequisites apply. Most delighted customers are happy to make introductions when asked, but unless someone is managing the relationship and doing the asking, they're far less likely to happen, and another opportunity to increase the return on that first sale's investment will go untapped.

The fourth way to grow that return links back to the earlier example of the operations director at the industry conference: promotion through joint marketing. A personal introduction with ringing endorsement from an esteemed peer is the gold-standard in marketing, but a shared platform at an event, on video or in written form, can be a fairly close second. It's particularly valuable when the marketing works for both parties, in the carer's case for instance, positioning the customer as an enlightened and outstanding employer of choice, and the non-profit as the invaluable partner that was instrumental in the achievement. It will generate interest, it will usually invoke a desire to find out more, and it establishes credibility and the potential for value beyond doubt.

Each of the disciplines I've covered in this chapter can help to transform a marginal proposition into a highly profitable one and help niche ideas to rapidly gain scale. Targeted and effective marketing, qualification and consultative selling, challenging procurement, delivering unique value and developing sticky, valuable relationships long after the sale has been made are the building blocks of the good sales cycle, but they don't come for free. There are investment implications, in both capacity and skills, and there are risks, particularly when challenging procurement processes. But without the investment in people and the confidence to take those risks, the potential reward will forever go unrealized.

The biggest, and most often underestimated implication, however, is for the leadership. Relationships take time to develop. Pushing back on poor procurement means overtly prioritizing impact and profit over revenue targets. The single biggest reason that consultative selling fails in any organization is a lack of leadership understanding. Setting targets and incentives that prioritize the number of proposals, for example, tells the team it's less important to get verbal agreement first, even if that takes several meetings, than it is to send a written pitch. Setting targets on revenue rather than on profit tells the team it's better to roll with a procurement team's demands and get a less profitable deal than it is to walk away and look for more financially sustainable business on better terms.

Becoming more successful through better sales and marketing means overcoming skills and capability challenges, but it also means overcoming leadership challenges: to get those skills into the organization, to develop the broader capabilities, and to set the expectations and the environment within which they can thrive.

## Endnotes

1  St Elmo Lewis, E (1908) *Financial Advertising: For commercial and savings banks, trust, title insurance, and safe deposit companies, investment houses,* Garland Publishing, New York

2  Aristotle (1991) *The Art of Rhetoric,* Book 1 Chapter 2, trans Hugh Lawson-Tancred, Penguin Classics, London

3  Belfort, J (2007) *The Wolf of Wall Street,* Bantam Books, New York; Belfort's original memoir, written after his conviction and imprisonment for fraud, was adapted into the 2013 film of the same name starring Leonardo DiCaprio.

4  *Glengarry Glen Ross* (1992) Zupnik Enterprises, based on the 1984 Pulitzer Prize-winning play by David Mamet

5  Rackham, N (1988) *SPIN Selling,* McGraw-Hill, New York

6  Eades, K M (2003) *The New Solution Selling: The revolutionary sales process that is changing the way people sell,* McGraw-Hill, New York

7  Dixon, M and Adamson, B (2011) *The Challenger Sale: Taking control of the customer conversation,* Portfolio Penguin, London

# 08

# Leading the charge

## Shaking off the cultural shackles

In his 2008 book, *Uncharitable*,[1] Dan Pallotta took issue with the way that the public views charity, and the constraints that such a view places on the potential of the sector. His 18-minute TED talk[2] on the same topic from 2013, entitled 'The way we think about charity is dead wrong', had been watched over four million times as of 2019. Pallotta's central thesis is that charities are being denied the powerful tools of capitalism: to be able to pay high salaries to professional workers; to invest heavily in infrastructure, advertising and fundraising campaigns; and as a result, all they can do is alleviate, rather than solve, society's deep and complex problems.

Pallotta's philosophy, that the outcomes justify the tactics however aggressive or expensive they may be, is not without risk as we've seen earlier, and a strong ethical framework, even if only to protect reputation, is essential for established charity brands. But his central observation, that charities could achieve more if unshackled from those limiting preconceptions, is entirely correct. Pallotta traces the source of the US sector's impoverished conservatism to the *Mayflower* puritans. Earlier I used the Victorian ethos phrase to paint a similar touchpoint for the UK, but in truth, the moral polarization between money and virtue goes back millennia, from threading camels through the eyes of needles to the ascetic route to spiritual enlightenment embedded in many of the world's oldest surviving belief systems.

Unpicking thousands of years of embedded doctrine at a population-wide level is a laudable ambition, but it is neither public perception nor legislation that prevents charities from picking up the tools of commerce. It is the internal belief in those same preconceptions, and the lack of a sufficiently strong narrative to push through them, that provides the constraint. It's not illegal for charities to do highly profitable work, to advertise heavily, to spend a great deal of their income on fundraising, nor to pay high salaries; nor must it necessarily provoke public outrage.

When the Wellcome Trust moved its investment funds from outside management to an internal team, it engaged its own professionals to manage the fund, paying over £3.7 million to its highest earner in 2017.[3] The financial rationale and accompanying narrative for that move was unarguable and, as far as I'm aware, no trustees have been taken into police custody, there's been no great public outcry, and Euston Road remains clear of bonfires and pitchforks. Wellcome Trust may have fewer public stakeholders than many other charities, but the logic was clear, the story compelling, and the response, where not muted, was entirely positive.

Charities cannot hope to change the public expectation unless they can first throw off their own mental chains. A strong, compelling narrative can be extremely effective, not only in helping to shed those internal shackles, but also in proactively mitigating any potential impact on donors, supporters and volunteers. Media loves a sensation, and as Terry Pratchett was certainly not the first to observe, 'A lie can run around the world before the truth has got its boots on',[4] so the greater the head-start that truth has, the better the outcome is likely to be. And the prize, in the acquisition and development of talent, in dramatically improved infrastructure, in the ability to rapidly scale both income and impact, is worth the effort, if that effort is primarily in overcoming our own inherited prejudices and fears about what others might say.

The role of the leader is to make and catalyse that effort. Whether the aim is the adoption of a more commercial approach to the work, or simply to step-change professionalism and performance, the leader's role is to initiate and embody the required change in attitude, to help the organization break itself out of the 'traditional charity' shackles, by personally changing the collective beliefs and behaviours of all the people within it. It is a big task, but the playbook is well established.

Narrative is the starting point for change, but the driving force is observed behaviour. Culture is shaped by the visible actions of the leaders: not by what they say, but by what they do after they have said it, and by how well those two things match up. What leaders choose to focus on, to take an active interest in, and ask repeated, probing questions about, is a key factor in establishing expectations and behaviour patterns throughout an organization. This is the 'updraft effect'.

If a CEO asks to see reports, whether on progress, performance or gender pay splits, on a monthly basis and not from finance or HR, but directly from divisional heads, it creates an updraft, drawing information and attention from the frontline teams right up to the executive. After a few months of tough questions, responses will already be prepared for the inquisition that will come back down the line, and pre-emptive actions to address anomalies will already be in place before they're requested. Everyone very quickly starts to learn the new playbook and acts accordingly, because nobody wants to be caught out a second time falling short of expectations with no credible plan to close the gap.

This is how the beliefs, behaviour and ultimately the self-perception of any organization actually change. Posters on walls articulating slogans and values may be all the rage, but as a tool for shaping culture, deliberately or inadvertently, the updraft effect that derives from leadership focus and reaction is the biggest single lever, particularly when paired with consequences, both positive and negative.

The strongest statement a leader can make about culture is through the behaviours they reward, the exemplars they promote, the personalities they hire and the renegades they fire. Bad culture develops when people in authority avoid negative consequences, thereby seeming to accept poor behaviour, and it absolutely thrives when those behaviours become so common that people stop seeing them. The problems that leaders ignore quickly become the standards they're seen to endorse.

I've run many workshops and seminars with senior leaders on performance and culture change, and a question I've often asked is: 'Have you ever fired anyone too soon?' Not once has anyone said yes, but there's always a plethora of painful recollections of when they'd waited too long. There's a reason we delay firing people whom we know need to go, the scientific evidence for which is extensive. Behavioural economists have nattily entitled it 'hyperbolic discounting', which essentially means we all have a subtle but powerful in-built preference for smaller immediate rewards over slower, longer-term gains, however poor those choices may seem in retrospect.

The benefits of not having to deal with that horrible conversation, the potentially tortuous HR process, the vacancy it will immediately introduce seem far more attractive than the positive, long-term benefits of removing a poor performer or even a culturally corrosive high-performing one. The short-term anxiety outweighs the long-term opportunity, right up until the problem escalates so much that it demands immediate action. But the reality is this: every day of delay costs engagement, performance and potentially the organization's best talent. Every occasion of implicit endorsement by not addressing the issue eats away at the culture and values of the organization and permanently undermines the credibility of the leader.

This is not a call for leaders to start firing dissenters in some sort of totalitarian purge. The best teams have a rich diversity of views and perspectives, and in most situations, if the narrative for culture change is sufficiently compelling, if it's spoken about regularly and the desired behaviours modelled consistently by the leadership, and if the updraft effect is consciously deployed with visible reward and robust challenge, people will buy in, behaviour will change, and performance will dramatically improve without any blood being spilt. The point is, however, that leaders must be prepared to act when they need to, because the accountability for the culture that exists within an organization sits squarely and entirely on the shoulders of its leadership.

In 1990, John W Gardner wrote arguably one of the most insightful leadership books ever written,[5] fittingly entitled simply *On Leadership*. In it, Gardner explores the entire field, from leadership in community activism to the pinnacles of business and politics; from the attributes of leaders in context and their symbiotic relationship with constituents to the dilemmas of morality and power. Gardner describes six aspects that distinguish leaders in any context: thinking longer-term; understanding the organization's relationships with other entities and the wider world; influencing beyond their own jurisdiction; emphasizing the intangibles of vision, values and motivations; adeptly balancing conflicting political requirements; and thinking in terms of organizational renewal rather than simply operation. But above all of these, Gardner puts accountability: 'The concept of accountability is as important as the concept of leadership.'

Accountability is the *sine qua non* of organizational performance, and it is the bedrock of a commercial culture. One cannot be developed without the other.

Jacob Tas, the CEO of Royal Netherlands Sea Rescue Institution, spent the first half of his career in the shipping industry, rising to Global Operations Director on the Board of P&O Nedlloyd. The second half of his career began in 2006 at the Prince's Trust, followed by three years at Action for Children, then five as CEO of the social justice charity Nacro. In his final weeks at Nacro in May 2019, I met with Tas and asked about the importance of a commercial culture for charities in the services sector. He said:

> We have charitable objectives and they are crucial, they're why we exist and
> what drives our outcomes and behaviour. But we are a social business operating
> in tough competitive markets, so we have to be very commercial. We've all
> seen what happened to Lifeline, Tomorrow's People, Working Links, Interserve

and Carillion. It doesn't matter if you're a business or a charity, working in service delivery with intense competition and very tight margins is not easy.

We have central and local government, at times irresponsibly pushing low-value contracts that realistically can't be delivered; there have been organizations irrational enough to take them on, who will probably fail; and there's a whole supply chain, including many medium and small charities, who don't have the capability or the awareness to do all the due diligence they need to, who end up doing the work and risk not getting paid for it if something goes wrong. I have a huge amount of sympathy for them, but we all have to be more hard-nosed commercially if we want to keep doing what we do.

Tas went on to speak about performance, about their process for strategy that cascaded the overall objectives of 'changing lives' right down to individual targets, and went on to talk about the critical importance of accountability:

> I don't think it's just Nacro, I think it's across the sector: there's a passiveness around performance, people thinking: 'If I can explain what has happened, that is all I can realistically do.' It's not from lack of effort or passion, I think it's cultural, and we needed to really improve the accountability and professionalism around performance. Stopping the decline in income was essential for us to begin with: we had lost three or four million in grants for policy and research from the Ministry of Justice a few years before I started, and that meant we had to lose a lot of good people. Our revenue fell as low as £38 million at one point. It's back up to about £66 million now.

That phrase 'If I can explain what has happened, that is all I can realistically do' is central to the concept of accountability. With the right support, our youngest son has thrived in mainstream education despite his diagnoses of autism and ADHD, but at least once a year we're asked to attend school because in one of his subjects there has been an issue in class. Invariably it's in a class that has recently appointed a new teacher. We ask if the teacher has been briefed on his needs, and invariably we receive the answer that it's all on the system that new teachers are required to use. We get the teacher briefed and the issues disappear, but it illustrates a far deeper issue within the school. The Special Needs team primarily sees its accountability as liaising with parents on the adaptations required, then entering them in the system for others to deliver. They will carry the baton to the edge of their organizational box, then toss it over the departmental wall, assuming someone else will catch it. They have accountability for part of a process, but not for how effective that process is, nor, it would seem, for the outcomes it is intended to deliver.

This is the same issue that customer service organizations have solved by giving explicit accountability to call centre operators to resolve a customer issue entirely, empowering them to do whatever they need to resolve it, including changing internal processes, however far-reaching the consequences. Their accountability does not end at the edge of their organizational box – it ends at the edge of that customer's experience. The biggest single feature on any organizational chart is the empty space in between the boxes, which, unsurprisingly, is where most organizational issues emerge. Individuals working within a process need to be given that 'outcome level' of accountability, the authority to deliver on it, and to have their performance appraised on that basis if the organization as a whole is to perform as it should. As Tas observed, this gap in performance accountability is not a Nacro thing, it is a pervasive cultural issue for most organizations that are in the business of doing good.

Performance and accountability have been at the centre of many of my conversations across the sector. In one of the first Charity CEO breakfast events I hosted, back in 2015, I asked the group what challenges they faced in improving performance. One of the most experienced of all the CEOs present said this: 'It feels like there's a moral offset sometimes in our sector; because we know we're doing something inherently good, we seem to think it's less important that we do it as well as it can be done. It's as if we think that "doing things well" matters less than in other sectors.' As the room fell quiet, she finished with this thought: 'What if we put as much passion into improving the way we work and the quality of our delivery as we put into championing our cause?'

And it's true. Even outside of the commercial income domain, if we were to put a fraction of the energy into developing a high-performance, high-accountability culture as we put into our programmes and campaigns, those programmes and campaigns would be far better funded and far more effective than could ever be achieved with passion alone.

## Crossing the capability chasm

Alongside culture, capability is the biggest gap that needs to be overcome for most established non-profits in the pursuit of commercial performance. I've talked in earlier chapters about the capabilities required in the strategy and innovation processes, and in Chapter 7 about the business-critical areas of marketing and sales. But defining those capabilities is one thing; getting them into a non-profit organization can often be another challenge entirely. Generically, there are three options: rent, build or buy.

**Renting** capability, whether through consultants, contractors or interims, can provide a powerful kick-start for internal change. By itself, it's not a long-term solution to a capability gap, but it can help enormously with building internal talent if it's set up with the right structure and incentives to transfer skills and embed new practices.

**Building** the internal talent has many merits. It's often easier to have a willing and able technical expert coached for a few months to help them learn professional sales, than it is to recruit a professional salesperson and have to teach them the breadth of subject-matter expertise from within the organization that will be required to credibly challenge a customer's preconceptions. But willingness is the key. Often people resist change, as we have seen.

**Buying** in commercial talent from outside and helping them to adapt to a mission-led environment can often be the fastest and most reliable method for bringing in new skills and catalysing rapid cultural change. Indeed, when cultural resistance is high, bringing in a robust outsider may be the only viable route to change, someone who, unlike many trustees from industry, will not leave their 'business head' at the door, but will bring it with them, leading the way and breaking a new trail for the organization.

Mark Hislop is the Director of Commercial Services for Scouts and is responsible for around two-thirds of the Association's £34 million annual income. Prior to 2007, Hislop's CV was as commercial as they come, with 16 years at Marks & Spencer followed by senior roles at Tesco and B&Q, culminating in the MD role at Habitat. His migration into the third sector was propelled by a year-long stint as Interim Retail Development Director for the National Geographic Society, a Washington-based non-profit whose strategic aims are to: 'Inspire people to place greater value on the natural world and its people; secure the natural systems essential for all life on Earth; and drive innovation that helps create a planet in balance.'

I asked Hislop about his experience of moving into the charity sector:

National Geographic was an education in the application of commerce for social benefit. One part of the organization was entirely focused on the mission: education, awareness, funding exploration and discovery and so on. The other part was entirely focused on generating the profit to fund that work.

Whether retail, products or licensing, it was completely and overtly commercial, and it worked really well.

After National Geographic, I was offered a job in a new role as Commercial Director at the Somerset House Trust. That was a much tougher cultural shift. The financials weren't great; it took over two years just to turn things around and get a more commercial approach working, and there was a lot of internal resistance. The Chair and CEO were fully bought-in, but I think, to begin with, most of the other people there thought I was the Antichrist; that I was going to commercially pollute the mission and detract from the art.

The first step was to get cafés and restaurants open that could generate a profit from visitors to the galleries and exhibitions. It wasn't easy; I was constantly having to say to the rest of the team, 'Look, I promise I won't tell you how to run your exhibitions, so don't tell me how to run a restaurant.' But it wasn't until they were up and running, when people could see how good they looked and how they were being received, and that they were bringing in money to fund the art programme, that most people finally got on board.

Having gained in credibility and support, Hislop was able to build his team, recruiting more people with a commercial background, going on to create the non-profit hub I described in Chapter 3 to generate more income from unused assets through a customer-centric approach. And over time, the Somerset House culture evolved to accept the essential marriage of commerce and mission that would secure its financial future.

Buying in talent with a background such as Hislop's can make a huge difference to the pace of change, and it's no surprise that over a quarter of the sector leaders I interviewed during the research for this book had similarly extensive backgrounds in the private sector. But buying high-level talent is not cheap, and as things stand with sector pay, it often depends on their willingness or ability to take a significant cut in income.

Recruiting people much earlier in their career and training them in the commercial disciplines would be far more cost-effective, but there are challenges there too. There may be some truth in the perception that millennials are driven more by mission than money, but the potential for personal development and skills acquisition is a big priority for anyone in the early stages of their career, as is the inescapable need to earn a half-decent living.

Earlier in the chapter I mentioned the conversation I had with Jacob Tas, in which, as with most CEO conversations, the challenge of attracting talent came up. 'I personally was lucky,' says Tas. 'I got a good pay-out which gave my family a financial buffer and allowed me to take a really great third-sector role to make a difference for the country. And Nacro is doing well, we have a good brand, strong track record on delivery, exciting growth story, but it's still hard to attract true talent and I think it's even harder for others in the sector.'

He illustrated the issue with a recollection:

> A colleague from another charity was doing the university milk round. They had put him in a corner but he's very charismatic and had still drawn a big crowd. But then he realized from their questions that they all assumed he was a volunteer, so he asked them, and none of them thought he got paid. These were very smart undergraduates, and none of them realized they could have a well-paid career in the charity sector and make a profound difference to civil society. One girl actually cried because she'd already accepted a job at an accounting firm. It's like my wife said to me: '*We leave the toughest problems in society to the organizations in a weak position to solve them, because most of the best talent goes off to the City, McKinsey, Google or wherever.*' I think this is the sector's and the country's biggest challenge.

Non-profits therefore have two big hurdles to overcome in attracting talent. The first is the common perception that most charity work is voluntary, and that it's not a place where one can earn a decent living. The second is the related perception that the sector is 'sleepy and unchallenging';[6] that it's not a place to develop oneself or one's career, it's the place to take the skills developed elsewhere once the money has been earned and the career aspirations fulfilled.

There's no doubt that the non-profit community can create better roles and personal development pathways, but the biggest gap is not between what the sector offers and what it could offer; it's between what the sector offers and what the public thinks it offers. There are many fantastic roles within the sector, and many inspiring leaders and role models to learn from. Better roles and career development would, of course, be highly desirable, but they're not a silver bullet for recruitment. This is not simply a process problem; it's a problem of public awareness and attitudes.

The irony is that non-profits have an exceptional track record in raising awareness, in changing public attitudes, in educating and influencing opinion. It would benefit the sector immeasurably if a slice of that same expertise were put to work in educating the public, from school age upwards, to raise awareness and change attitudes about what non-profits actually are, how they operate and what they're like to work for.

Conversations with young people need not stop at activism, volunteering and donating; they can lay the foundation for compelling career aspirations. Every representative of a charity who walks into a school or university to talk about their cause has a huge opportunity to shift the dynamic, to unpick the preconception, to narrow the gap between perception and reality. These are the leadership attributes Gardner described as understanding the broader external environment and influencing far beyond the prescribed jurisdiction, attributes one might hope the sector would have in abundance, but which individual leaders need to deploy far more deliberately in overcoming the perception hurdle to talent acquisition.

Meanwhile, to address the career development hurdle, investing in skills and capabilities is an inescapable need, not just for attracting younger talent but, more importantly, for building the capabilities of the people already in the organization. To quote Alex Skailes, Director at the Centre for Charity Effectiveness at Cass Business School: 'It's not a popular thing to say, but the charity sector has for too long been a net importer of talent. It doesn't invest as much as I think it would like to in its people, partly because of financial constraints, and also because it's not what donors want to pay for.'

Cass is one of the few UK universities that have a dedicated education arm for charity professionals. It offers a programme of professional development courses and five specialist Executive MSc degrees. In 2019, it was the first to get a Master's-level course accredited specifically for non-profits, which could be funded from their apprenticeship levies. I asked Skailes what she thought would need to happen for charities to be able to develop more talent of their own, perhaps to the point of being able to export talent to other sectors:

> The tide is beginning to turn, and we now increasingly see examples of charitable organizations investing in their people either through formal education and professional development routes or through innovative initiatives such as shadowing placements and internal coaching programmes. And it's not only within the larger organizations; some funders are recognizing the correlation between delivering sustained social value, and the skills, competencies and resilience needed from charity leaders. The two-year leadership programme we recently delivered for charity leaders in the legal advice sector was funded by the Barings and J Paul Getty Junior Foundation, and that's just one example of funder-led schemes.

Any non-profit that wants to improve performance, that wants to become more efficient and have more impact and income, will inevitably need most of the people within it to develop new skills and adopt new behaviours. The former can be achieved through training, for which there is thankfully an increasing variety of options, but the latter can be far more challenging. This is where cultural resistance often kicks in, not around learning new skills, but in changing working practices and changing behaviours to make the most of those skills, and that resistance happens primarily for one reason: people 'fear the dip'.

A friend of mine recently started taking lessons with a golf coach to improve his game. I'm one of those unenlightened people who see golf as a good walk spoilt, but in a rare show of interest I asked how much he'd improved. His reply surprised me: 'It's getting better now, but in the first few weeks it went off a cliff.'

Apparently, the reason he'd been struggling was down to his grip. The coach got him to change it and, to start off with, it made things worse. He stuck with it and, after a couple of weeks of coaching, his game got back to where it was before, only now it had the potential to get much better. 'I had to go through the dip to get to the other side', he explained. 'That's why you get a coach. If I'd been on my own, I'd have given up and gone back to my old grip, and I'd never have improved.'

Most people are perfectly comfortable doing what they do, if they're skilled at their task, and they derive no small degree of personal self-esteem and confidence from their professional success. Asking them to do something very different, or to radically change how they do what they do, is often unsettling because, to begin with, they will inevitably be less successful, and when working with beneficiaries that prospect can be enormously unsettling.

The perception that their performance will dip, and the emotional impact on confidence, self-esteem and belief in the organization's direction, can emerge in a variety of unhealthy and unhelpful ways. The most common result is the desire to back out of the dip through various conscious and unconscious aversion behaviours, whether covert or overt, which leads to blame, tension and stress, and sometimes even to the emergence of factionalism and cliques.

Some people embrace the challenge that comes with major change, particularly if they've been through the dip a few times in the past and they know what to expect and how to feel about it. But for most, it is far from sufficient to simply send them on a course, then expect them to adopt, or worse, to engender, a far-reaching change in behaviour or approach. No non-profit would expect that of its beneficiaries, because it knows only too

FIGURE 8.1 Crossing the capability chasm

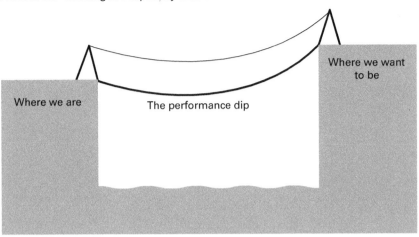

well that the social and emotional context into which they return can make that behavioural change almost impossible for one individual to maintain, so why would it expect anything different from its staff?

Commercial capability, performance improvement and culture change go hand in hand, and therefore require an integrated approach. In Chapter 1, I used Skills for Care as a great example of commercial focus, but the organization's aim for that project was broader: it was to explore social entrepreneurship, and as CEO Sharon Allen explained in a video recorded shortly after the project, she recognized that it meant a '... move from being a fairly typical bureaucratic organization involved in delivering government agendas, to trying to do that alongside being almost a Lean Start-up'.

As an organization specializing in workforce development, it's little surprise that the CEO and her team already had a deep understanding of the type of process required for change, and flowing straight out of the strategy design was a capability development project that would support the desired shift in culture towards agility and enterprise. That process began with a group training and coaching programme for the CEO, the executive team and a number of key senior managers, which included all the principles and techniques of consultative selling and marketing. The learning was then cascaded down the rest of the organization through training and coaching delivered by the senior management themselves, explicitly endorsed and supported by the executive.

When I returned, almost three years later, and asked Allen which aspects of the work had stood the test of time, commercial skills and consultative selling were the first things she described. 'We talk about it all the time; it's just a part of the everyday language now', she explained, and the near doubling of their trading company's income over the ensuing three years is testament to how effectively the carefully choreographed introduction of those skills has enabled the cultural change that she envisaged to permanently embed.

Whether the approach to crossing the capability chasm is to rent, build or buy, or a combination of all three, the essential ingredients in every case are the senior leadership's involvement, their explicit and ongoing support, and their willingness to invest, not just in training or bringing in external expertise, but in the time, effort and planning it takes to minimize the dip and get everyone safely across.

## The disciplines of agile delivery

As we saw in Chapter 6, the process of innovation can be iterative, sometimes messy, and does not lend itself to formal project management techniques. Detailed activity plans are fine for the first few weeks, but as soon as customers start to feed back, those plans generally go out of the window.

This challenge exists for almost any form of innovation but is especially apparent with technology. Twenty years ago, the standard approach for information systems development was to send out a cohort of business analysts to sit down with a system's potential users and customers, to capture all of their needs, and to design the architecture of a new system for which the software engineers could then spend the next couple of years writing code.

By the time the system was ready to roll out, often those needs had changed, the world had moved on, and the solution was already out of date. But even where the needs were unchanged, what technology businesses found, time and again, was that as soon as users got onto the system, they started asking to be able to do different things, and many of the original functions they'd requested, which may have taken months to develop, were never even used. People are very poor predictors of their future behaviour and needs, or, as Steve Jobs put it, they don't know what they want until you show it to them.

This challenge, of meeting indistinct and often changeable needs, led technology businesses to invent a new approach to project management. Out went the two-year plans with detailed tasks and milestones, and in came the 'agile' methodology. Agile offered a way of running projects faster and more flexibly; it was a way to accelerate the process of software innovation and ensure it delivered what users actually wanted, not just what they said they wanted.

The agile approach is built on developing very early prototypes, getting them in front of users, often in multiple groups each with slightly different versions of the software. From that mini-launch, the team watches and tracks user behaviour, what they actually do when they're using the system, and listens to their experiences and feedback before starting the next development 'sprint'. It has many big advantages over the big-plan approach: it gets something usable out far more quickly, it empowers teams to make rapid decisions and course corrections, it enables them to quickly learn what actually works for customers and to adapt their approach to that learning, as opposed to relying entirely on predictions made at the design stage and making customers wait years for the solution.

These strengths make the agile approach ideally suited to the early stages of just about any innovation, from consumer products to entire business models. Thus, over the years, 'agile working' has escaped the IT environment and been increasingly applied across a wide spectrum of innovation projects. Its philosophy sits at the heart of the Lean Start-up concept and the innovation process I described in Chapter 6. But along the way, 'agile' has also acquired a mystique and an allure far beyond the innovation space.

Leaders know that the pace of change in the world around them is accelerating, that organizations need to get closer to customer needs, to be better able to adapt, and to change more rapidly as circumstances and expectations evolve, which sounds very much like the things the agile approach delivers on innovation. And so, that need for speed, flexibility and customer responsiveness, at a whole-business level, has increasingly been termed 'organizational agility', leading to the unfortunate misconception that a methodology that works well at a project level can simply be expanded across all aspects of an organization to create a faster, more responsive whole. Sadly, that's not how life works. Running a standalone innovation project in an agile way, and enabling a large, complex, mature organization to become more responsive to changing demands, are two very different challenges indeed, as many of the new wave of technology companies have discovered.

In a 2010 interview[7] with Business Insider, Facebook CEO Mark Zuckerberg described his mantra for the organization as: 'Move fast and break things. Unless you are breaking stuff, you are not moving fast enough.'

What he intended the phrase to do was to give full licence to his developers to try their ideas; to make Facebook as fast and agile as it could possibly be.

Rather than mandating that every software release worked perfectly, he saw each release as a learning opportunity. The faster Facebook could iterate and test new ideas, the further it would move away from the competitors trying to chase it down, and if that chaotic approach meant breaking the product on occasion, it was a price worth paying. In April 2014, under pressure from users and advertisers who'd been increasingly putting up with buggy software, system downtime and chaotic responses from support, Zuckerberg launched a new mantra: 'Move Fast with Stable Infrastructure'.[8]

As Zuckerberg himself explained, 'What we realized over time is that it wasn't helping us to move faster because we had to slow down to fix these bugs… It might not have the same ring to it and might not be as catchy… but it helps us build better experiences for everyone we serve and how we operate now.' Agility is great, up to a point, but discipline is essential for delivery, and maintaining core areas of stability is critical in a complex organization.

Facebook tried to scale up an agile innovation approach to its entire organization and, unsurprisingly, within a few years, all those sprints, refinements and changes in direction from myriad semi-autonomous teams created a web of complexity that took Facebook years to unpick. At an organizational level, being agile requires a huge amount of coordination and control, and it needs a great deal of discipline to succeed. It requires a core skeleton of stability, an infrastructure of systems, processes and programmes that are rock solid and reliable, around which the individual muscles of innovation can be free to flex.

In practice, this means that organizations will always have a mix of core work that needs a more formal, classical management approach, and innovation programmes that need agile, empowered teams. Scenario planning can help in shaping the split, as it can provide a sense of what is likely to change in the future, but also what is likely to remain broadly the same across a variety of scenarios. Defining the boundaries between the stable and the fluid and managing those different sub-cultures within a single organization, while at the same time allocating and moving projects and resources between them, is therefore a key leadership skill that's invariably required for improving the overall agility of an organization.

At a higher level, achieving a sustainable shift in pace and responsiveness, becoming more agile as an organization, requires the adoption of a much more flexible leadership vision, one that is defined by the outcomes the organization intends to achieve, rather than by the specific things it intends to do or the shape it intends to adopt. Both of the latter may change significantly over time, but the former should stay as firm as a rock. A strong fix on the outcomes but complete flexibility on the route is the hallmark of an agile approach to organizational strategy.

Irrespective of how far an organization embraces the concept of agility, discipline around delivery will always be important, and there are five pairs of disciplines that I've found to be critical to implementation success:

- **Ownership and accountability**: Each project or agile initiative needs accountable leadership, and the targets for delivery, milestones and decision points need to be clearly owned by an individual. The flexibility of agile initiatives changes the nature of accountability, from tasks to results, but the management disciplines remain: asking what needs doing, giving permission to do it, and following up to make sure it is done.

- **Priority and visibility**: The updraft effect I described earlier means that, in simplistic terms, people do what the CEO pays attention to. It means the leadership needs to ask about, talk about, and give every bit as much quality time and attention to the strategic agenda as they do to the urgent, tactical issues bubbling up from below. It is the cadence of these conversations, and the behaviours they create outside the meetings, that drives organizational focus on what's important.

- **Transparency and objectivity**: The leadership and Board need to know they are getting transparent and honest information. On traditional projects that might be on progress and budgets; for agile ones it will be about metrics and milestones, but the key to both is objectivity. Whether a gloss is applied deliberately or subconsciously is irrelevant; an independent reporting mechanism is essential to avoid nasty surprises.

- **Consistency and stability**: Once accountabilities have been allocated and teams have been formed, the leadership's job is essentially to get out of the way, and to keep things as stable as possible around the teams. Constant interference, changes and restructures can set initiatives back months, so if change is going to be required, a short, sharp transition and a rapid return to stability is the least disruptive option for the teams.

- **Communication and reward**: There are three elements to great communication: story, repetition and success. Story explains and exemplifies why the organization is doing what it's doing, and how the initiatives are rooted in its mission. Repetition is about using every conversation, in every meeting, every day of the week, to reinforce those stories and the messages they're intended to convey. Success is the heartbeat that drives motivation around the organization, so it needs to be recognized, rewarded and celebrated as publicly as possible at every available opportunity.

## The role of the leader

There have been libraries of books written on leadership, promoting an array of approaches and archetypes for those who wish to attain the role or who find themselves thrust into it, so there is little value in my adding to the debate on styles, characteristics and prerequisites. The models most in vogue, whether charismatic, autocratic, servant, coach or authentic, seem to change by the season, and yet, from my own observations, the most effective style for any individual tends to depend largely on circumstance. But there are a few key concepts that are worth sharing under any circumstance, and these are as follows.

Most fundamentally, a leader's job is to 'lead', not to 'do'. Sir Alex Ferguson never scored a single goal, made a single assist or saved a single shot when he was at Manchester United, but the teams he selected, nurtured and developed topped the English Football League in 13 of his 27 seasons in charge. The quality of a team is judged on the results they achieve, but the quality of a leader is judged on the team they build, the talent they produce, and the legacy of strength in depth they leave behind. In fact, there are only two things leaders can't delegate: the big strategic decisions and the big team decisions.

The one thing that cuts across both of those non-delegable areas is culture. The development of culture can't be left to chance. As I've demonstrated throughout this book, culture is key: for change management; for performance improvement; for effectiveness, impact and commercial success. The role with the greatest influence on organizational culture is the CEO and everything the CEO is seen to do: what's interesting and irrelevant, what's tolerated and what isn't, the rewards and the consequences, the personal language and everyday behaviours, all send a continual cultural message across the organization.

The best leaders have an eye for talent. They delegate a great deal, because they have trust in their teams to do a better job than they could themselves, but they keep an appraising watch on how that delegation is working out and act swiftly if it's not. That approach frees up their time to look outside of the organization; to engage with others across and beyond the sector; to lead the thinking about what the future may bring; to consider and take the big decisions; to help the team form a shared vision; to craft a compelling narrative around it; and to set an ambitious pace for moving in the direction of where the puck is going to be.

Not all leaders are good on their feet, not all can pull off the 'Chief Engagement Officer' role, but they do need to be able to engender passion, enthusiasm and self-confidence, and to create an urgent desire within their team to stretch themselves and their colleagues, to strive for better. Above all, they need to recognize their weaknesses, and fill those gaps with the skills of others, both internal and external, and through deliberate self-development. Great leaders don't fear talent in others, nor do they hesitate to draft in help for themselves.

In the same way that the preconceptions about what a charity should be can become deeply self-limiting, the perception that asking for help is a sign of weakness can be deeply debilitating. It not only takes courage to ask for help, it takes self-confidence and a strong sense of self-worth. Many leaders, both in business and non-profit, will watch sporting events and witness world champions surrounded by their coaches, but don't think they can justify even a fraction of that investment in themselves.

The reason for this cognitive disconnect is usually subconscious. Often, it's the fear of exposing a weakness, even to oneself. In many cases, the desire to 'struggle and overcome', to get through a challenge purely using one's own resources and fortitude, is really driven by a deeper sense of self-doubt. The confidence that can come from such self-reliant success-against-the-odds can be of great personal value, but in a leadership role it comes at a cost to others. The inability to ask for help is a classic leadership blind-spot about which parables and fables have been told for millennia, with good reason: while a leader is struggling to overcome a challenge alone, it is everyone around them who is affected by the consequences, and it is their endeavour that is put at risk.

A leader's self-development is not a nice-to-have, nor is their asking for help a luxury or a cop-out, it is a rational and pragmatic way to make a greater difference. Just as a non-profit has a duty to its beneficiaries to continually strive to improve what it does, a non-profit leader has the same duty to their team and trustees, to invest time and, if necessary, resources in their own improvement and development, in their ability to better lead the organization.

Marshall Goldsmith has probably done more for the profile of executive coaching than anyone else. In his 2007 bestseller[9] *What Got You Here Won't Get You There*, he lays out his thesis, developed over decades of personally coaching top executives. In his view, as leaders climb higher up the organizational ladder, the qualities and capabilities necessary for their continued success change profoundly. For example, their technical and professional expertise, so important in their previous roles, becomes far less important than some of the interpersonal behaviours of which they may be only vaguely aware, and to which they may personally attach very little import.

The capabilities that got us here, for instance: managing big teams, innovating services, revitalizing departments, are not the ones that will take us from being a competent manager or executive to becoming an outstanding CEO. Incremental improvement in them might help us get to the top of our current game, but to succeed at the next level requires a different game plan, a paradigm shift in our self-development. And that's not just true when moving up through the ranks; it can also be true for moving between different organizations, and, indeed, between different stages of the journey of change within a single organization.

The role of a leader is to achieve certain outcomes, and throughout this chapter I have highlighted the most important ones:

- a clearly defined future direction for the organization, where it will play, how it will behave, and how it will succeed;
- a powerful and compelling narrative, constantly sold within and without the organization, to colleagues, supporters, funders, partners and customers;
- the continual development of better people and leaders, across the team and throughout the organization;
- and finally, the execution of the strategy and, through it, the delivery of the greatest possible social value for beneficiaries.

Before reacting to any given situation, wise leaders will ask themselves: what is the outcome I wish to achieve? And therefore, what is the right response, the right course of action, the right behaviour to display, in order to secure that outcome from this unique situation? Having the judgement and self-discipline in the moment, to consciously make that choice, and to behave in a way most conducive to the outcome desired, is the epitome of good leadership.

Thus, the challenge for you as a leader is not to become the leader that you want to be, nor the leader that any particular author or adviser tells you that you should be, but to discern and become the leader your people need you to be, in the situation they find themselves, right here, right now.

# Endnotes

1   Pallotta, D (2008) *Uncharitable: How restraints on nonprofits undermine their potential*, Tufts University Press, Medford, MA

2   Pallotta, D (2013) The Way We Think about Charity Is Dead Wrong, *TED*, https://tedsummaries.com/2015/03/16/dan-pallotta-the-way-we-think-about-charity-is-dead-wrong/ (archived at https://perma.cc/58UR-6B5C)

3   Kay, L (2017) Wellcome Trust Paid Its Highest Earner More Than £3.7 Million Last Year, *Third Sector*, www.thirdsector.co.uk/wellcome-trust-paid-its-highest-earner-37m-last-year/finance/article/1452792 (archived at https://perma.cc/6TD9-9DWG)

4   The quote is from Pratchett, T (2000) *The Truth*, Doubleday, London; earlier versions of the saying date back at least to 1710 when Jonathan Swift wrote the following in *The Examiner*: 'Falsehood flies, and the Truth comes limping after it; so that when Men come to be undeceiv'd, it is too late; the Jest is over, and the Tale has had its Effect.'

5   Gardner, J W (1990) *On Leadership*, Free Press, New York

6   Cooney, R (2019) Let's Debunk the Myths about Working for Charities, Says Macmillan Recruitment Head, *Third Sector*, www.thirdsector.co.uk/lets-debunk-myths-working-charities-says-macmillan-recruitment-head/management/article/1580367 (archived at https://perma.cc/G4BG-SUDW)

7   Blodget, H (2010) Facebook Strategy Revealed: Move Fast And Break Things!, *Business Insider*, www.businessinsider.com.au/henry-blodget-innovation-highlights-2010-2 (archived at https://perma.cc/A8ZR-M9W8)

8   Zuckerberg, M (2014) Keynote Presentation, *F8 Developers Conference*, www.youtube.com/watch?v=0onciIB-ZJA (archived at https://perma.cc/GB67-VVJ8)

9   Goldsmith, M (2007) *What Got You Here Won't Get You There: How successful people become even more successful*, Hyperion, New York

# Epilogue

## *The charity of business*

Throughout this book I have demonstrated a multitude of ways in which expertise and approaches from the commercial sector can be adapted and adopted to greatly benefit modern non-profits, but it would be deeply misguided to assume that the opportunities for that transfer flow only in one direction. There is a wealth of value that business can gain from adopting some of the principles and practices found in the third sector, some of which I touched upon in earlier chapters.

The specialist technical expertise within many non-profits, from the scientific to the pragmatic, from research and insights to practices and protocols, all offer significant potential value to businesses, as many charities are beginning to realize, and charge for. Most of those areas will be entirely on-mission for the non-profits, as illustrated by some of the examples I've used, for example in medical research; in establishing an environmentally friendly supply chain; in cause-related marketing campaigns; or in practices and expertise around inclusion, both social and economic.

With social inclusion, businesses have a critical role to play in providing inclusive products, services and environments that are accessible to people with different needs. For many in the construction, retail, hospitality or leisure industries, for example, disabled accessibility still equates to adding a ramp to a doorway, even though wheelchair users are merely the visible tip of a much larger, far more diverse disability iceberg. Criticizing institutions and businesses and applying pressure through campaigning is one thing, but partnering with them, providing education, training and consultancy, based on a clear commercial value case, can dramatically improve the practical outcomes of those campaigns for beneficiaries.

The same is true for economic inclusion, for finding employment or starting up a business as a way to escape poverty, isolation and the deep social issues that can take hold and fester in deprived communities at home and abroad. In both of those aspects of inclusion, the solutions that the non-profit community alone can provide will always be limited in scale unless they can be adopted within the mainstream. A charity's social enterprises can only employ so many refugees. Home automation for someone with severe disability will be far less expensive to develop and far easier to scale if it works through Siri or Alexa, rather than through something a charity has developed by itself.

It's not merely that it's possible for businesses to learn from charities' expertise; in order to achieve broader social outcomes, it is often a prerequisite.

Outside of the technical arena, there are other pragmatic things that business can learn from the non-profit world. The relevance of theory of change methodology to commercial marketing and the person-centred approach to service delivery both have wide potential application within business. A service that uniquely and measurably improves the lives of a particular section of society will engender a great deal of loyalty, stickiness and advocacy within that community, all of which has tangible commercial value. Similarly, the approaches that the most successful international non-profits have developed for adapting to cultural context, for marrying global reach with extreme localization in delivery, have enormous commercial relevance.

At a higher level, in areas such as leadership, governance and ethics, the non-profit world has the potential to offer individual learning to a wealth of aspiring business executives through trustee and advisory roles. This is not merely an opportunity for non-profits to engage talent within their boards; it is an opportunity to export their values and philosophy into a business community that is increasingly searching for a purpose beyond profit.

There exists a visibly growing and widely reported desire, across an increasing number of businesses, to find some higher form of mission, to engage with society in a more sustainable way, or in the words of Simon Sinek,[1] whose TED talk is regularly quoted as the third most popular of all time, to 'Find your Why'. It is a trend often attributed to more socially conscious millennials swelling the managerial and executive ranks of companies, but there are equally pragmatic, commercial reasons driving the shift.

Purpose-driven charities and non-profits have an unparalleled ability to engage. Employees are extraordinarily passionate and loyal to the sector, and the public freely and voluntarily give it vast amounts of their time, money, expertise and voice. Nobody donates to Tesco or volunteers for a few hours at their local HSBC. Businesses see that engagement, and the loyal communities that form around a clear social purpose, and unsurprisingly they want a slice of that action. But it would be cynical and misguided to suggest that's as far as it goes.

Business leaders are people, just like anyone else, and for each one who's in it purely for the money, there are many more who want to use their positions and wealth to benefit their employees, the communities they serve, and society at large – to build a legacy that reaches far beyond a healthy balance sheet. Were that not the case, there would be no such thing as philanthropy, nor would any charity maintain a fundraising team dedicated to major donors.

Unilever, under the leadership of Paul Polman and Keith Weed, has probably done more than any other organization to put the ethical business model on the global map, but the growing cadre of B Corporations and self-identified profit-with-purpose businesses illustrates a wider momentum. The increasing prevalence of compelling concepts such as the Triple Bottom Line, as popularized by John Elkington,[2] has added further impetus to the trend, but arguably the greatest single driver of uptake of these more caring forms of capitalism is that, commercially, they work.

Ethical consumers are on the rise, and they are more engaged by ethical brands because they care about what happens to their money once it goes into the till. Employees care as well, as do potential recruits, and corporate ethics is an increasingly important element in distinguishing an employer of choice. Shareholders in some quarters are starting to get it too; there is a growing perception that corporate social responsibility (CSR), particularly around the environment considering the predictions of climate scientists, is essential to the long-term sustainability of any business.

It is in this area that the transfer of culture and expertise from the third sector into the business sector has perhaps the greatest potential to make a profound and systemic impact, because while the desire may be there, the knowledge and skills are often absent.

In January 2019, Gillette launched an advert heralding a new direction for the organization and calling for its customers to become 'The Best Men Can Be'. The aim was for the video[3] to go viral, and it did, but not in a good way. The advert was widely viewed but deeply divisive, with customers and observers alike branding it as offensive, patronizing, and more than a little hypocritical coming from Gillette, a brand that had perhaps done more than most to reinforce macho stereotypes for generations. The backlash on social media was immediate. Within 24 hours, the YouTube release had been viewed five million times, gathered 100,000 likes, 400,000 dislikes and an avalanche of negative comments, with 'virtue signalling' a common theme. In Aristotelian terms, their logos may have been valid, but their pathos was polarizing and their ethos almost entirely lacking.

Gillette may be an extreme case, but right across the ethical business spectrum there remains a lack of understanding and expertise in what it means to develop genuine credibility by delivering social good. In areas such as environmental impact and sourcing, businesses are making progress, and most often it's by learning either directly or indirectly from the high-profile non-profits who've been working in those spaces for years. But in other areas, businesses are still decades behind non-profits. Some recognize this, and I mentioned earlier the decision by Belu to essentially outsource their social impact to WaterAid, in a move that proved extremely beneficial for both organizations. But that recognition is rare. Most businesses genuinely don't know what 'good' looks like in the sphere of social purpose.

The broader opportunity for businesses is to move beyond 'tipping their hat' to social impact by bolting on a CSR team, or by cascading a set of ethical requirements to suppliers, or even by committing themselves to carbon neutrality. The opportunity is for them to understand the true meaning of social impact, what it really looks like and the mechanisms by which it can be brought about. The opportunity is for outcome-led cross-sector partnerships; collaborations that don't simply mitigate the potential damage of a business's footprint, or pay for a couple of years of projects and campaigns, but instead aspire to create material, positive and sustainable outcomes at a population level. The desire, in many cases, is already there; what they lack are the tools for the job and the partners to show them the way; and in the business world more than any other, where leaders lead, the rest invariably follow.

In this book I have laid out how non-profits can harness and reshape business concepts and techniques to improve the situation for both themselves and their beneficiaries. For the most ambitious and far-seeing non-profits, however, there may also be a greater opportunity: to engage businesses not just with their expertise, but with their very mission. Not merely to grasp the tools of capitalism, but to guide and shape the aims and actions of capitalism itself, through leadership by influence and example, to harness the engines of industry to transform our collective ability to change the world for good.

## Endnotes

1 Simon Sinek (2009) *Start with Why: How great leaders inspire everyone to take action*, Portfolio, Penguin

2 John Elkington (1997) *Cannibals with Forks: The triple bottom line of 21st century business*, Capstone/John Wiley

3 We Believe: The Best Men Can Be | Gillette (Short Film) published on YouTube 13 January 2019

# FURTHER READING

Chan Kim, W and Mauborgne, R (2005) *Blue Ocean Strategy: How to create uncontested market space and make the competition irrelevant*, Harvard Business School Press, Brighton, MA

Chang, A M (2018) *Lean Impact: How to innovate for radically greater social good*, John Wiley & Sons, Hoboken, NJ

Cialdini, R B (1984) *Influence: The psychology of persuasion*, HarperCollins, London

Collins, J (2001) *Good to Great: Why some companies make the leap and others don't*, Random House Business, London

Covey, S R (1989) *The 7 Habits of Highly Effective People: Powerful lessons in personal change*, Simon & Schuster, New York

Crutchfield, L R and McLeod Grant, H (2012) *Forces for Good: The six practices of high-impact nonprofits*, Jossey-Bass, San Francisco, CA

Dixon, M and Adamson, B (2011) *The Challenger Sale: Taking control of the customer conversation*, Portfolio Penguin, New York

Drucker, P F (2006) *Managing the Nonprofit Organization*, HarperBusiness, New York

Eades, K M (2003) *The New Solution Selling: The revolutionary sales process that is changing the way people sell*, McGraw-Hill, New York

Elkington, J (1997) *Cannibals with Forks: The triple bottom line of 21st century business*, Capstone/John Wiley, Oxford

Gabor, A (2000) *The Capitalist Philosophers: The geniuses of modern business – their lives, times and ideas*, Three Rivers Press, New York

Gardner, J W (1990) *On Leadership* (1990) Free Press, New York

Gladwell, M (2000) *The Tipping Point: How little things can make a big difference*, Little Brown, New York

Godin, S (2003) *Purple Cow: Transform your business by being remarkable*, Penguin, Harmondsworth

Goldsmith, M (2007) *What Got You Here Won't Get You There: How successful people become even more successful*, Hyperion, New York

Gunther McGrath, R (2013) *The End of Competitive Advantage: How to keep your strategy moving as fast as your business*, Harvard Business Review Press, Brighton, MA

Kellman Baxter, R (2015) *The Membership Economy: Find your superusers, master the forever transaction and build recurring revenue*, McGraw-Hill Education, Maidenhead

Khaneman, D (2012) *Thinking Fast and Slow*, Penguin, Harmondsworth

Martin, R and Lafley, A G (2013) *Playing to Win: How strategy really works*, Harvard Business Review Press, Brighton, MA

Maurya, A (2012) *Running Lean: Iterate from plan A to a plan that works*, O'Reilly, Farnham, Surrey

McLeod, L E (2013) *Selling with Noble Purpose: How to drive revenue and do work that makes you proud*, John Wiley & Sons, Hoboken, NJ

Osterwalder, A and Pigneur, Y (2010) *Business Model Generation*, John Wiley & Sons, Hoboken, NJ

Pallotta, D (2008) *Uncharitable: How restraints on nonprofits undermine their potential*, UPNE, Lebanon, NH

Peters, T and Waterman, H Jr (2004) *In Search of Excellence: Lessons from America's greatest companies*, updated edn, Profile Books, London

Pink, D (2009) *Drive: The surprising truth about what motivates us*, Riverhead Books, London

Pink, D (2012) *To Sell is Human: The surprising truth about persuading, convincing and influencing others*, Canongate, Edinburgh

Porter, M E (1985) *Competitive Advantage: Creating and sustaining superior performance*, Free Press, New York

Rackham, N (1988) *SPIN Selling*, McGraw-Hill, New York

Radcliffe, S (2012) *Leadership Plain and Simple*, Pearson Education, Harlow

Reiss, E (2011) *The Lean Startup: How constant innovation creates radically successful businesses*, Penguin, Harmondsworth

Rumelt, R (2011) *Good Strategy/Bad Strategy: The difference and why it matters*, Profile Books, London

Schein, E H (2010) *Organizational Culture and Leadership*, 4th edn, Jossey-Bass, San Francisco, CA

Setili, A (2014) *The Agility Advantage: How to identify and act on opportunities in a fast-changing world*, Jossey-Bass, San Francisco, CA

Sinek, S (2009) *Start with Why: How great leaders inspire everyone to take action*, Portfolio Penguin, London

Stephens, D (2017) *Reengineering Retail: The future of selling in a post-digital world*, Figure 1 Publishing, Vancouver

Thaler, R and Sunstein, C (2009) *Nudge: Improving decisions about health, wealth and happiness*, Penguin, Harmondsworth

Toffler, A (1970) *Future Shock*, Random House, New York

Villeneuve-Smith, F and Blake, J (2016) *The Art of the Possible in Public Procurement*, E3M Publications, London

Weiss, A (2008) *Value-Based Fees: How to charge – and get – what you're worth*, 2nd edn, Pfeiffer, Hoboken, NJ

Yunus, M (2010) *Building Social Business*, Perseus, New York

# INDEX

CPSIA information can be obtained
at www.ICGtesting.com
Printed in the USA
LVHW071516150821
695367LV00018B/795